TALKING
FROM 9 TO 5

TALKING
FROM 9 TO 5

How Women's and Men's
Conversational Styles Affect
Who Gets Heard,
Who Gets Credit,
and What Gets Done
at Work

Deborah Tannen, Ph.D.

WILLIAM MORROW AND COMPANY, INC.
New York

TO ADDIE AND AL MACOVSKI

Library of Congress Cataloging-in-Publication Data

Tannen, Deborah, Ph.D.
    Talking from 9 to 5: How women's and men's conversational styles affect who gets heard, who gets credit, and what gets done at work / Deborah Tannen, Ph.D.
        p. cm.
    Includes index.
    ISBN 0-688-11243-9
    1. Business communication. 2. Communication in management.
    3. Communication—Sex differences. 4. Interpersonal relations.
    5. Sex differences (Psychology) 6. Language and languages—Sex differences. 7. Women—Language.   I. Title.
    HF5718.T36   1994
    651.7—dc20   94-4966
                                                                    CIP

Printed in the United States of America

First Edition

1 2 3 4 5 6 7 8 9 10

ACKNOWLEDGMENTS

This book could not have been written without the generosity of many companies and innumerable individuals who opened their doors and their lives to me. I talked to so many people at so many companies that it is impossible to mention them all by name, yet I want to express heartfelt appreciation to every one. Some of the companies that I can name, because they chose not to remain anonymous, are Ben & Jerry's, Chevron Overseas Petroleum Inc., Corning Inc., Essex County A.R.C., and Rohm and Haas. At all these and the other companies where I talked to people and observed interaction, I was deeply impressed and moved by the intelligence, dedication, and spirit of those who trusted me with their own stories and conversations. My greatest debt is to all of them.

ACKNOWLEDGMENTS

Many generous colleagues and friends read drafts of the manuscript and offered comments. For their time, attention, and wisdom I am grateful to Carolyn Adger, A. L. Becker, Susan Faludi, Rom Harré, Shari Kendall, Keller Magenau, Sally McConnell-Ginet, Susan Philips, Dave Quady, Lucy Ray, Cynthia Read, Ron Scollon, Suzanne Scollon, Naomi Tannen, David Wise, Haru Yamada, and Keli Yerian. I may not have always listened to their suggestions, but the book is surely a better one for the times I did.

Three research assistants helped me examine the voluminous transcripts of conversation I had amassed: Shari Kendall, Keller Magenau, and Keli Yerian. Their insights greatly enriched my thinking.

My students are always a source of inspiration as I work out the ideas I am writing about. The students in my seminars during the year of final writing were especially helpful: Lena Gavruseva, Kunihiko Harada, Itoko Kawakami, Shari Kendall, Keller Magenau, Melanie Metzger, Gabriella Modan, and Keli Yerian. Over the years, Japanese students have taught me a great deal about the Japanese communication system, which has helped me understand the American system by setting it in relief. This is especially true of those whose dissertations I directed: Yoshiko Nakano, Shoko Okazaki, Suwako Watanabe, and Haru Yamada.

Many people offered examples or helped me see new perspectives in formal interviews, casual conversation, or unsolicited letters. I cannot possibly name everyone who has contributed to my understanding in these and other ways, but some I can name are listed here. Though I group them together, I know that each made a unique contribution, for which I earnestly offer my thanks: Madeleine Adkins, Susan Baer, Lisa Beattie, James Clovis, Frances Conley, Linda Convissor, Elton Couch, Florian Coulmas, Bertrand de Coquereaumont, Elizabeth Devereaux, David Downs, Craig Dunham, Beecher Eurich, Ralph Fasold, Ed Finegan, Geoff Freter, Richard Giannone, Karl Goldstein, Tracey Groomes, Sally Helgesen, Mark Curtis Jones, Beth Kobliner, Linda Lagace, Iris Litt, Mary Maggini, Anne Mancini, Judy Mann, Joanne Martin, Barbara Mathias, Richard Matzke, Maire McAuliffe, Adrienne

McClenny, Steve McFarland, Patricia McGuire, Marie McKee, David McMullen, Barbara Meade, Kathleen Much, Manjari Ohala, Livia Polanyi, Juliet Porch, Dave Quady, Linda Raedeke, Erle J. Rappaport, Cynthia Read, Adele Reinhartz, Julie Richardson, Kathleen Curry Santora, Carole Schaefer, Nahum Schneidermann, Robert Scott, Catherine Shaw, Elaine Showalter, Elizabeth Solernou, Charles Tatum, Gordon Ting, Bill Watson, Mona Wexler, Lenny Winter, Clare Wolfowitz, Sharon Young, and Stan Yunick.

My own study of doctor-patient communication that I draw from in Chapter Five was done at the Georgetown University Child Development Center. I am grateful to the staff and especially to the mother and doctor for their permission to analyze and quote from their interaction.

Some of the research for this book was done while I was a Fellow at the Center for Advanced Study in the Behavioral Sciences in Stanford, California. In addition to the luxury of a quiet office with a lovely view and no telephone (but access to e-mail), and the ministrations of a large and uniformly helpful staff, the center provided the opportunity for enlightening discussions with other Fellows. Particularly helpful to me were conversations with George Cowgill, Dorothy Ross, Susan Watkins, and Richard Yarborough. I shall always be grateful for this yearlong taste of academic heaven, and for the financial support provided by the National Science Foundation SES-9022192 to the center.

Working with my editor, Sally Arteseros, was a revelation and a joy. I came to admire and trust her unfailingly wise and prompt editorial judgment. As always, my agent, Suzanne Gluck, has been a tireless advocate at every step.

My family is a continuing a source of strength. My sisters Miriam and Naomi provided specific discussions of their own experiences as well as general encouragement, and Naomi read an early draft and offered invaluable comments. My parents, Dorothy and Eli Tannen, also made comments on parts of the manuscript, about which my mother commented, with characteristic pithiness, "I read it for enjoyment; Daddy sits down with a pencil and paper to see what he can correct." Both his corrections and her enjoyment were of great value to me; my abiding appreciation for differing styles begins with them.

My husband, Michael Macovski, has been a companion and supporter in every way. It would be redundant to dedicate book after book to him, yet he is the one who has accompanied me on each of these journeys, during the nine years we have been together. I dedicate this book to his parents, for the love and unquestioning support they have shown me, and for having helped make their son who he is.

CONTENTS

PREFACE

In my mind, this book is the third in a series. In *That's Not What I Meant!: How Conversational Style Makes or Breaks Your Relations With Others,* I laid out the framework of conversational style that I have spent the last two decades researching. That framework is a linguistic approach to understanding relationships: People have different conversational styles, influenced by the part of the country they grew up in, their ethnic backgrounds and those of their parents, their age, class, and gender. But conversational style is invisible. Unaware that these and other aspects of our backgrounds influence our ways of talking, we think we are simply saying what we mean. Because we don't realize that others' styles are different, we are often frustrated in conversations. Rather than seeing the culprit as differing styles, we attribute troubles to others' intentions (she doesn't like me), abilities (he's stupid), or character (she's rude, he's inconsiderate), our own failure (what's wrong with me?), or the failure of a relationship (we just can't communicate).

In *You Just Don't Understand: Women and Men in Conversation*, I narrowed the focus to patterns of conversational style influenced by gender. Based on the assumption that we learn styles of interacting as children growing up, and that children tend to play in sex-separate groups in which very different styles are learned, practiced, and reinforced, the book proceeded from the metaphor of male-female conversation as cross-cultural communication.

The two earlier books are about private speaking, focusing primarily (though not exclusively) on one-on-one conversations between intimates and friends. This book is concerned with private speaking in a public context—the talk that goes on at work, particularly in offices. It is private in the sense that many of the conversations I analyze are still one-on-one, except for meetings and presentations. They are also "private" compared to the public contexts of speaking on radio or television, or giving a lecture. Yet the work setting is public, in that most of the people you talk to at work are not family you know intimately, nor friends or partners you have chosen, but strangers into whose midst you have been thrown by the circumstances of your job. Another way that work mixes public and private is simply a matter of time: Although our private relationships with family and friends are the center of our emotional lives, many of us spend more hours of our lives at work with colleagues and co-workers, some of whom eventually become friends or even family.

There is another sense in which talk at work is public. No matter how private a conversation is, in most work settings your performance will be evaluated at some point, by a boss, a board, a client, a colleague, or a subordinate. Conversations at work can be, in a sense, like a test. What we say as we do our work can become evidence on which we are judged, and the judgments may surface in the form of raises (or denials of raises), promotions (or their lack or their opposite), and favorable (or unfavorable) work assignments.

These three books make up what social scientists call an implicational hierarchy. Everything I said in *That's Not What I Meant!* applies to the two books that follow, and everything I wrote in *You Just Don't Understand* applies here, even though I obviously cannot repeat those books as a preface to this one. Although I may talk about "women" and "men," I am always aware, and remind readers to be aware, that—as *That's Not What I Meant!* shows in detail—gender is only one of many influences on conversational style. Each individual has a unique style, influenced by a personal history of many influences such as geographic region, ethnicity, class, sexual orientation, occupation, religion, and age— as well as a unique personality and spirit. Patterns that I describe are always a matter of degree, of a range on a continuum, not of absolute difference, when it comes to gender as well as the other influences and affiliations I just mentioned. In other words, our ways of talking are influenced by every aspect of our communities, so no two women or two men are exactly alike, any more than any two New Yorkers or Spaniards or forty-year-olds are necessarily alike. Yet understanding the patterns of influence on our styles is crucial to understanding what happens to us in our conversations—and our lives.

Although I am aware of the many influences on conversational style and have spent most of my career studying and writing about them, in this book, as in *You Just Don't Understand,* style differences influenced by gender receive particular attention. This is not only because these are the differences people most want to hear about (although this is so and is a factor), but also because there is something fundamental about our categorization by gender. When you spot a person walking down the street toward you, you immediately and automatically identify that person as male or female. You will not necessarily try to determine which state they are from, what their class background is, or what country their grandparents came from. A secondary identification, in some places and times, may be about race. But, while we may envision a day when a director will be able to cast actors for a play without reference to race, can we imagine a time when actors can be cast without reference to their sex?

Few elements of our identities come as close to our sense of who we are as gender. If you mistake people's cultural background—you thought they were Greek, but they turn out to be Italian; you assumed they'd grown up in Texas, but it turns out they're from Kentucky; you say "Merry Christmas" and they say, "we don't celebrate Christmas; we're Muslim"—it catches you off guard and you rearrange the mental frame through which you view them. But if someone you thought was male turns out to be female—like the jazz musician Billy Tipton, whose own adopted sons never suspected that their father was a woman until the coroner broke the news to them after his (her) death—the required adjustment is staggering. Even infants discriminate between males and females and react differently depending on which they confront.

Perhaps it is because our sense of gender is so deeply rooted that people are inclined to hear descriptions of gender *patterns* as statements about gender *identity*—in other words, as absolute differences rather than a matter of degree and percentages, and as universal rather than culturally mediated. The patterns I describe are based on observations of particular speakers in a particular place and time: mostly (but not exclusively) middle-class Americans of European background working in offices at the present time. Other cultures evince very different patterns of talk associated with gender—and correspondingly different assumptions about the "natures" of women and men. I don't put a lot of store in talk about "natures" or what is "natural." People in every culture will tell you that the behaviors common in their own culture are "natural." I also don't put a lot of store in people's explanations that their way of talking is a natural response to their environment, as there is always an equally natural and opposite way of responding to the same environment. We all tend to regard the way things are as the way things have to be—as only natural.

The reason ways of talking, like other ways of conducting our daily lives, come to seem natural is that the behaviors that make up our lives are ritualized. Indeed, the "ritual" character of interaction is at the heart of this book. Having grown up in a particular culture, we learn to do things as the people we encounter do them, so the vast majority of our decisions about how to speak become automatic. You see someone you know, you ask "How are you?," chat, then take your leave, never pausing to ponder the many ways you could handle this interaction differently—and would, if you lived in a different culture. Just as an American automatically extends a hand for a handshake while a Japanese automatically bows, what the American and Japanese find it natural to say is a matter of convention learned over a lifetime.

No one understood the ritual nature of everyday life better than sociologist Erving Goffman, who also understood the fundamental role played by gender in organizing our daily rituals. In his article "The Arrangement Between the Sexes," Goffman pointed out that we tend to say "sex-linked" when what we mean is "sex-class-linked." When hearing that a behavior is "sex-linked," people often conclude that the behavior is to be found in every individual of that group, and that it is somehow inherent in their sex, as if it came hooked to a chromosome. Goffman suggests the term "genderism" (on the model, I assume, of "mannerism," not of "sexism") for "a sex-class linked individual behavioral practice." This is the spirit in which I intend references to gendered patterns of behavior: not to imply that there is anything inherently male or female about particular ways of talking, nor to claim that every individual man or woman adheres to the pattern, but rather to observe that a larger percentage of women or men *as a group* talk in a particular way, or individual women and men *are more likely* to talk one way or the other.

That individuals do not always fit the pattern associated with their gender does not mean that the pattern is not typical. Because more women or men speak in a particular way, that way of speaking becomes associated with women or men—or, rather, it is the other way around: More women or men learn to speak particular ways *because* those ways are associated with their own gender.

15

And individual men or women who speak in ways associated with the other gender will pay a price for departing from cultural expectations.

If my concept of how gender displays itself in everyday life has been influenced by Goffman, the focus of my research—talk—and my method for studying it grow directly out of my own discipline, linguistics. My understanding of what goes on when people talk to each other is based on observing and listening as well as tape-recording, transcribing, and analyzing conversation. In response to my book *You Just Don't Understand,* I was contacted by people at many companies who asked whether I could help them apply the insights in that book to the problem of "the glass ceiling": Why weren't women advancing as quickly as the men who were hired at the same time? And more generally, they wanted to understand how to integrate women as well as others who were historically not "typical" employees into the increasingly diverse workforce. I realized that in order to offer insight, I needed to observe what was really going on in the workplace.

I approached this in a number of ways. At some companies, I followed individuals around, sitting in on formal interactions like meetings as well as informal ones like chats at the coffee machine and lunch. At other companies, I undertook more formal research in which individuals volunteered to tape-record their conversations. I was not present at these tapings, so my presence would not interfere with what was going on (although I realize that the presence of a tape recorder can be an intrusion that results in distortion too). I also spent time shadowing the individuals, to become familiar with the settings they worked in and who was who, and to get my own impressions of the situation and the people. Later, I had the taped conversations transcribed, and then I examined the transcripts and listened to the tapes.

Finally, at all these companies, and in other companies and contexts, I talked at length to individuals and in many cases tape-recorded our conversations. In a sense, these were interviews, but I did not go in with a list of questions. There were, however, certain questions I usually asked, such as "What are your impressions of

PREFACE

the people you work with?"; "What is your idea of a good manager?"; and "Looking back on your work life, what were some of your best and worst experiences with managers or with people you managed?" I also drew on my own experience and the experiences of friends, family, and chance acquaintances who happened to tell me incidents from their own lives.

My students, too, are invaluable sources of examples and insights. I have drawn (always with acknowledgment) on material they provided in class assignments, term papers, and notebooks I ask them to keep in which they record experiences and their analyses of them. Finally, I refer to the research of others. I have not attempted to give a comprehensive review of the literature (such an endeavor would constitute a book in itself), but have simply selected a few studies that dramatize points I consider important. I offer apologies to the many researchers who have done relevant studies that I have not cited.

Since the publication of *You Just Don't Understand,* I have often been told, "Your book saved my marriage." Clashing conversational styles can wreak havoc at the conference table as well as at the breakfast table, with consequences as frustrating and even more dangerous, since people's welfare and even lives can be at stake. Everyone's frustration will be reduced, and companies as well as individuals will benefit, if we all begin to understand and accept each other's styles. In this spirit, I hope this book will give similar support to people who are struggling with co-workers, with jobs, and with companies. That is the reason I now turn my attention to talking at work.

A NOTE ON NOTES
AND TRANSCRIPTION

Since my training is as a scholar, I believe it is important to give credit whenever I write something that was informed or inspired by someone else's writing, and to tell readers how they can track down my references or get more information on a topic that interests them. This requires footnotes. I have followed the convention of trade books and include notes at the end of the book, but these notes are not flagged by numbers in the text. I know this will frustrate those readers who want to know whenever a statement is accompanied by a note; to them I offer apologies and the following explanation: A majority of readers find little numbers distracting; many feel compelled to interrupt their reading and search for the note, then feel tricked when the note offers only bibliographical information about which they care little. For those who do care, whenever I quote someone, I provide information on where that source is to be found in notes and/or references. If the source is a book or article and I am citing only one book or article by a partic-ular author, I simply include the source in the References section at the end of the book. Since the References are listed alphabetically by author, finding sources there should be easier than searching for the right page for notes.

A word also is in order on transcription. Conversational tran-scripts are the stock in trade of sociolinguists, and we have devel-oped conventions intended to capture, as much as possible, how the dialogue sounded. Three dots separated by spaces (. . .) show that something has been omitted, but three unspaced dots (...) indi-cate a slight pause. When a bit of talk was inaudible, it is repre-sented by a question mark in slashes: /?/. Uncertain transcription is also surrounded /by slashes/. Words are always written as the speaker spoke them, without correcting for written "grammar."

ONE

Women and Men
Talking on the Job

Amy was a manager with a problem: She had just read a final report written by Donald, and she felt it was woefully inadequate. She faced the unsavory task of telling him to do it over. When she met with Donald, she made sure to soften the blow by beginning with praise, telling him everything about his report that was good. Then she went on to explain what was lacking and what needed to be done to make it acceptable. She was pleased with the diplomatic way she had managed to deliver the bad news. Thanks to her thoughtfulness in starting with praise, Donald was able to listen to the criticism and seemed to understand what was needed. But when the revised report appeared on her desk, Amy was shocked. Donald had made only minor, superficial changes, and none of the necessary ones. The next meeting with him did not go well. He was incensed that she was now telling him his report was not acceptable and accused her of having misled him. "You told me before it was fine," he protested.

Amy thought she had been diplomatic; Donald thought she had been dishonest. The praise she intended to soften the message "This is unacceptable" sounded to him like the message itself: "This is fine." So what she regarded as the main point—the needed changes—came across to him as optional suggestions, because he had already registered her praise as the main point. She felt he hadn't listened to her. He thought she had changed her mind and was making him pay the price.

Work days are filled with conversations about getting the job done. Most of these conversations succeed, but too many end in impasses like this. It could be that Amy is a capricious boss whose wishes are whims, and it could be that Donald is a temperamental employee who can't hear criticism no matter how it is phrased. But I don't think either was the case in this instance. I believe this was one of innumerable misunderstandings caused by differences in conversational style. Amy delivered the criticism in a way that seemed to her self-evidently considerate, a way she would have preferred to receive criticism herself: taking into account the other person's feelings, making sure he knew that her ultimate negative assessment of his report didn't mean she had no appreciation of his abilities. She offered the praise as a sweetener to help the nasty-tasting news go down. But Donald didn't expect criticism to be delivered in that way, so he mistook the praise as her overall assessment rather than a preamble to it.

This conversation could have taken place between two women or two men. But I do not think it is a coincidence that it occurred between a man and a woman. This book will explain why. First, it gives a view of the role played by talk in our work lives. To do this, I show the workings of conversational style, explaining the ritual nature of conversation and the confusion that arises when rituals are not shared and therefore not recognized as such. I take into account the many influences on conversational

22

style, but I focus in particular on the differing rituals that typify women and men (although, of course, not all individual men and women behave in ways that are typical). Conversational rituals common among men often involve using opposition such as banter, joking, teasing, and playful put-downs, and expending effort to avoid the one-down position in the interaction. Conversational rituals common among women are often ways of maintaining an appearance of equality, taking into account the effect of the exchange on the other person, and expending effort to downplay the speakers' authority so they can get the job done without flexing their muscles in an obvious way.

When everyone present is familiar with these conventions, they work well. But when ways of speaking are not recognized as conventions, they are taken literally, with negative results on both sides. Men whose oppositional strategies are interpreted literally may be seen as hostile when they are not, and their efforts to ensure that they avoid appearing one-down may be taken as arrogance. When women use conversational strategies designed to avoid appearing boastful and to take the other person's feelings into account, they may be seen as less confident and competent than they really are. As a result, both women and men often feel they are not getting sufficient credit for what they have done, are not being listened to, are not getting ahead as fast as they should.

When I talk about women's and men's characteristic ways of speaking, I always emphasize that both styles make sense and are equally valid in themselves, though the difference in styles may cause trouble in interaction. In a sense, when two people form a private relationship of love or friendship, the bubble of their interaction is a world unto itself, even though they both come with the prior experience of their families, their community, and a lifetime of conversations. But someone who takes a job is entering a world that is already functioning, with its own characteristic style already in place. Although there are many influences such as regional background, the type of industry involved, whether it is a family business or a large corporation, in general, workplaces that have previously had men in positions of power have already established male-style interaction as the norm. In that sense, women, and others whose styles are different, are not starting out equal, but are at a disadvantage. Though talking at work is quite similar to talking in private, it is a very different enterprise in many ways.

WHEN NOT ASKING DIRECTIONS IS
DANGEROUS TO YOUR HEALTH

If conversational-style differences lead to troublesome outcomes in work as well as private settings, there are some work settings where the outcomes of style are a matter of life and death. Health-care professionals are often in such situations. So are airline pilots.

Of all the examples of women's and men's characteristic styles that I discussed in *You Just Don't Understand,* the one that (to my surprise) attracted the most attention was the question "Why don't men like to stop and ask for directions?" Again and again, in the responses of audiences, talk-show hosts, letter writers, journalists, and conversationalists, this question seemed to crystallize the frustration many people had experienced in their own lives. And my explanation seems to have rung true: that men are more likely to be aware that asking for directions, or for any kind of help, puts them in a one-down position.

With regard to asking directions, women and men are keenly aware of the advantages of their own style. Women frequently observe how much time they would save if their husbands simply stopped and asked someone instead of driving around trying in vain to find a destination themselves. But I have also been told by men that it makes sense not to ask directions because you learn a lot about a neighborhood, as well as about navigation, by driving around and finding your own way.

But some situations are more risky than others. A Hollywood talk-show producer told me that she had been flying with her father in his private airplane when he was running out of gas and uncertain about the precise location of the local landing strip he was heading for. Beginning to panic, the woman said, "Daddy! Why don't you radio the control tower and ask them where to land?" He answered, "I don't want them to think I'm lost." This story had a happy ending, else the woman would not have been alive to tell it to me.

Some time later, I repeated this anecdote to a man at a cocktail party—a man who had just told me that the bit about directions was his favorite part of my book, and who, it turned out, was also an amateur pilot. He then went on to tell me that he had had a similar experience. When learning to fly, he got lost on his first solo flight. He did not want to humiliate himself by tuning his radio to the FAA emergency frequency and asking for help, so he flew around looking for a place to land. He spotted an open area that looked like a landing field, headed for it—and found himself de-planing in what seemed like a deliberately hidden landing strip that was mercifully deserted at the time. Fearing he had stumbled upon an enterprise he was not supposed to be aware of, let alone poking around in, he climbed back into the plane, relieved that he had not gotten into trouble. He managed to find his way back to his home airport as well, before he ran out of gas. He maintained, however, that he was certain that more than a few small-plane crashes have occurred because other amateur pilots who did not want to admit they were lost were less lucky. In light of this, the amusing question of why men prefer not to stop and ask for directions stops being funny.

The moral of the story is not that men should immediately change and train themselves to ask directions when they're in doubt, any more than women should immediately stop asking directions and start honing their navigational skills by finding their way on their own. The moral is flexibility: Sticking to habit in the face of all challenges is not so smart if it ends up getting you killed. If we all understood our own styles and knew their limits and their alternatives, we'd be better off—especially at work, where the results of what we do have repercussions for co-workers and the company, as well as for our own futures.

To Ask or Not to Ask

An intern on duty at a hospital had a decision to make. A patient had been admitted with a condition he recognized, and he recalled the appropriate medication. But that medication was recommended for a number of conditions, in different dosages. He wasn't quite sure what dose was right for this condition. He had to make a quick decision: Would he interrupt the supervising resident during a meeting to check the dose, or would he make his best guess and go for it?

What was at stake? First and foremost, the welfare, and maybe even the life, of the patient. But something else was at stake too—the reputation, and eventually the career, of the intern. If he interrupted the resident to ask about the dosage, he was making a public statement about what he didn't know, as well as making himself something of a nuisance. In this case, he went with his guess, and there were no negative effects. But, as with small-plane crashes, one wonders how many medical errors have resulted from decisions to guess rather than ask.

It is clear that not asking questions can have disastrous consequences in medical settings, but asking questions can also have negative consequences. A physician wrote to me about a related experience that occurred during her medical training. She received a low grade from her supervising physician. It took her by surprise because she knew that she was one of the best interns in her group. She asked her supervisor for an explanation, and he replied that she didn't know as much as the others. She knew from her day-to-day dealings with her peers that she was one of the most knowledgeable, not the least. So she asked what evidence had led him to his conclusion. And he told her, "You ask more questions."

There is evidence that men are less likely to ask questions in a public situation, where asking will reveal their lack of knowledge. One such piece of evidence is a study done in a university classroom, where sociolinguist Kate Remlinger noticed that women students asked the professor more questions than men students did.

As part of her study, Remlinger interviewed six students at length, three men and three women. All three men told her that they would not ask questions in class if there was something they did not understand. Instead, they said they would try to find the answer later by reading the textbook, asking a friend, or, as a last resort, asking the professor in private during office hours. As one young man put it, "If it's vague to me, I usually don't ask. I'd rather go home and look it up."

Of course, this does not mean that no men will ask questions when they are in doubt, nor that all women will; the differences, as always, are a matter of likelihood and degree. As always, cultural differences play a role too. It is not unusual for American professors to admit their own ignorance when they do not know the answer to a student's question, but there are many cultures in which professors would not, and students from those cultures may judge American professors by those standards. A student from the Middle East told a professor at a California university that she had just lost all respect for one of his colleagues. The reason: She had asked a question in class, and the offending professor had replied, "I don't know offhand, but I'll find out for you."

The physician who asked her supervisor why he gave her a negative evaluation may be unusual in having been told directly what behavior led to the misjudgment of her skill. But in talking to doctors and doctors-in-training around the country, I have learned that there is nothing exceptional about her experience, that it is common for interns and residents to conceal their ignorance by not asking questions, since those who do ask are judged less capable. Yet it seems that many women who are more likely than men to ask questions (just as women are more likely to stop and ask for directions when they're lost) are unaware that they may make a negative impression at the same time that they get information. Their antennae have not been attuned to making sure they don't appear one-down.

This pattern runs counter to two stereotypes about male and female styles: that men are more focused on information and that women are more sensitive. In regard to classroom behavior, it seems that the women who ask questions are more focused on information, whereas the men who refrain from doing so are more focused on interaction—the impression their asking will make on others. In this situation, it is the men who are more sensitive to the impression made on others by their behavior, although their concern is, ultimately, the effect on themselves rather than on others. And this sensitivity is likely to make them look better in the world of work. Realizing this puts the intern's decision in a troubling perspective. He had to choose between putting his career at risk and putting the patient's health at risk.

It is easy to see benefits of both styles: Someone willing to ask questions has ready access to a great deal of information—all that is known by the people she can ask. But just as men have told me that asking directions is useless since the person you ask may not know and may give you the wrong answer, some people feel they are more certain to get the right information if they read it in a book, and they are learning more by finding it themselves. On the other hand, energy may be wasted looking up information someone else has at hand, and I have heard complaints from people who feel they were sent on wild-goose chases by colleagues who didn't want to admit they really were not sure of what they pretended to know.

The reluctance to say "I don't know" can have serious consequences for an entire company—and did: On Friday, June 17, 1994, a computer problem prevented Fidelity Investments from calculating the value of 166 mutual funds. Rather than report that the values for these funds were not available, a manager decided to report to the National Association of Securities Dealers that the values of these funds had not changed from the day before. Unfortunately, June 17 turned out to be a bad day in the financial markets, so the values of Fidelity's funds that were published in newspapers around the country stood out as noticeably higher than those of other funds. Besides the cost and inconvenience to brokerage firms who had to re-compute their customers' accounts, and the injustice to investors who made decisions to buy or sell based on inaccurate information, the company was mightily embarrassed and forced to apologize publicly. Clearly this was an instance in which it would have been preferable to say, "We don't know."

Flexibility, again, is key. There are many situations in which it serves one well to be self-reliant and discreet about revealing doubt or ignorance, and others in which it is wise to admit what you don't know.

NEGOTIATING FROM THE INSIDE OUT OR THE OUTSIDE IN

Two co-workers who were on very friendly terms with each other were assigned to do a marketing survey together. When they got the assignment, the man began by saying, "I'll do the airline and automobile industry, and you can do the housewares and direct-mail market." The woman was taken aback. "Hey," she said. "It sounds like you've got it all figured out. As a matter of fact, *I'd* like to do airlines and autos. I've already got a lot of contacts in those areas." "Oh," he said, a little chagrined and a lot surprised. She continued, "I wish you wouldn't come on so strong." "Well, how would you have started?" he asked. She said, "I wouldn't have just said what I wanted to do. I would have asked, 'What parts do you want to do?' " This made no sense to him. "Then what are you complaining about? If you had asked me what parts I wanted to do, I would have said, 'I'll do the airlines and autos.' We would have ended up in the same place anyway."

The woman saw his point. But if the conversation had gone that way, she still would have been frustrated. To her, the question "What parts of the survey would you like to do?" is not an invitation to grab the parts he wants and run away with them. It's an invitation to talk about the various parts—which ones interest him, which he has experience in, which he would like to learn more about. Then he would ask, "What do you want to do?" and she would say what interests her, where her experience lies, and where she'd like to get more experience. Finally, they would divvy up the parts in a way that gave them both some of what they wanted, while taking advantage of both their expertise.

Making decisions is a crucial part of any workday. Daily, weekly, monthly, decisions must be made with never enough information and never enough time. People have very different ways of reaching decisions, and none is clearly better than others. But when two people with different styles have to make decisions together, both styles may have worse results than either would have if their styles were shared, unless the differences are understood and accommodated.

Beginning by stating what you will do is a style of negotiating that starts inside and works its way out. If others have different ideas, you expect them to say so, and you'll negotiate. Opening with a question like "What would you like to do?" or "What do you think?" is a style that begins by being vague and works its way in. It specifically invites others to express their perspective. Either style can work well. What makes the machine go TILT! is the difference in styles. Someone who expects negotiation to proceed from the inside and work its way out hears a vague question as an invitation to decide; someone who tends to negotiate from the outside in hears a specific claim as a nonnegotiable demand. In this sense, both styles are indirect—they depend on an unspoken understanding of how the subsequent conversation is expected to go. This is a sense in which conversation is ritualized: It follows a preset sequencing scheme that seems self-evidently appropriate.

WHEN IS THE WAGE GAP A COMMUNICATION GAP?

There are those who claim that what's really important is economic issues like the salary gap—equal pay for equal work. Why do women still make less than men, on the average, and why, if efforts are made to equalize salaries in a given setting, is it only a few years before the women's pay once again falls behind? This too can be a matter of ways of speaking, since anything you get depends on talking.

Marjorie and Lawrence Nadler suspected that getting raises, promotions, and other advantages depends on people's ability to negotiate, and that women might be at a disadvantage in this regard. They tested this by asking 174 students to role-play negotiations for salary, and sure enough, they found that the women in their study ended up with lower raises than men. The researchers turned up a slew of other fascinating results too: On the average, male students role-playing supervisors gave lower raises than females in the same role, even though the males started out by offering more than the females. In other words, the women playing supervisors raised their offers much more as a result of negotiation. Even more interesting, and more worrisome, male students playing supervisors ended up giving higher raises to male student-subordinates, though this may be related to the fact that male student-subordinates made higher initial demands than females did. In the end, the lowest raises were negotiated by female students playing subordinates in negotiation with males as bosses.

This does not mean that differences in ways of speaking are the only reason for the salary gap. Nadler and Nadler found not only that men in their role-plays ended up with higher raises than women as the outcome of negotiation, but that men were offered higher raises *to start with, before* negotiation. Most distressing, the lowest initial offers were made by female students playing supervisors negotiating with females as subordinates. It could be that the women started with low offers to women because they knew they would raise the offers as a result of negotiation. In the end, the researchers found that higher final offers were made when the negotiators were of the same sex.

A real-life incident sheds light on another phenomenon that could affect relative wages. Doreen had advanced gradually but inexorably up the ladder in her company, until she held one of the highest positions in the firm. She had advanced at each stage along with Dennis, who had been hired at the same time as she. It seemed that the executives at the top were reluctant to give her a promotion or raise unless they felt that Dennis merited the same recognition, even though their jobs were by now quite different, and hers

31

involved more responsibility as well as a higher operating budget. At one point, when she asked for a raise to bring her salary up to that of the other managers who had jobs comparable to hers, she was told that the firm couldn't manage raises for her and Dennis at that time. Doreen was taken aback by the reference to Dennis; she had simply asked about her own salary. But she was also enlightened; this tipped her off that her bosses regarded the two of them together and did not feel they could let her salary get ahead of his.

It may well be that some people have a gut-level, not-logically-thought-out sense that women should get less, either because they are expected to have lower abilities, or because they do not display their abilities, or because their rank and salaries are being measured against those of other women rather than their male peers. There may also be an unarticulated sense that women need less: Whether or not an individual woman is self-supporting or the main or sole support of her family, the image of a woman does not readily suggest "breadwinner."

All of this is to say that results like the salary gap may result from a range of factors, including ways of speaking as well as preconceptions about women and men.

MORE ON NEGOTIATING STYLES

The managers of a medium-size company got the go-ahead to hire a human-resources coordinator, and two managers who worked well together were assigned to make the choice. As it turned out, Maureen and Harold favored different applicants, and both felt strongly about their preferences. Maureen argued with assurance and vigor that the person she wanted to hire was the most creative and innovative, and that he had the most appropriate experience. Harold argued with equal conviction that the applicant he favored had a vision of management that fit with the company's, whereas her candidate might be a thorn in their side. They traded arguments for some time, neither convincing the other. Then Harold said that hiring the applicant Maureen wanted would make him so uncomfortable that he would have to consider resigning. Maureen respected Harold. What's more, she liked him and considered him a friend. So she felt that his admission of such strong feelings had to be taken into account. She said what seemed to her the only thing she could say under the circumstances: "Well, I certainly don't want you to feel uncomfortable here; you're one of the pillars of the place. If you feel that strongly about it, I can't argue with that." Harold's choice was hired.

In this case, the decision-making power went not to the manager who had the highest rank in the firm (their positions were parallel) and not necessarily to the one whose judgment was best, but to the one whose arguing strategies were most effective in the negotiation. Maureen was an ardent and persuasive advocate for her view, but she assumed that she and Harold would have to come to an agreement in order to make a decision, and that she had to take his feelings into account. Since Harold would not back down, she did. Most important, when he argued that he would have to quit if she got her way, she felt she had no option but to yield.

What was crucial was not Maureen's and Harold's individual styles in isolation but how their styles interacted—how they played in concert with the other's style. Harold's threat to quit ensured his triumph—when used with someone who would not call his bluff. If he had been arguing with someone who regarded this threat as simply another move in the negotiation rather than as a nonnegotiable expression of deep feelings that had to be respected, the result might have been different. For example, had she said, "That's ridiculous; of course you're not going to quit!" or "If that's how shallow your commitment to this firm is, then we'd be better off without you," the decision might well have gone the other way.

When you talk to someone whose style is similar to yours, you can fairly well predict the response you are going to get. But when you talk to someone whose style is different, you can't predict, and often can't make sense of, the response. Hearing the reaction you get, if it's not the one you expected, often makes you regret what you said. Harold later told Maureen that he was sorry he had used the argument he did. In retrospect he was embarrassed, even a bit ashamed of himself. His retrospective chagrin was like what you feel if you slam down something in anger and are surprised and regretful to see that it breaks. You wanted to make a gesture, but you didn't expect it to come out with such force. Harold regretted what he said precisely because it caused Maureen to back down so completely. He'd known he was upping the ante—he felt he had to do something to get them out of the loop of recycling arguments they were in—but he had not expected it to end the negotiation summarily; he expected Maureen to meet his move with a balancing move of her own. He did not predict the impact that personalizing his argument would have on her. For her part, Maureen did not think of Harold's threat as just another move in a negotiable argument; she heard it as a personal plea that she could not reject. Their different approaches to negotiation put her at a disadvantage in negotiating with him.

"HOW CERTAIN ARE YOU OF THAT?"

Negotiating is only one kind of activity that is accomplished through talk at work. Other kinds of decision-making are also based as much on ways of talking as on the content of the arguments. The CEO of a corporation explained to me that he regularly has to make decisions based on insufficient information—and making decisions is a large part of his work life. Much of his day is spent hearing brief presentations following which he must either approve or reject a course of action. He has to make a judgment in five minutes about issues the presenters have worked on for months. "I decide," he explained, "based on how confident they seem. If they seem very confident, I call it a go. If they seem unsure, I figure it's too risky and nix it."

Here is where the rule of competence and the role of communication go hand in hand. Confidence, after all, is an internal feeling. How can you judge others' confidence? The only evidence you have to go on is circumstantial—how they talk about what they know. You judge by a range of signs, including facial expression and body posture, but most of all, speech. Do they hesitate? Do they speak up or swallow half their words? Is their tone of voice declamatory or halting? Do they make bald statements ("This is a winner! We've got to go for it!") or hedge ("Um ... from what I can tell, I think it'll work, but we'll never know for sure until we try")? This seems simple enough. Surely, you can tell how confident people are by paying attention to how they speak, just as you can tell when someone is lying.

Well, maybe not. Psychologist Paul Ekman has spent years studying lying, and he has found that most people are very sure they can tell when others are lying. The only trouble is, most can't. With a few thus-far inexplicable exceptions, people who tell him they are absolutely sure they can tell if someone is lying are as likely to be wrong as to be right—and he has found this to be as true for judges as for the rest of us.

In the same way, our ability to determine how confident others are is probably quite limited. The CEO who does not take into account the individual styles of the people who make presentations to him will find it difficult, if not impossible, to make the best judgment. Different people will talk very differently, not because of the absolute level of their confidence or lack of it, but because of their habitual ways of speaking. There are those who sound sure of themselves even when inside they're not sure at all, and others who sound tentative even when they're very sure indeed. So being aware of differences in ways of speaking is a prerequisite for making good decisions as well as good presentations.

FEASTING ON HUMBLE PIE

Although these factors affecting decision-making are the same for men and women, and every individual has his or her own style, it seems that women are more likely to downplay their certainty, men more likely to downplay their doubts. From childhood, girls learn to temper what they say so as not to sound too aggressive—which means too certain. From the time they are little, most girls learn that sounding too sure of themselves will make them unpopular with their peers. Groups of girls, as researchers who have studied girls at play have found, will penalize and even ostracize a girl who seems too sure she's right. Anthropologist Marjorie Harness Goodwin found that girls criticize other girls who stand out by saying, "She thinks she's cute," or "She thinks she's something." Talking in ways that display self-confidence are not approved for girls.

It is not only peers who disapprove of girls talking in ways that call attention to their accomplishments. Adults too can be critical of such behavior in girls, as was a woman who wrote a letter that was published in a magazine. The letter-writer was responding to an article about a ten-year-old girl named Heather DeLoach who became a child celebrity by tap-dancing in a bee costume on a rock video. Heather was portrayed in the magazine as still being awed by others' fame ("I got to meet Pauly Shore and Janet Jackson, and I got Madonna's autograph, but I wasn't allowed to take pictures") and unawed by her own ("I see myself so much on TV that when the Bee Girl comes on, I just click right through the channel"). Sounding very much like other girls, she hedged when mentioning her good grades ("sort of like straight-A"). But she was also quoted as saying, "I'm extremely talented. I guess when the director first set eyes on me, he liked me. I try my best to be an actress, and I'm just great. I'm the one and only Bee Girl."

Although the article did not explain what question the interviewer asked to elicit Heather's truthful description of herself, the disapproving reader zeroed in on those words and admonished, "Heather DeLoach, the Bee Girl, describes herself as 'extremely talented' and 'just great.' Perhaps 10-year-old Heather should stop being a *bumble*bee and start being a *humble* bee." Not only did this reader tell the child star to start being more humble, but she also told her to stop being a bumblebee—that is, doing what she's so good at that it's bringing her attention, reward, and too much—or too obvious—self-confidence.

Reactions like these teach girls how they are expected to talk in order to be liked. It is not surprising that when she spoke in this guileless way, Heather DeLoach was ten. By the time she gets through junior high school and puberty, chances are she will have learned to talk differently, a transformation—and loss of confidence—that white middle-class American girls experience at that stage of their lives, according to a great deal of current research. But it is crucial to bear in mind that ways of talking are not literal representations of mental states, and refraining from boasting may not reveal a true lack of confidence. A pair of studies by a team of psychologists makes this clear.

Laurie Heatherington and her colleagues had student experimenters ask hundreds of incoming college students to predict how they thought their first year at college would go by forecasting the grades they expected to get. In some cases, the predictions were made anonymously: They were put in writing and placed in an envelope. In others, they were made publicly, either orally to the experimenter or by writing on a paper that the experimenter promptly read. The researchers found that women predicted lower grades for themselves than men did—but only when they made their predictions publicly. The predictions the women students made in private did not differ from the men's, just as the grades they actually earned as the year progressed did not differ from the men's. In other words, their lower predictions evidenced not lack of confidence but reluctance to reveal the level of confidence they felt.

The same researchers conducted a second study that captured women's characteristic balancing act between their own interests and those of the person they are talking to. In half the cases, the experimenters told their own grade-point averages to the students they interviewed, and the grades they claimed to have gotten were comparatively low. Lo and behold, when women students thought they were talking to someone who had gotten low grades, they lowered their predictions of what they expected their own grades to be. Whether or not the experimenter claimed to have gotten low grades did not affect the predictions made by men students.

The first of these ingenious experiments dramatizes that the social inhibition against seeming to boast can make women appear less confident than they really are. And the second study shows that part of the reason many women censor themselves from proclaiming their confidence is that they are balancing their own interests with those of the person they are talking to. In other words, they modify their speech to take into account the impact of what they say on the other person's feelings.

There may be something peculiarly white middle class and American about the cultural constraint against women boasting. Those who have studied the remarkable change in how girls talk about their own talents and prospects during the crucial junior high school years have noted that the pattern is not necessarily found, or is not as strong, among black American teenage girls. And anthropologist Thomas Kochman notes that talking about one's own accomplishments can be a highly valued source of humor for members of the cultural group he calls "community blacks," as illustrated by the widely publicized self-congratulatory verbal performances of the African-American prizefighter Muhammad Ali. But every culture makes distinctions that outsiders may miss. Kochman contrasts acceptable African-American "boasting" to the kind of self-aggrandizement that is negatively sanctioned by the same community as "bragging."[6]

To emphasize the cultural relativity of attitudes toward boasting, I should mention, too, the reaction of a British man who was certain that in his country, a boy who spoke like Heather DeLoach would be as likely as a girl to be chastised. Indeed, this Briton remarked, the British often find Americans annoyingly boastful.

For middle-class American women, though, the constraint is clear: Talking about your own accomplishments in a way that calls attention to yourself is not acceptable. This social constraint became both a source of criticism and a dodge for figure-skater Nancy Kerrigan when an inordinate amount of media attention was focused on her during the 1994 winter Olympics. *Newsweek* magazine called her "ungracious" for saying of her own performance, "I was flawless," and of her competitor's, "Oksana wasn't clean." But when a microphone picked up what Kerrigan thought was private grumbling about how "corny" and "dumb" it was to parade through Disney World with life-size cartoon characters, her "handlers" issued a statement that "she was referring merely to her mom's insistence that she wear her silver medal. She feared it would 'look like bragging.' "

The expectation that women should not display their own accomplishments brings us back to the matter of negotiating that is so important in the workplace. A man who owned a medium-sized company remarked that women who came to ask him for raises often supported their requests by pointing to a fellow worker on the same level who earned more. He considered this a weak bargaining strategy because he could always identify a different co-worker at that level who earned less. They would do better, he felt, to argue for a raise on the basis of how valuable their own work is to the company. Yet it is likely that many women would be less comfortable "blowing their own horn" than making a claim based on fairness.

FOLLOW THE LEADER

Similar expectations constrain how girls express leadership. Being a leader often involves giving directions to others, but girls who tell other girls what to do are called "bossy." It is not that girls do not exert influence on their group—of course they do—but, as anthropologists like Marjorie Harness Goodwin have found, many girls discover they get better results if they phrase their ideas as suggestions rather than orders, and if they give reasons for their suggestions in terms of the good of the group. But while these ways of talking make girls—and, later, women—more likable, they make women seem less competent and self-assured in the world of work. And women who do seem competent and self-assured are as much in danger of being negatively labeled as are girls. After her retirement, Margaret Thatcher was described in the press as "bossy." Whereas girls are ready to stick this label on each other because they don't think any girl should boss the others around, it seems odd to apply it to Thatcher, who, after all, was the boss. And this is the rub: Standards of behavior applied to women are based on roles that do not include being boss.

Boys are expected to play by different rules, since the social organization of boys is different. Boys' groups tend to be more obviously hierarchical: Someone is one-up, and someone is one-down. Boys don't typically accuse each other of being "bossy" because the high-status boys are expected to give orders and push the low-status boys around. Daniel Maltz and Ruth Borker summarize research by many scholars showing that boys tend to jockey for center stage, challenge those who get it, and deflect challenges. Giving orders and telling the others what to do are ways of getting and keeping the high-status role. Another way of getting high status is taking center stage by telling stories, jokes, and information. Along with this, many boys learn to state their opinions in the strongest possible terms and find out if they're wrong by seeing if others challenge them. These ways of talking translate into an impression of confidence.

The styles typical of women and men both make sense given the context in which they were learned, but they have very different consequences in the workplace. In order to avoid being put in the one-down position, many men have developed strategies for making sure they get the one-up position instead, and this results in ways of talking that serve them well when it comes to hiring and promotion. In relation to the examples I have given, women are more likely to speak in the styles that are less effective in getting recognized and promoted. But if they speak in the styles that are effective when used by men—being assertive, sounding sure of themselves, talking up what they have done to make sure they get credit for it—they run the risk that everyone runs if they do not fit their culture's expectations for appropriate behavior: They will not be liked and may even be seen as having psychological problems.

Both women and men pay a price if they do not behave in ways expected of their gender: Men who are not very aggressive are called "wimps," whereas women who are not very aggressive are called "feminine." Men who are aggressive are called "go-get-ters," though if they go too far, from the point of view of the viewer, they may be called "arrogant." This can hurt them, but not nearly as much as the innumerable labels for women who are thought to be too aggressive—starting with the most hurtful one: bitch.

Even the compliments that we receive are revealing. One woman who had designed and implemented a number of innovative programs was praised by someone who said, "You have such a gentle way of bringing about radical change that people don't realize what's happening—or don't get threatened by it." This was a compliment, but it also hinted at the downside of the woman's gentle touch: Although it made it possible for her to be effective in instituting the changes she envisioned, her unobtrusive style ensured a lack of recognition. If people don't realize what's happening, they won't give her credit for what she has accomplished.

Not only advancement and recognition, but hiring is affected by ways of speaking. A woman who supervised three computer programmers mentioned that her best employee was another woman whom she had hired over the objections of her own boss. Her boss had preferred a male candidate, because he felt the man would be better able to step into her supervisory role if needed. But she had taken a dislike to the male candidate. For one thing, she had felt he was inappropriately flirtatious with her. But most important, she had found him arrogant, because he spoke as if he already had the job, using the pronoun "we" to refer to the group that had not yet hired him.

I have no way of knowing whether the woman hired was indeed the better of these two candidates, or whether either she or the man was well suited to assume the supervisory role, but I am intrigued that the male boss was impressed with the male candidate's take-charge self-presentation, while the woman supervisor was put off by it. And it seems quite likely that whatever it was about his way of talking that struck her as arrogant was exactly what led her boss to conclude that this man would be better able to take over her job if needed.

41

This example brings to mind a small item in an unusual memoir: the autobiography of an Australian woman with autism. In her remarkable memoir *Somebody Somewhere,* Donna Williams explains that although her autism made it difficult for her to process language, she managed to function in the world by mimicking the speech she heard around her. However, she regarded her successful performances not as her own doing but as the work of two imaginary personas, Carol and Willie. Although there is no evidence that Williams herself thought of these two "characters" (as she called them) as female and male, when reading her account of the kinds of things they could say and do, I repeatedly noticed that Carol performed stereotypically female behavior (she cocked her head, filled the air with social chatter, and, above all, smiled), while Willie played the stereotypically male part (he was strong, detached, and accumulated facts to impress people). So it struck me as amusing, but also troubling, when I read in Williams's memoir that it was Willie who went for interviews but Carol who held down jobs. This is not to imply that men do not deserve the jobs they get, but that ways of talking typically associated with men are more likely to impress many job interviewers as well as those making decisions about promotions to managerial levels.

I believe these patterns explain why it is common to hear that a particular woman lacks confidence or that a particular man is arrogant. Though we think of these as individual weaknesses, underconfidence and arrogance are disproportionately observed in women and men respectively, because they result from an overabundance of ways of speaking that are expected of females and males. Boys are expected to put themselves forward, emphasize the qualities that make them look good, and deemphasize those that would show them in a less favorable light. Too much of this is called arrogance. Girls are expected to be "humble"—not try to take the spotlight, emphasize the ways they are just like everyone else, and deemphasize ways they are special. A woman who does this really well comes off as lacking in confidence. Ironically, those who learn the lessons best are most in danger of falling into traps laid by conversational conventions.

TWO

"I'm Sorry, I'm Not Apologizing": Conversational Rituals

Conversation is a ritual. We say things that seem the thing to say, without thinking of the literal meaning of our words any more than we expect the question "How are you?" to call forth a detailed account of aches and pains. On the job, the meat of the work that has to be done is held together, made pleasant and possible, by the ketchup, relish, and bun of conversational rituals. But people have different habits for using these rituals, and when a ritual is not recognized, the words spoken are taken literally. I have heard visitors to the United States complain that Americans are hypocritical because they ask how you are but aren't interested in the answer. And Americans in Burma are puzzled when Burmese ask, "Have you eaten yet?"—and show no sign of inviting them to lunch. In the Philippines, people ask each other, "Where are you going?"—which may seem rather intrusive to Americans, who don't realize that the only reply expected is, "Over there."

It is easy, and entertaining, to notice different rituals in foreign countries, as did the Briton who spent a year working in France and was amused that everyone ceremoniously shook hands and said *"Bonjour"* to everyone else when they arrived at work in the morning—and again when they left for lunch, returned from lunch, and left at the end of the day. He even observed elementary-school children shaking each other's hands in greeting when they met on their way to school. We expect rituals at points of transition like greetings, and we expect them to be different—and those differences to cause confusion—when we go to foreign countries. But we don't expect differences, and are far less likely to recognize the ritual nature of our conversations, among other Americans at work. Our differing rituals are even more problematic when we think we're all speaking the same language.

SAYING "I'M SORRY" WHEN YOU'RE NOT

One conversational ritual that can differ from one person to the next and cause trouble at work is apologizing.

I had been interviewed by a well-known columnist who ended our friendly conversation by giving me the number of her direct telephone line in case I ever wanted to call her. Some time later, I did want to call her but had misplaced her direct number and had to go through the newspaper receptionist to get through to her. When our conversation was ending, and we had both uttered ending-type remarks, I remembered that I wanted to get her direct number for the future and said, "Oh, I almost forgot—last time you gave me your direct number, but I lost it; I wondered if I could get it again." "Oh, I'm sorry," she came back instantly. "It's . . ." And she gave me the number. I laughed because she had just done something I had mentioned in our interview: said "I'm sorry" when an apology was not called for. She had done nothing wrong; I was the one who lost the number. But in fact she was not apologizing; she was just uttering an automatic conversational smoother to assure me she had no intention of rushing me off the phone or denying me her number.

In one of the conversations taped for me at an advertising company, a man had received a voice-mail message from which he understood that the caller, Vicki, had two things to discuss with him. He returned her call, and she told him about one matter, but she did not have a second item to discuss. When he questioned her about this, she said, "Oh I'm sorry. Uh ... that must have been me just being unclear." In addition to (apparently) apologizing and taking blame for being unclear, Vicki spoke in a self-deprecating way.

Sometimes a tone of self-deprecation is heard as an apology even without the word "sorry" being spoken. In another tape of a conversation recorded for me, a manager named Kristin was explaining to a computer-support manager named Herb why she invited him to a meeting, even though she wasn't sure he was the right person:

Kristin: Just 'cause, you know, I'd worked with him and then you came and I—I didn't know ... what his schedule was. And I wasn't sure who [laughing] the head of that group was! [Herb also laughs.] To tell you the truth! So ...
Herb: No, don't—don't apologize.

Many women are frequently told, "Don't apologize" or "You're always apologizing." The reason "apologizing" is seen as something they should stop doing is that it seems synonymous with putting oneself down. But for many women, and a fair number of men, saying "I'm sorry" isn't literally an apology; it is a ritual way of restoring balance to a conversation. "I'm sorry," spoken in this spirit, if it has any literal meaning at all, does not mean "I apologize," which would be tantamount to accepting blame, but rather

"I'm sorry that happened." To understand the ritual nature of apologies, think of a funeral at which you might say, "I'm so sorry about Reginald's death." When you say that, you are not pleading guilty to a murder charge. You're expressing regret that something happened without taking or assigning blame. In other words, "I'm sorry" can be an expression of understanding—and caring—about the other person's feelings rather than an apology.

That an apology can be a routinized way of taking the other person's feelings into account becomes clear in the following example. When professional pool player Ewa Mataya, who is regarded as one of the top female pool players in the world, was being bested in a tournament by amateur Julie Nogiac, Mataya said of Nogiac, "She's very sweet. She kept apologizing." I doubt Nogiac actually regretted that she was beating the champion; she was simply expressing her awareness that her doing so must have been making Mataya feel bad.

This is not to say that "I'm sorry" is never an apology. But when it is, in the sense of accepting responsibility for something that went wrong, it is often assumed to be the first step in a two-step ritual: I say "I'm sorry" and take half the blame; then you take the other half. A secretary told me she liked working for her boss because, if he said, "When you typed this letter, you missed this phrase that I inserted," and she said, "Oh, I'm sorry. I'll fix it," he would usually follow up, "Well, I wrote it so small it was easy to miss."

Admitting fault can be experienced as taking a one-down position. When both parties share the blame, they end up on an equal footing. That is the logic behind the ritual sharing of blame in response to an apology. It's a mutual face-saving device. Someone who feels that an apology requires a ritualized sharing of blame might even make up a fault to admit, in order to seal off the interchange in an appropriate way. And those who share an understanding of the ritual will not take that admission of fault literally, but will simply appreciate it as an attempt to save face for them. Put another way, it is a courteous way of not leaving the apologizer in the one-down position.

Someone, on the other hand, who does not use apologies ritually may well take them all literally. And this can lead to resentment on the part of the ritual apologizer. If I say "I'm sorry" and you say "I accept your apology," then my attempt to achieve balance has misfired, and I think you have put me in a one-down position, though you probably think I put myself there. (Sensing this, people sometimes make a joke of preserving the imbalance following an apology: "Okay, just make sure it doesn't happen again." It's funny because it is obvious that is not the way the exchange is supposed to go.)

Ritual apologies—like other conversational rituals—work fine when both parties share assumptions about their use. But people who utter frequent ritual apologies when others don't may end up seeming to be taking blame for mishaps that are not their fault. When they are partly at fault, they come out looking entirely so. There are cultural as well as gender influences on how likely people are to use apologies in this way, but research on Americans by Nessa Wolfson and on New Zealanders by Janet Holmes shows that women are more likely to do it than men. Holmes found that women uttered the most apologies to other women and far fewer to men, while men uttered very few to other men and slightly more to women.

My own observations support this. In a meeting I sat in on at an insurance company, the sole woman in the group, whom I will call Helen, said "I'm sorry" or "I apologize" repeatedly. For example, at one point she said, "I'm thinking out loud. I apologize." At another, she relinquished the floor and then thought of something to add and said, "I'm sorry. I guess I'm still sleeping," referring to the early hour. In fact, whenever she changed course, stumbled, or wanted to add something to what she had said before, she said "I'm sorry" or "I apologize." Yet the meeting was intended to be an informal brainstorming session, and everyone made similar self-corrections and additions. The men in the room never apologized, nor did any of them have any reason to—any more than she did.

The reason Helen's frequent apologies stood out was that she was the only person in the room issuing so many. And the reason I was concerned about them was that Helen felt that the bonus she had just received did not fairly reflect the work she had done. As outside corroboration, everyone I interviewed in her group had volunteered that Helen was one of the best group members in terms of both skills and collegiality. Yet when bonuses were announced, she got one of the lowest. I wondered, though I could not be sure, whether her ritual use of apologies was part of a speech style that masked her true competence, or at least did not display it.

The negative impression created when someone apologizes frequently at work is the result of two patterns of behavior: that this person apologizes often and that others don't. Those who are attuned to anything that might put them in a one-down position will be likely to avoid apologizing. A CEO at one small company was so averse to apologizing that one of his vice presidents spent a great deal of time making the rounds after the boss had offended people, apologizing on his behalf. Another man had his wife call and apologize for him after he had inappropriately lost his temper.

Whether or not people apologize seems to be as much (or more) a function of their individual styles as of the apportionment of blame in particular events. To catch this process in action, I compared the incidence of apologies in the talk of four managers whose workplace conversations I had on tape. I identified two individuals who tended to use apologies ritually and two who didn't. One of those who did was Kristin, whom I quoted above. Another who did I'll call Charlene. For example, Charlene said "sorry" whenever her taping a conversation seemed to intrude. She also said it to a recent employee after scheduling an evaluation: "I'm— I'm really apologetic, Bruce, that I laid this on you so, uh, soon but I had no idea that this had to be done." In another, she apologized when someone visited her at an inconvenient time. After explaining that she was frantically preparing for an important meeting that was about to take place, she said, "Boy, I'm really sorry about this rush rush." When someone called and asked for information she didn't have, she referred him to someone else and added,

"Yeah, I'm sorry that I don't have, uh, you know I can't really give you the information you need on it, but he's very involved with it, actually, so he probably is your best source, okay?" Finally, she apologized for returning to an earlier topic after the person she was talking to had moved on to something else: "Uh, sorry, Bruce, can we back up a minute?"

Interestingly, sometimes Charlene's speech was taken for apology when she didn't utter the words: When asking a subordinate to do something, she said, "I hate to impose on you like that," and he restored the balance by saying, "No problem, my time is yours." I should note that Charlene was very highly placed in her organization; her frequent use of "sorry" clearly had not held her back. This may be because she used it to manage the coming and going of social interaction, not in the context of her own expertise or the nitty-gritty of her work.

In contrast to Charlene's ubiquitous "sorrys," a man I call Sid never apologized explicitly in nine hours of taping. Another woman, Evelyn, did so only four times in eighteen hours of taping. Once she said, "Sorry, can't help it," when it was not clear from the audiotape what had happened. Another time she seemed to have taken someone by surprise upon entering her office: "Knock knock," she said, laughing, then added, "I'm sorry, I didn't mean to startle you." A third time she said "sorry" when she used the wrong word as a slip of the tongue. Finally, when a subordinate pointed out that a question she asked about a chart indicated she was making an incorrect interpretation, she said, "Okay. Okay, that's what I thought, I'm sorry."

There were, however, numerous instances in which Evelyn seemed to be apologizing, even though she didn't actually say "I'm sorry." For example, at one point she found in her briefcase some documents that others who reported to her had been looking for:

Evelyn: Are these yours?
Manny: Ohhhh, that's what we've been lookin' for!
Evelyn: I cleaned out—I'm embarrassed, I cleaned out—
Manny: That's okay. That's great.

Evelyn: I cleaned out my briefcase this weekend and I thought, "Ahh, I bet I know what those are!"

Manny: When you talk to Vivian this morning, if you can tell her?

Evelyn: I'll tell her. Yeah. You gave 'em to me last time and I put 'em in my briefcase and completely forgot about it. I kept wondering why my briefcase was so heavy.

Although she does not utter the words "sorry" or "apologize," Evelyn shows contrition, which is a form of apology. But she did not use "sorry" as a ritual to grease the conversational wheels.

Although all the individuals I observed who used apologies ritually were women, the case of Evelyn shows that not all women do this. Since many women use ritual apologies, it is possible that women are expected to, so those who do not use them may be seen as somehow hard-edged.

If appearing contrite can come across as an apology without the words "sorry" or "apologize" being spoken, it is equally possible to utter these words without sounding contrite, effectively canceling the apology even as it spoken. The word "sorry" can be pronounced in a tone (soh-REE!) that implies a complaint has been unjustified, or at least exaggerated, and "I'm sorry I hurt your feelings" expresses regret about the effect of an action without regretting the action or accepting fault. A woman I'll call Mary felt an inexplicable unease after a telephone conversation with another woman, Elizabeth, who chaired a board. Mary had called Elizabeth to seek an explanation (and, she expected, an apology) for an offense committed by one of the board's members. Elizabeth said, "Well, I apologize" in a tone that did not sound the least bit apologetic, so Mary continued to explain why her feathers had been ruffled. Elizabeth said in a stony voice, "I'll apologize for the second time," but went on to explain why she thought the board member had done nothing wrong and why Mary's call was causing her trouble. As the conversation proceeded, Elizabeth said, "I'll apologize for the third time," and later, "I'll apologize for the fourth time." Ironically, each time Elizabeth repeated this icy phrase with a larger number, she seemed to be implying that Mary was at fault for pressing her complaint, which Mary continued to do precisely because the apologies did not sound apologetic—and hence did not work as apologies. Rather than smoothing her ruffled feathers, each nonapologetic apology ruffled them more.

TAKING BLAME AND INFLUENCING PEOPLE

Assigning and assuming blame is a delicate balancing act that can be achieved with or without uttering apologies.

Sociolinguist Keller Magenau tape-recorded and studied the talk of a woman who worked in the central office of a large insurance company. The woman, Karie, was responsible for approving insurance policies referred to her by underwriters. In one taped segment, Karie had received a policy from Lisa that she could not approve because it lacked a critical piece of information that Lisa should have provided. Instead of saying, "Lisa, you haven't given me all the information you're supposed to," Karie began, "I'm just a little confused." When she pointed out the problem, Lisa took responsibility for it: "No, I should have reworded that," and went on to clarify. Karie did not lose face by claiming confusion, because Lisa took the blame back on herself. If Karie put herself in a one-down position, it was only fleeting, because Lisa quickly pulled her back up. It is only when others do not do their part to restore the balance that ritual self-deprecation leaves the speaker in a one-down position.

In her analysis, Magenau explained that Karie and many of the women who sent her policies for approval had been friends for many years; they started work in the company at roughly the same time, advanced through the ranks at more or less the same pace, and had maintained friendly social relations over breaks and lunch. Karie's new job, however, gave her the authority to question their work and point out errors. Magenau suggests that it was because of their friendship and near-equal status that Karie down-played her authority when talking to Lisa. In a sense, she put her-self in a one-down position ("I'm confused") to avoid appearing to act one-up. Or perhaps her friendship with Lisa freed her to take the ritual one-down position because she knew Lisa would not ex-ploit it.

In conversations with another underwriter, one who was much younger, less experienced, and with whom she had neither familiarity nor friendly relations, Karie spoke in a far less self-deprecating way. It is also worth noting that this other underwriter was a young man. This may have been a factor influencing Karie's style when she spoke to him, but Magenau also points out that Karie was less mitigative with women she knew less well who were lower in rank.

I once observed with amazement the reverse strategy: avoid-ing blame that is really deserved. I was involved in a fairly complex negotiation for which I had to have a lawyer represent me. The lawyer arranged a conference call with the lawyer and principal for the other side. I sat in an office with him while the voices of the other parties came into the room on a speaker phone. At one point, my lawyer accidentally elbowed the telephone, and the call was cut off. When his secretary got the parties back on again, I fully ex-pected him to say what I would have said: "Sorry about that. I knocked the phone with my elbow. Where were we?" Instead, he said, "Hey, what happened? One minute you were there, the next minute you were gone!" He spoke as if he had no idea how the call got cut off. The other lawyer made a joke like, "Yeah, yeah, you probably didn't like what we said, so you cut us off." "That's right," my lawyer played along, and built on the joke. Everyone had a good laugh, and no harm was done. But for me it was one of those pivotal moments when you realize that the world you live in is not the one everyone lives in, and the way you assume is *the* way to talk is really only *one* way, quite different from how others might talk in the same situation. My lawyer seemed to have a knee-jerk impulse not to admit fault if he didn't have to. When I thought about it, I realized that this could be a very adaptive strategy in many settings.

GIVING CRITICISM

A woman who co-wrote a report together with a male colleague was hurt when she read to him a rough draft of the introduction and he leaped into his critical response—"Oh, that's too dry! You have to make it snappier!"—with more alacrity than she would have, and without hedging and softening. She would have been more likely to say, "That's a really good start; of course you'll want to make it a little snappier when you revise."

Whether criticism is best given "straight" or best tempered to avoid seeming too harsh is also a matter of convention. I noticed the difference when talking to an editor at a newspaper about a short opinion essay I had written that was about to be published in the paper. While going over changes she wanted me to make, she said, "There's one other thing. I know you may not agree with me. The reason I noticed it is that your other points are so lucid and elegant." She went on for several more sentences hedging what she was about to say until I jumped in to put her out of her misery: "Do you want to cut that part?" I asked. "That's okay. I'm not wedded to it." But I appreciated her tentativeness. Her approach contrasted sharply with the styles of other newspaper editors I had worked with, who asked for cuts in few words with no softeners, saying, for example, "That's not needed. You already made your point." I even recalled a (male) colleague of hers who had summarily rejected an idea for an opinion essay and added, "Call me when you have something new to say."

Those who prefer criticism given straight are operating on a conventionalized agreement that says, "This is business; feelings have no part in it. Here's the dope; I know you're good; you can take it." Those who are used to ways of talking that soften the impact in consideration of the feelings of the person addressed may find it hard to deal with right-between-the-eyes criticism. Both styles have their own logic. I expressed my appreciation to the editor who had hemmed and hawed before telling me to cut a section from my essay. In response (and in ritual self-abnegation to balance my compliment), she said that she found it difficult to deal with authors who become angry when she tampers with their prose. I would guess that such authors are less problematic for the editor who could bark, "Call me when you have something new to say!" On the other hand, I wondered how many potential authors would not venture another call to an editor who spoke that way.

"THANKS FOR NOTHING!"

Charlene, the manager who frequently said "sorry," also frequently said "thanks." She often began and ended meetings by thanking people for coming. Just two examples give a feel for the way many of Charlene's telephone and face-to-face conversations ended. The first came at the end of a telephone conversation in which Charlene set up a meeting with a subordinate named Russell:

Charlene: Plan for say eight o'clock. Let's plan for eight, okay?
Russell: Okay.
Charlene: Yeah.
Russell: Okay.
Charlene: Thanks so much.
Russell: Bye.
Charlene: Bye-bye.

The next example is the end of another telephone conversation, also setting up a meeting with a subordinate, this one named Stuart:

Charlene: Why don't we meet in the morning, at nine.
Stuart: Okay.
Charlene: How's that.
Stuart: That's perfect.
Charlene: Okay, good, I'll put it down. Thanks so much.

Stuart: Okay.
Charlene: Bye-bye.

Since Charlene was the boss setting up necessary meetings with subordinates, she obviously did not say "thanks" because she felt grateful for a favor they had done her; rather, it seems to be a ritualized way for her to bring a conversation to a close. Russell and Stuart seemed to take it that way, as they responded simply by saying "Okay" and "Bye."

Evelyn, the manager who did not apologize ritually, did frequently thank people. For her too, "thanks" seemed to be a ritual conversational closer, like "okay," as in this conversation with her assistant about the preparation of some forms:

Renee: So this one will have to be—this one you wanted
         redone.
Evelyn: Yeah. Yep. But, we don't need to do it in bold, it's
         just fine like that. And this one is okay the way it is.
         Good!
Renee: Okay.
Evelyn: Thanks.

That Evelyn used "thanks" as a ritual way of ending an encounter became even clearer in a segment of a conversation she taped for me when her boss, John, brought her with him to a meeting with his boss, but it turned out that John's boss did not think Evelyn needed to be there. In making her exit, she said—what else?— "Thanks."

Evelyn: You don't need me then?
John: Uh, /?/.
Evelyn: Okay.
John: It's just—
Evelyn: [She laughs.] Should I stay or should I leave?
John: I think not. I think— I'll get it done today because
         it's /?/.
Evelyn: Okay. Thanks. [She leaves.]

Since no one had done anything for Evelyn, her saying "Thanks" could not be literal; it could only be a ritual way of making her exit.

The fourth person, Sid, who rarely said "Sorry" also rarely said "Thanks." He simply ended conversations with "Okay." (But this in no way made him sound impolite, as we will see in the next chapter.)

Just as a ritual apology is expected to trigger a balancing apology, so a ritual thanks is expected to trigger an in-kind response. When that response doesn't come, the result can be annoyance, since the thanker is left in a one-down position.

A novelist who prided herself on her efficiency and attention to detail received a fax from an assistant in the publicity office at her publishing house; it contained suggested catalog copy for her latest novel. She immediately faxed him her suggested changes, and when he later faxed his revision, she called him right back with her response. When they were done going over the changes, she said, "Thanks for running this by me," fully expecting him to say, "Thanks for giving me such a quick response." Instead, he said, "You're welcome." Suddenly, instead of an equal-appearing exchange of mutual pleasantries, she found herself positioned as the one-down recipient of a favor. This made her feel like responding, "Thanks for nothing!"

Whenever something spoken automatically as part of a ritual does not receive the expected response, feelings can be hurt. The author's expression of gratitude, "Thanks for running this by me," was such a ritual. Her contract with the publisher prescribed that she had to approve catalog copy, so the publicity assistant wasn't doing her a favor; he was doing his job. But she regarded exchanging thanks as a pleasant and common way of ending a conversation. In fact, when she thought about it, she realized that she had come to expect to be thanked by employees of presses when she got back to them almost immediately, since such promptness was apparently not usual. Her thanking him was probably a way of trying to trigger the thanks she expected of him.

The rituals of apologizing, softening criticism, and thanking can be used by women or men. But they are more often found in the speech of women. And all these rituals depend on mutuality. If one person apologizes and the other simply accepts the apology, or if one person is doing all the thanking, then the result is an imbalance—and a loss of face. Many of the rituals typical of women's conversations depend on the goodwill of the other not to take the self-abnegation literally and to restore the balance. When the other speaker does not do that, the woman may feel like someone on a seesaw whose partner suddenly abandoned the other end. Instead of balancing in the air, she has plopped to the ground, wondering how she got there.

RITUAL FIGHTING

If these are some rituals common among women that are often taken literally by men when used in a work setting, what are some rituals common among men at work that are often taken literally by women? One is ritual opposition.

In his book *Fighting for Life: Contest, Consciousness and Sexuality,* cultural linguist Walter Ong (who happens to be a Jesuit priest) shows that males are more likely than females to use "agonism"—a warlike, oppositional format—to accomplish a range of interactional goals that have nothing literally to do with fighting. Public debate is a prime example: Each debater takes one side of the argument and tries to muster all the arguments he can think of for that side, while trying his damnedest to undercut and attack the arguments for the other side. This is done regardless of his personal convictions, and regardless of his ability to see the other's point of view, just as lawyers are supposed to make the best argument they can for their client and try to undercut the opponent's case by whatever means they can. From such ritual opposition is supposed to come truth, or, in the case of the legal system, justice. In such contests, the role of language is particularly powerful. As Gregory Matoesian puts it in a book about rape trials, "The legal system is not necessarily about truth and falsity, but winning and losing, and that, in turn, depends largely on which side can best manipulate language."

A woman told me she watched with distaste and distress as her office-mate heatedly argued with another colleague about whose division would suffer necessary cuts in funding, but she went into shock when, shortly after this altercation, the two men were as friendly as ever. "How can you pretend that fight never happened?" she asked the man who shared her office. He responded, "Who's pretending it never happened?," as puzzled by her question as she was by his behavior. "It happened," he said, "and it's over." She mistook their ritual fighting for real.

The level of expression of emotion that accompanies opposition is also culturally relative. The British think Americans are extremely excitable, which is just what Americans think of Mediterraneans. The other side of the coin is that Mediterraneans think Americans are cold, just as Americans tend to regard the British.

Among Americans, many people expect the discussion of ideas to be a ritual fight—that is, explored through verbal opposition. When presenting their own ideas, they state them in the most certain and absolute form they can and wait to see if they are challenged. Their thinking is that if there are weaknesses, someone will point them out, and by trying to argue against those objections, they will find out how their ideas hold up. In this spirit, literary theorist Stanley Fish, who as chair of an academic department instituted many controversial changes, explained in an interview, "I would announce changes and see if anyone said anything. No one ever did." He took their silence as a go-ahead. The question is, how many of the professors in his department felt that complaining after the fact was an option, and how many thought that a policy already announced was nonnegotiable?

Those who expect someone who disagrees to challenge them openly may also respond to a colleague's ideas by challenging—questioning, trying to poke holes and find weak links—as a way of helping the colleague see whether the proposal will pan out. Although cultural background is an important influence as well, fewer women than men engage in ritual opposition, and many women do not like it. Missing the ritual nature of verbal opposition, they are likely to take such challenges as personal attacks. Worse, they find it impossible to do their best in a contentious environment.

The logic behind ritual opposition is that knowing your ideas will be scrutinized by others should encourage you to think more rigorously in advance. When you are publicly challenged, you rise to the occasion: Adrenaline makes your mind grow sharper, and you get ideas and insights you would not have thought of without the spur of battle. But if you are not accustomed to ritual opposition, or simply do not thrive on it, you will have a very different response. Knowing you are likely to be attacked for what you say, you begin to hear criticism of your ideas as soon as they are formed. Rather than making you think more clearly, it makes you doubt what you know. When you state your ideas, you hedge in order to fend off potential attacks, making your arguments appear weak. Ironically, this is more likely to invite attack from agonistic colleagues than to fend it off. When you feel attacked, emotion does not sharpen your wits, but rather clouds your mind and thickens your tongue, so you can't articulate the ideas that were crystal clear before. Speakers with this style find their creative juices flowing in an atmosphere of mutual support but stopped up in the face of ritual opposition. People like this (many of whom are women) are not able to do their best work in the very environment that is bringing out the best in many of their co-workers—those who not only thrive in an agonistic climate but are probably helping to create it.

Not all companies encourage a style of verbal opposition; each company has its own distinctive culture, developed over time. Different companies tend to encourage more or less verbal opposition and argument. But within each company, there are people who are more or less given to the oppositional style. And in any conversation, those who are comfortable with open opposition have an advantage over those who do not. Regardless of which style is rewarded in a given company, it will be hard for those whose styles are different to do their best work.

At work, women often take it personally when someone disagrees with them or openly argues. An engineer who was the only woman among four men in a small company found that she had to be willing to take her colleagues on in animated argument in order to be taken seriously. Once she had done that, they seemed to accept and respect her. A similar discovery was made by a physician attending a staff meeting at her hospital who became more and more angered by a male colleague arguing against a point of view she had put forth. Her better judgment told her to hold her tongue, to avoid making an enemy of this senior colleague. But finally her anger got the best of her, and she rose to her feet and delivered an impassioned attack on his position. She sat down in a panic, certain she had permanently damaged her relationship with this powerful colleague and probably alienated others allied with him. To her amazement, he came up to her after the meeting and said, "That was a great rebuttal. I'm really impressed. Let's go out for a beer after work and hash out our approaches to this problem."

These different ways of doing the same interactional work were dramatized for me by two different journalists who interviewed me.

A man interviewed me for a feature article in a newspaper. His questions were challenging to the point of belligerence. He brought up potential criticisms of my work with such eagerness that I was sure his article would make me look terrible. To my amazement, he wrote a very flattering portrait, with no hint of the belligerence he had used to get information from me. Rather than repeating the potential criticisms, he used only my responses. By confronting me, he had been giving me an opportunity to present myself in a positive light.

On another occasion, I was interviewed by a woman who talked to me as if she were talking to a friend. She spent several hours in my home and revealed a lot of personal information about herself, which encouraged me to be similarly self-revealing. Nothing in her manner led me to suspect she would write anything but a favorable article, and I began to blather on, confident that I was on safe turf. The article that resulted from this interview surprised me as much as the other one, but in the opposite way. She used the information I had given her to write a piece that cast me in an unflattering light. Whereas I was pleasantly relieved to see that the first article was more favorable than I expected, I felt betrayed and tricked by the second. I thought the woman who wrote it had misled me, pretending to take the stance of a friend so I would reveal more vulnerable sides of myself. In retrospect, I could see that both journalists were using routine conversational formats to encourage self-revelation. He tried to provoke an uncensored response by challenging, she by establishing rapport. Both were ways of getting me to let down my guard—which is, after all, a journalist's job. Both spoke in ways designed to direct the conversation along ritualized lines.

I suspect it was not coincidental that it was a man who positioned himself as my opponent to get me to let down my hair, and a woman who positioned herself as my friend. Another woman journalist told me that the part of her job she dislikes most is having to ask confrontational questions in interviews, challenging people by repeating to them the worst things others have said about them. Yet a man she worked with told her that was the part of the job he enjoyed the most.

"What Do You Think?"

Another conversational ritual is asking others for their opinions before making a decision. It is the antithesis of the style that simply assumes anyone who disagrees will volunteer opposition, so silence can be taken as assent.

In a company where employees regularly evaluate their supervisors, a manager was taken aback when one of her subordinates complained that she didn't listen to him. She was especially surprised because she made a point of soliciting the opinions of everyone in her group on every major decision and listening carefully to what they said. She sat down with this man to find out what could account for their so-different views. It turned out that it was her very habit of soliciting his opinion that led to his complaint that she didn't listen. He had taken her requests for his opinion as requests for advice. He thought she was literally asking him to make decisions for her. Then, when she did what she thought best, which often was not what he had recommended, he felt betrayed: She had asked him to decide and then did not "listen to" him.

Many people ask those they work with for their opinions ("What do you think we should do about this?") to get a range of opinions, to make others feel involved, and to create the appearance, or the reality, of making decisions by consensus. But consensus does not mean (obviously, it can't mean) that all those who express opinions will get their way. It means only that everyone gets heard. In the end, ideally, a decision is made that satisfies as many people as possible while accommodating others' needs as much as possible. Those whose recommendations are not followed, by this arrangement, go along with the consensus because they know their input was considered and trust that the best decision was made. But someone not accustomed to this arrangement may well interpret the request for an opinion as a literal invitation to make the decision and therefore feel misled when the advice is not taken. Such a person may even feel manipulated or tricked: "You're trying to make me feel like it's my decision, but you're going to do what you want anyway, so why pretend by asking me?"

The practice of asking others what they think is especially risky at work, where talk is not only a way to get work done but also, and always, a means of evaluation: At the same time that people are listening for what you mean, they are also judging you as a person and as a worker. (One executive reported that his own mentor had told him, when she hired him, "Start noticing who's good now, so when your time comes to promote and hire, you'll be ready.") Everything you say becomes evidence of your competence, or lack of it. Most jobs, especially high-level ones, involve the need to make decisions. Someone who appears to need help making decisions can easily be judged negatively: "It's her responsibility, but she's trying to get others to decide for her. Maybe she doesn't have the confidence to make decisions herself."

Once again, ways of talking intended to show consideration of others can end up making the speaker appear to lack confidence. To avoid such a result, it might be wise to discuss style with co-workers, in other words, to "meta-communicate"—talk about communication. In some cases, it might be helpful to say explicitly, "I'm going to make the decision myself, but I'd like to know your opinion." In the case of the manager whose subordinate told her she didn't listen, talking about their style differences solved the problem. They agreed that since they respected each other, if either felt the other was behaving annoyingly, they would bring it up and talk about it.

MIXING BUSINESS AND NONBUSINESS TALK

I was sitting in the waiting area of a car dealership while my car was being fixed. Gradually, I let the book I was reading fall to my lap, as I became engrossed in the friendly conversation taking place among three salesmen who had gathered around the coffeemaker that was placed in the same lounge where customers waited. They were exchanging humorous stories about having to work late and return home to disgruntled wives. They gossiped about how late another salesman worked and joked that it was a wonder his wife hadn't left him. Suddenly, I saw the sole woman who worked in sales in this dealership approaching the men. I thought, how nice, she's going to join them. I was eager to see how her entrance into the conversation would affect it. But it immediately became clear she was not going to join them. As soon as the men saw her approaching, the conversation stopped, and everyone went stiff. It was as if a chill had rippled through the air. She asked one of the men a question, got an answer, and went away. I have no way of knowing what accounted for the particular relations between this woman and the men she worked with. But regardless of the reasons, I could imagine how difficult it had been for her to break through that sheet of ice to ask her question. And I thought how much less pleasant it must be for her to go to work each day than it is for them.

Talk at work is not confined to talk about work. Many moments are spent in casual chat that establishes the friendly working environment that is the necessary backdrop to getting work done. It is easier to approach someone with a work-related issue if you are comfortable in each other's presence and the lines of communication are open. A major way such working relationships are established is through informal, nonwork talk. Both men and women engage in nonwork chat at work, but what they are likely to talk about, and how, are often different.

Many women mix business with talk about their personal lives and expect other women to do so too; they may see women who do not engage in personal chat as cold, aloof, or "not a people person." Men are more likely to mix business talk with banter about sports or politics. (Even though the car salesmen were talking about how their late hours affect their home lives, they were still in a way talking about work—the pressure of hours demanded by their jobs—and doing so in a humorous, joking tone.) Everyone can see the interest value of the type of small talk they themselves engage in, but they are likely to regard as "trivial" the type of small talk they don't happen to enjoy. It's common to hear men complain about or mock women's interest in talking about clothes and personal details, and common to hear women complain about or mock men's interest in sports.

Both women and men know that their small talk is just that— "small" compared to the "big" talk about work—but differences in small-talk habits can become very big when they get in the way of the easy day-to-day working relationships that make us feel comfortable at work and keep the lines of communication open for the big topics when they arise. A man who regularly finds himself left out of lively conversations about clothes or haircuts or family problems, or a woman who regularly finds herself left out of lively conversations about sports or hunting, may also find themselves out of the friendly loop in which important as well as unimportant information goes around the office.

Small talk is not just an aid but a necessity—the grease that keeps the gears running in an office. This discovery was made by a woman who was hired as the chief editor of a magazine. When she got into the top slot, she tried to run the office as her predecessor had: no time for small talk; get right down to business. After a while, she began to hear rumblings that the women in the office were unhappy with her. They felt she was cold and aloof, that power had gone to her head and made her arrogant. She had to modify her style, taking some time to talk, to check in with people about their personal lives and exchange pleasantries. The feeling that their bosses are interested in them personally may be common to many people, but women are more likely to expect it to be displayed as interest in their lives outside of work—especially by other women.

A woman who works with men might find it useful to learn something about sports to take part in those conversations. One woman said that she learned she could have a pleasant interchange with men in her office by saying, "Hey, wasn't that an incredible game last night?" She would get an animated response, even if she had no idea what game they thought she was referring to. Another woman, however, commented that although she was an avid sports fan who always knew exactly what game was played the night before, she still couldn't take part in the men's conversations about them. I would not discount the possibility that the men she worked with might simply have not wanted her to take part—either because she was a woman or because they didn't like her. But it is also possible that the way she thought it was appropriate to talk about sports was not the way they were used to. Sports talk, like any conversational ritual, has to be done in an agreed-upon way. For many men, sports talk is a playful game in itself, composed of attack, counterattack, and teasing. "Wasn't Jones incredible?" "Jones?! You like that creep?! I can't believe they keep him on the team! It was Smith who won that game." "Smith?! Are you for real? That turkey couldn't catch a ball if it was handed to him!"

How much small talk is expected, and when, is also a matter of individual style. There are people who find it appropriate to call someone on the telephone and jump right to the point of the call rather than "waste time"—or stand on ceremony—with long-winded greetings. The very fact of omitting a greeting can imply, "We're on such good terms we can dispense with the niceties that people who know each other less well are bound by." But not everyone agrees that this is appropriate; to some people it is rude. A new employee called his boss and started right in with what he needed so as not to impose on her time any more than necessary. "Frank," she said, cutting him off. "First of all, good morning." That made it clear that she was not someone who liked to dispense with small talk.

GIVING PRAISE

Giving praise is also a conversational ritual, and here too there are cultural as well as gender patterns, as the next two examples show.

Lester had been on his new job only six months when he heard that some of the women reporting to him were deeply dissatisfied. When he talked to them, they erupted; two were on the verge of quitting, they said, because they weren't happy working for someone who didn't appreciate their work. They were convinced that Lester didn't think they were doing a good job, and they preferred to quit rather than wait to be fired. Lester was dumbfounded. He believed they were doing a fine job and had never thought otherwise. Surely, he had said nothing to give them the impression he didn't like their work. And indeed he hadn't. That was the problem. He had said nothing. The women expected him to praise their work if he liked it, and to show interest in what they were doing by asking about it from time to time. When he said nothing about the job they were doing, they assumed he was following the adage "If you can't say something nice, don't say anything." He thought he was showing confidence in them by leaving them alone. To him, everything was fine unless he corrected them. To them, unless he told them everything was fine, there must be a problem.

Vince had a similar experience by which he learned there is no right amount of praise and attention to give. He supervised a group of eight people who reported directly to him. He believed in keeping in touch with his group, so he made a point of checking in with each one, even if briefly, at least once a day. Certain he was being a responsible and caring boss, he was shocked when a new system of soliciting evaluations from subordinates was instituted. Though there were some who were pleased with his style of management, the complaints of others ranged from, "He's always looking over my shoulder; he doesn't seem to trust me to do the work" to "He rarely shows any interest in what I'm doing; he doesn't seem to care about it, so why should I care?" It turned out that checking once a day was too much attention for some in his group and too little for others. Those who saw his visits as too brief were interpreting them in terms of power: He's my superior, he's checking on me. Those who saw them as too brief were interpreting them in terms of rapport: He's not interested enough to spend more time. In Vince's case, it turned out that those who took the first tack were men, and those who took the second were women.

Praise is a very special form of feedback. Although I heard many men and women mention that they got more thanks and praise from women than from men, I never heard anyone say they resented receiving praise. I frequently heard from men that they did not mind not getting feedback; if they didn't hear anything, they felt they were doing okay. But when they had a boss who praised them often, they always said they liked it. "It's a problem," one man joked, "because it's habit-forming. The more praise you get, the more you want!"

"I don't know where I stand with you," a woman complained to her boss. "You're not giving me any signals." This is a complaint I heard frequently from women who worked for men. But I also heard it from many men who work for women. I suspect it is not a matter of women or men not sending out signals, but of their sending different signals, which are more likely to be missed by those of the other gender. Another possibility is that many men feel women don't tell them directly enough if they are doing something wrong, and many women feel that men don't tell them directly enough if they are doing well.

"THANKS FOR THE COMPLIMENT"

Compliments are a conventionalized form of praise, and exchanging compliments is a common ritual, especially for many women. Both Nessa Wolfson and Janet Holmes have studied complimenting and concluded that women offer compliments far more than men do, and they offer them far more often to other women than to men. A mismatch in expectations regarding this ritual created problems for a woman I will call Deirdre.

Deirdre and her colleague William both gave presentations at a national conference. On the way back to their home city, Deirdre told William, "That was a great talk!" "Thank you," he said. Then she asked, "What did you think of mine?" and he told her—in the form of a lengthy and detailed critique. Although she found it uncomfortable to listen to his criticism, she assured herself that he meant well, and that his honesty was a signal that she too should be honest when he asked for a parallel critique of his performance. As a matter of fact, she had noticed quite a few ways in which he could have improved his presentation. But she never got a chance to tell him because he never asked. An unpleasant feeling of having been put down came over her. Since she didn't tell him how he could have done better but only complimented him, she felt she had left him with the impression that his performance had been flawless. Somehow she had been positioned as the novice in need of his expert advice. The worst part was that she seemed to have only herself to blame, since she had, after all, asked what he thought of her talk.

But had Deirdre really asked for William's critique? When she asked what he thought of her talk, she wasn't expecting a critique but a compliment. In fact, her question had been an attempt to repair a ritual gone awry. When Deirdre complimented William, she was simply uttering a pleasant remark she felt was more or less required following anyone's talk, and she had assumed he would respond with a matching compliment about hers. When William did not offer the expected compliment, Deirdre prompted him by asking directly. But he responded instead with criticism, so she figured, "Oh, he's playing 'Let's critique each other' rather than 'Let's pat each other on the back.' " The game "Let's critique each other" would be another symmetrical ritual, not the one she would have initiated but one she was willing to play. Had she realized William was going to give her a literal answer and not ask her to reciprocate, she would never have asked the question in the first place.

It would be easy to assume that Deirdre was insecure, whether you interpret her question as fishing for a compliment or soliciting a critique. But she was simply talking automatically, performing one of the many conversational rituals that allow us to get through the day. William may have sincerely misunderstood Deirdre's intention and taken the question literally because exchanging compliments is not a ritual he was in the habit of performing. Or perhaps he had been lying in wait for the opportunity to put her in a one-down position. But even if the latter were the case, it was her attempt to spark an exchange of compliments that gave him the invitation to launch his critique.

This interchange could have occurred between two men or two women, and yet it does not seem coincidental that it happened between a woman and a man. For one thing, as linguist Janet Holmes discovered, the pattern for giving compliments is similar to the one her research had shown for apologies: Women give them more than men, especially to other women. Furthermore, fewer men would be likely to ask, "What did you think of my talk?"—for whatever reason—as they might sense that this could invite an unwanted critique. Men are more likely to be on guard to prevent themselves from being put in a one-down position, because of the social structure of the peer groups in which they grew up. Because boys' groups tend to be more obviously hierarchical than girls', and the lives of the low-status boys can be made quite miserable, many men learn to avoid the one-down position and develop strategies for making sure they get the one-up position instead. In contrast, many women learned from their experience as girls that human relationships should maintain the appearance of equality, and no one should take the one-up position in too obvious a way. This means women are less likely to have learned to avoid talking in ways that could give someone else the chance to put them in the one-down position. Quite the contrary, many of the rituals they have learned involve taking the one-down position but depending upon the other person to round off the ritual and pull them back up.

In this framework, it is easy to see how the opportunity to offer Deirdre suggestions for improvement could have appealed to William. Giving a critique was something he probably felt quite pleased to do, since it positioned him as the expert speaker, the one who had the tips to give, as teacher or trainer to student or trainee. So comfortable was William in this role that the next time they both presented at a conference, he did compliment Deirdre—on how well she had learned the lessons he taught her. "You did much better this time," he soothed.

This example also shows how women's and men's characteristic styles, though equally logical and valid in themselves, often put women at a disadvantage in interactions with men. If one person is trying to keep everyone equal and working hard to save face for the other, while another person is trying to maintain the one-up position, the person seeking the one-up position is very likely to get it, and to succeed in assigning the one-down position to the person who has not been expending effort to stay out of it. The fact that women often take (or accept) the role of the one seeking advice reinforces the expectation that women will take this role.

COMPLAINING AS SOLIDARITY

Another conversational ritual is "troubles talk," which can be a form of "rapport talk." In other words, one way to establish rapport with someone is to commiserate: You tell about a problem (this is especially good because it shows you are "just folks," not someone who appears to have it all), and the other person responds by telling about a matching problem. (This response is good because it keeps you both on an apparently equal footing.) Because troubles talk is more common among women than men, many men are likely to take the statement of a problem as a request to solve it. A reader wrote to offer an example of troubles talk that was overheard by teachers at a nursery school between a little girl and a little boy:

Girl: Hey, Max, my baby's not feeling good.
Boy: So sorry. I'm not the person who fixes sick babies.
Girl: I wasn't telling you to fix her, I was just telling you.

Another woman told me that the troubles-talk impasse accounted for one source of frustration she experienced with her office-mate. Her example also showed how difficult it is to change these habitual patterns. She would frequently initiate what she thought would be pleasant complaint-airing sessions, in which she'd talk about situations that bothered her just to talk about them, maybe in order to understand them better. But her office-mate would begin to tell her what she could do to improve the situation. This left her feeling condescended to and frustrated. Upon reading my description in *You Just Don't Understand,* she thought, "Aha! That's it!" She showed the section on troubles talk to her office-mate and said, "I think this is what's happening with us." He read the section and was similarly impressed. "That's amazing," he said. "She's right. That's the problem. How can we solve it?" Then they both laughed, because the same thing had happened again: He short-circuited the detailed discussion of their different styles and cut to the chase of finding a solution.

Once again, the equal-opportunity fallout from these differences in style can have unequal consequences for women and men at work. A particular danger for women who engage in "troubles talk" is that men who work with them may hear their complaints as literal. Such a woman may get a reputation for being a chronic malcontent with a bad attitude. Furthermore, if talking about troubles gives the impression that problems are worse than they are, she may be seen as not up to solving the problems that arise on the job.

"WHAT'S SO FUNNY?"

A man called in to a talk show and said, "I have worked for two women in my life, and neither one of them had a sense of humor. You know, when you work with men, there's a lot of joking and teasing." The talk-show host and guest (both women) took his comment at face value, and assumed that the women this man worked for had no sense of humor. The guest said, "Isn't it sad that women don't feel comfortable enough with authority to see the humor?" The host said, "Maybe when more women are in authority roles, they will be more comfortable with that power." But although it may be the case that the two women this man worked for took themselves too seriously and lacked a sense of humor, it is just as likely that they had senses of humor, maybe even terrific ones, but the way their humor expressed itself was different from the way he was used to. They may have been like the woman who wrote to me, "When I am with men, my wit or cleverness seems inappropriate (or lost!) so I don't bother. When I am with my women friends, however, there's no hold on puns or cracks and my humor is fully appreciated."

The types of humor women and men tend to prefer differ. Research has shown that the most common form of humor among men is razzing, teasing, and mock-hostile attacks. In contrast, the most common form of humor among women is self-mocking. Women often mistake men's teasing and mock attacks as genuinely hostile and personal, and men often mistake women's mock self-deprecation as truly putting themselves down. Both women and men are inclined to scoff at the other's characteristic forms of humor.

One woman told me she was taken more seriously when she learned to joke with the guys—especially if her jokes were off-color. Although others have told me they get better results by not joining such conversations (especially if it does not come naturally to them), sociolinguist Keller Magenau noticed an exchange in the insurance company she studied that seemed to fit that description. Karie, the woman who taped her conversations for Magenau, had been out to lunch with three young men in their late twenties to early thirties: Lane, who worked in her department, and two of his friends. In her fifties, Karie was old enough to be their mother. Since she was tape-recording her conversations, she had clipped the microphone to her jacket lapel. As she walked with the young men from the restaurant to the car, someone commented that it would be difficult for the microphone to pick up their voices. Lane quipped, "This is good stuff you're missing. From now on, talk directly into Karie's chest." Everyone laughed. They laughed even harder after Karie retorted by suggesting they talk into her "left one."

Karie didn't initiate the sexually tinged humor, but she played along with it; in fact, she upped the ante of innuendo: If Lane used "chest" to suggest "breast" without using the word, Karie's reference to the "left one" made that connection even clearer. Magenau reports that such suggestive banter did not come naturally to Karie, but she had been rather pleased that she had been able to play along, probably because it gave her the feeling of fitting in with the three young men.

In many cases where a woman reported "fitting in" with men, she was participating in this sort of humor. Sociolinguist Keli Yerian taped the conversation of a woman she called Maven who worked at a government agency. Maven told Yerian that she felt she got along better with the men in her office than the women. After examining the tapes of Maven's talk at work, Yerian concluded that Maven's style of humor seemed to mesh better with that of the men, and it worked well to give her a means of entry into the men's banter.

At one meeting Maven attended with two men and another woman, the men began reminiscing about playing football in college. The other woman said nothing during this segment, but Maven tried to take part. Her first few attempts to say something about her own college experience were ignored, but when she broke in with a playful insult, the men responded with affectionate indulgence:

> Kevin: I started as a defensive right halfback.
> Started—played Texas. Played all of /?/ all of those
> teams. That's just a long—another /?/
> Joe: Well you—you played a lot. Let me tell you /?/
> Maven: In *my* undergrad school, the football players
> majored in "duhh."
> Kevin: Ohh, I *knew* you were going to say that.
> Joe: Oh, Maven!

By playfully implying that football players are stupid, Maven was able to take part in the men's conversation and provoke a display of mock-annoyed affection toward her.

In a factory where I observed, there was one woman about whom everyone raved. I heard only enthusiastic, superlative comments about Gayle from everyone who worked with her, including subordinates, peers, and superiors. In the tapes and transcripts of meetings and conversations in which she participated, one sign of the affection her male co-workers felt for her was that they frequently teased her, as in the following example.

The setting was a routine meeting of the factory management. As the computer-services supervisor responsible for the inventory-tracking program, Gayle had pointed out that problems were created because the factory was operating too close to deadlines. She argued that they should produce inventory earlier in the month, but the production manager, Harry, insisted he had to keep inventories to a minimum, to make sure they did not produce more than they could sell. The operations manager, Paul, pointed out that another problem with working so close to deadlines was that it didn't allow time to correct errors. Then he teased Gayle by threatening to fire her. In fact, Gayle had recently been promoted and assigned to a new job, in a place called Valen, and they both made reference to that fact:

Paul: What—what it comes down to is it really comes down to doin' it right the first time, but what it does—'cause it means you gotta—you gotta do things at the last minute, which really requires almost error-free work.
Harry: Yup.
Sam: Boy, does that sound familiar. [He laughs.]
Paul: Either that or get rid of the—rid of the computer-services supervisor, not count that stuff anymore. [Gayle and some men laugh.] Send her off to see—send her off to Valen or somethin'.
Harry: You know there—there—there's a—
Gayle: Just remember, I'm trainin' my replacement before I go!

It is clear from the transcripts, as well as from interviews with everyone involved, that this bantering style was typical of Gayle's interaction with the men at the factory, and that she enjoyed it as much they did. (She even drops the 'g' in words ending in "ing" as the men do.)

The same style of humor that can allow a woman to fit in with the men may set her off from some women. This was not the case with Gayle, but it could be part of what was happening with Maven, the woman in Keli Yerian's study who felt she got along better with men than women. It certainly accounts for the following, final example, which also comes from Yerian's analysis of humor at work. Although not on tape, the conversation was reported to Yerian by a teacher who had gone to a national conference along with seven other teachers (mostly women), a group of school principals, and the school district's superintendent (Dwight) and assistant superintendent (Eric). The teacher had a friendly relationship with the administrators but did not know the other attendees. At the conference, she was annoyed that the administrators always found reasons to leave boring seminars, while the teachers felt they had to stay and take notes, no matter how useless the seminar. One evening, when the group met at a bar in the conference hotel, Eric asked her how one such seminar he had left turned out. She retorted, "As soon as you left, it got much better." This is how she described the response she got:

> I remember Dwight and Eric laughing out loud at that; the other men laughing, but less loudly, and the women hardly at all. . . . I knew Eric and Dwight would appreciate that kind of "ballsy" humor from a teacher to an assistant superintendent. . . . The comment created a wedge right away, though. . . . The women had little to say to me after that—I felt like an alien among them.

The very type of humor—a playful insult—that appealed to the men alienated the women. No doubt the fact that by using this humor the teacher was aligning herself with the administrators also played a role in setting her off from the other teachers.

"WHICH WAY IS RIGHT?"

Someone who is told, "Stop apologizing" rarely thinks of replying, "It's just a ritual; you should say, 'I'm sorry' more. It would make you more likable." She is more likely to say, or think, "What's wrong with me? Why do I apologize all the time?" Our understanding of language inclines us to look for literal rather than ritual meanings in words. And many of us are also inclined to look for individual psychological problems to explain the way we talk. It is easy to make someone who has spoken indirectly feel guilty: "Why do I do that? What's wrong with me?" But few people wonder why they speak as they do when they are talking to others who share their conversational rituals. It's only when our rituals fail that we question them.

I have described in this chapter a number of conversational rituals (by no means all) that can differ from one person to the next. Many readers will wonder, "Which way is best?" There is no one best way. Any style of speaking will work just fine in some situations with those who share the style. The most common culprit is style differences. (This is not to imply that misunderstandings or other tensions will never arise when styles are shared. Discord can result from ill intentions or conflicts of interest, and all styles have built-in liabilities that can cause problems in some situations.) But all styles will at times fail with others who don't share or understand them, just as your language won't do you much good if you try to speak it to someone who doesn't know that language. It's not that you are no longer speaking a good language; it will still work fine to express your ideas. But if what you're after is not just self-expression but communication—getting others to understand what you say—then it's not enough for language to be right; it has to be shared—or at least to be understood.

THREE

"Why Don't You Say What You Mean?": Indirectness at Work

Auniversity president was expecting a visit from a member of the board of trustees. When her secretary buzzed to tell her that the board member had arrived, she left her office and entered the reception area to greet him. Before ushering him into her office, she handed her secretary a sheet of paper and said, "I've just finished drafting this letter. Do you think you could type it right away? I'd like to get it out before lunch. And would you please do me a favor and hold all calls while I'm meeting with Mr. Smith?" When they sat down behind the closed door of her office, Mr. Smith began by telling her that he thought she had spoken inappropriately to her secretary. "Don't forget," he said, *"you're* the president!"

Putting aside the question of the appropriateness of his admonishing the president on her way of speaking, it is revealing—and, I think, representative of many Americans' assumptions—that the indirect way in which the university president told her secretary what to do struck him as self-deprecating. He took it as evidence that she didn't think she had the right to make demands of her secretary. He probably thought he was giving her a needed pep talk, bolstering her self-confidence.

I challenge the assumption that talking in an indirect way reveals powerlessness, lack of self-confidence, or anything else about the character of the speaker. Indirectness is a fundamental element in human communication. It is also one of the elements that varies the most from one culture to another, and one that can cause confusion and misunderstanding when speakers have different habits with regard to using it. I want to dispel the assumption that American women tend to be more indirect than American men across the board. Women and men are both indirect, but, in addition to differences associated with their backgrounds—regional, ethnic, and class—they tend to be indirect in different situations and in different ways.

INDIRECTNESS IS NOT INSECURITY

At work, we need to get others to do things. Different people have different ways of accomplishing this, and any individual's ways will vary depending on who is being addressed—a boss, a peer, or a subordinate. At one extreme are bald commands. Mark, a manager at a meeting that was taped for me, issued twenty-five directives in about five hours of meetings, of which only four were significantly softened by indirectness. For example, in suggesting a way to rewrite something, he told a subordinate, "because that's who you mean, that's what you oughtta say. It's—it will confuse people." At the other extreme are requests so indirect that they don't sound like requests at all, but are just a statement of need or a description of a situation. Another manager whose talk was taped, Kristin, tended to tell people what to do in this softened way. For example, in the following conversation with a subordinate, Charles, about the draft of a report he had written for the director, Miller, about the company's sales in a foreign country, it is clear that Kristin thought Charles should put the conversion rate from the foreign currency to dollars into his report. But she had to repeat her suggestion several times, in increasingly direct ways, as Charles either resisted making the change or missed her indirect way of suggesting it.

> Kristin: And that works out to 2.50 per FFB [local currency].
> Charles: 2.50 per FFC, right.
> Kristin: Per FFB ... FFC yeah right. [She laughs.] Excuse me. [She laughs again.]
> Charles: Yeah that's in then current dollars.
> Kristin: Okay. It might be useful—I'm not sure we're gonna show that.
> Charles: Yeah. Well, like I—y'know I saw—I thought I'd like to have an arsenal. [Kristin: Yeah] Or a sort of y'know collection of things [Kristin: Yeah] from which we could pick and choose.
> Kristin: This would be good in the arsenal, absolutely, yeah. Go for it.
> Charles: Okay.
> Kristin: Yeah. You might want to also— Well, w-would he—would Miller know that twelve—twelve dollars per unit is the same as twenty FFC?
> Charles: Um, actually it's fifteen dollars, it's more like this number that we were quoted before. Um, it's fifteen—this is fifteen and a half. [Kristin: Oh, okay.] Fifteen or sixteen depending on how you measure it. Uh, top-of-the-line or bottom-of-the-line. It's fifteen dollars a unit [Kristin: Okay.] for before tax, which is five dollars an FFC.

Kristin: You know—you might put in parentheses you know, to—yeah—you—you—you could put dollars per unit, and then in parentheses put, you know, dollars per FFC.

Charles: Okay.

Kristin: Just for /?/ for people like me who are not that quick with the conversions. [She laughs.] That would be good.

Kristin first tried to suggest that Charles put in the conversion rate from local currency to dollars when she said, "It might be useful—I'm not sure we're gonna show that." She seems to have started to say, "It might be useful to put the conversion rate in" but stopped midsentence and substituted a general statement: "I'm not sure we're gonna show that." Charles did not respond to her suggestion, so she took another crack at it: "You might want to also— Well, w-would he—would Miller know that twelve—twelve dollars per unit is the same as twenty FFC?" Again she seems to have started to say, "You might want to put the conversion rate in your report," but she cut herself off and expressed the idea more indirectly, by asking whether the director would know the conversion rate. She apparently assumed Charles would infer that the director might not know it, so the information should be provided. But Charles ignored this and continued talking about what the conversion was, ignoring the issue of whether or not to include it in his report. Only then did Kristin actually tell him to put it in. Even so, her instructions were mitigated: She said, "You might put in parentheses" rather than "Put that in parentheses," and toned down the suggestion by hesitations and "you know." Then, as a final softener, she added a reason for her instructions, a reason that put herself down: "Just for /?/ for people like me who are not that quick with the conversions," when she could just as easily have laid it on the director ("Just in case Miller isn't that quick with the conversions"). She also capped her request with laughter and words of approval ("That would be good").

Notice too that when Charles was talking, Kristin inserted frequent supporters like "Yeah" and "Okay," even though he wasn't addressing the issue she was raising. Also, she ratified his (military) metaphor of "an arsenal" by repeating it approvingly before steering the conversation back to the point she was trying to make. And throughout, she laughed—not loudly, as at a joke, but softly, in a good-natured way, as if to show goodwill and lack of animosity. Her frequent laughter was not joined by Charles's; he left her to laugh alone.

All of this verbal behavior gave Kristin's style a "soft touch" (a description I heard about her from a number of her colleagues). The kernel of her style was the indirect way in which she told Charles what to do.

Some people will find Mark's direct commands more appropriate; others would find them abrasive. Some would find Kristin's indirect directives congenial; others would find them irritating. One woman told me that she enjoyed working for a boss who tended to say things like, "I have a problem. I really have to get this report done, but I can't do it myself. What do you think?" Predictably, the employee would offer to write the report, to help her boss out. This woman preferred being given the opportunity to volunteer rather than being directly asked or even ordered, but someone who expected to be told directly might resent rather than appreciate this indirectness.

People with direct styles of asking others to do things perceive indirect requests as manipulative—if they perceive them as requests at all. But "manipulative" is often just a way of blaming others for our discomfort with their styles. This boss's way of allowing her employee to offer to write the report is no more "manipulative" than making a telephone call, asking, "Is Rachel there?" and expecting whoever answers the phone to put Rachel on. Only a child is likely to answer "Yes" and continue holding the phone—not out of orneriness but because of inexperience with the conventional meaning of the question. (A mischievous adult might do it to tease.) Those who feel that indirect orders are illogical or manipulative do not recognize the conventional nature of indirect requests.

INDIRECTNESS CAN BE POWERFUL

Some readers may have noticed that the manager who issued bald commands, Mark, was male, whereas the one who was indirect, Kristin, was female. But not all the managers whose talk I observed at companies across the country fell into this gendered pattern. One male manager, Sid, never gave unmitigated directives. He typically asked his secretary to do things by assuming she had already thought of doing them. For example, when Sid and his secretary, Rita, were discussing preparations for the impending visit of several high-level managers from a regional office, he said:

Sid: Oh and I was meaning to ask you about that. When I meet them Sunday, I'll have the invi—invitation for Sunday night's activities, and also I'll have an agenda, for the following day? In fact an agenda for the following week, for them—to give them, is that right?
Rita: Well, we can—we can do that.
Sid: So that—so that that night they can plan on, they can just look down through the agenda and see where they're going the next day, and we don't just present it to them Monday morning first thing.
Rita: That's a very good idea. I'll, uh—
Sid: And, uh, if it could just be in an envelope or something for each one of them and when I give them the invitation I can give them also the agenda showing them what the—what is going to happen for not only Monday but Tuesday and Wednesday, they've got the whole three days laid out.

. . .

Rita: That's a very good idea. Okay we'll see if we can have a whole lot of things for you to present to them.
Sid: Okay. All right, yep, that's a good idea.

Sid never directly told Rita to make up a schedule for the visitors' entire week and have it ready in an envelope for each one by Sunday night when they arrived. He spoke as though he presumed she would have it ready ("I'll have the invi—invitation for Sunday night's activities, and also I'll have an agenda, for the following day?") But it is clear from Rita's response that she was hearing this idea for the first time and took it as a request with which she would comply ("Well, we can—we can do that"). He also told her indirectly to put each one in an envelope, using the word "if" ("if it could just be in an envelope or something for each one of them").

Sid's indirect way of speaking to his secretary comes across as polite, yet he didn't say "thank you" at the end. In fact, Sid almost never said "thank you" in the week's worth of talk that I examined. This puzzled me at first, but then I realized that it went along with his never making direct requests but maintaining the appearance that Rita was going to do these things anyway. Saying "thank you" would imply that she had just agreed to do something for him, whereas his way of speaking avoided that implication.

The common assumption that asking people to do things indirectly, in a polite way, shows powerlessness and lack of security flies in the face of this and many other examples from Sid's speech. He always spoke this way when asking his secretary or other support staff (all were women) to do things. (He was more direct, though he still used many mitigating strategies, when talking to the managers who reported to him, all of whom were men.) And yet nothing about Sid gave the impression of powerlessness or lack of confidence. This brings us to the realization that issuing orders indirectly can be the prerogative of those in power.

Imagine, for example, a master who says, "It's cold in here" and expects a servant to make a move to close a window, while a servant who says the same thing is not likely to see his employer rise to correct the situation and make him more comfortable. Indeed, a Frenchman raised in Brittany tells me that his family never gave bald commands to their servants but always communicated orders in indirect and highly polite ways. This pattern renders less surprising the finding of David Bellinger and Jean Berko Gleason that fathers' speech to their young children had a higher incidence than mothers' of both direct imperatives such as, "Turn the bolt with the wrench" *and* indirect imperatives like, "The wheel is going to fall off."

The use of indirectness can hardly be understood without the cross-cultural perspective. Many Americans find it self-evident that directness is logical and aligned with power whereas indirectness is akin to dishonesty and reflects subservience. But for speakers raised in most of the world's cultures, varieties of indirectness are the norm in communication. This is the pattern found by Japanese sociolinguist Kunihiko Harada in his analysis of a conversation between a Japanese boss and a subordinate.

In the conversation Harada recorded and analyzed, the markers of superior status were clear. One speaker was a Japanese man in his late forties who managed the local branch of a Japanese private school in the United States. His conversational partner was a Japanese-American woman in her early twenties who worked at the school. By virtue of his job, his age, and his native fluency in the language being taught, the man was in the superior position. Yet when he addressed the woman, he frequently used polite language and almost always used indirectness. For example, he had tried and failed to find a photography store that would make a black-and-white print from a color negative for a brochure they were producing. He let her know that he wanted her to take over the task by stating the situation and allowed her to volunteer to do it. (The conversation took place in Japanese, so this is a translation.)

> On this matter, that—that—on the leaflet? This photo, I'm thinking of changing it to black-and-white and making it clearer. . . . I went to a photo shop and asked them. They said they didn't do monochrome. I asked if they knew any place that did. They said they didn't know. They weren't very helpful, but anyway, a place must be found, the negative brought to it, and the picture developed.

Harada observes, "Given the fact that there are some duties to be performed and that there are two parties present, the subordinate is supposed to assume that those are his or her obligation." It was precisely because of his higher status that the boss was free to choose whether to speak formally or informally, to assert his power or to downplay it and build rapport—an option not available to the subordinate, who would have seemed cheeky if she had chosen a style that enhanced friendliness and closeness.

Exactly the same pattern was found by Chinese sociolinguist Yuling Pan in a meeting of the staff of a neighborhood youth center. All staff members spoke in ways that reflected their place in the hierarchy. A subordinate addressing a superior always spoke in a deferential way, but a superior addressing a subordinate could either be authoritarian, demonstrating his power, or friendly, establishing rapport. The ones in power had the option of choosing which style to use. In this spirit, I have been told by people who prefer their bosses to give orders indirectly (in their minds, politely—but what is regarded as polite varies with conversational style) that those who issue bald commands must be pretty insecure; otherwise why would they have to bolster their egos by throwing their weight around?

I am not inclined to accept that those who give orders directly are really insecure and powerless, any more than I want to accept that judgment of those who give indirect orders. The conclusion to be drawn is that ways of talking should not be taken as obvious evidence of inner psychological states such as insecurity or lack of self-confidence. Nor is this to say that no one is insecure or underconfident. It is simply that, considering the many influences on conversational style, individuals have a wide range of ways of getting things done and expressing their emotional states. Personality characteristics such as insecurity cannot be linked to ways of speaking in an automatic, self-evident way.

"YES, SIR!"

Those who expect orders to be given "politely" are offended when directives come unadorned. One woman said that when her boss gives her instructions, she feels she should click her heels, salute, and say, "Yes, boss!" His directions strike her as so imperious as to border on the militaristic. Yet I received a letter from a man telling me that indirect orders were a fundamental part of his military training. He wrote:

Many years ago, when I was in the Navy, I was training to be a radio technician. One class I was in was taught by a Chief Radioman, a regular Navy man who had been to sea, and who was then in his third hitch. The students, about twenty of us, were fresh out of boot camp, with no sea duty, and little knowledge of real Navy life. One day in class the Chief said it was hot in the room. The students didn't react, except perhaps to nod in agreement. The Chief repeated himself: "It's hot in this room." Again there was no reaction from the students.

Then the Chief explained. He wasn't looking for agreement or discussion from us. When he said that the room was hot, he expected us to do something about it—like opening the window. He tried it one more time, and this time all of us left our work benches and headed for the windows. We had learned. And we had many opportunities to apply what we had learned.

This letter especially intrigued me because "It's hot in here" is the standard sentence used by linguists to illustrate an indirect way of getting someone to do something—as I used it earlier. In this example, it is the very obviousness and rigidity of the military hierarchy that makes the statement of a problem sufficient to trigger corrective action on the part of subordinates.

A man who had worked at the Pentagon reinforced the view that the burden of interpretation is on subordinates in the military—and he noticed the difference when he moved to a position in the private sector. He was frustrated when he'd say to his new secretary, for example, "Do we have a list of invitees?" and be told, "I don't know; we probably do" rather than "I'll get it for you."

Indeed, he explained, at the Pentagon, such a question would likely be heard as a reproach that the list was not already on his desk.

What prompted the letter from the former navy technician was my perspective on "troubles talk." I had written about the frustration that often results when a woman wants to talk about a problem or situation, but when she brings it up for discussion, the man she tells it to offers a solution. The letter writer pointed out that a man who responds to troubles talk by trying to solve the problem is operating on a system of indirectness. The woman did not ask, "So what do you think I could do to solve this problem?" Yet he concludes she wants a solution because he assumes that she wouldn't bother telling him about the problem if she didn't want something from him—and he surmises that what she wants must be a solution. The gender difference lies not in the ability to interpret indirectness, but in whether or not one expects indirectness in a given situation. In the case of troubles talk, exchanging talk about problems is a ritual more common among women than men, and it is unfamiliarity with the ritual that leads some men to look for an indirect meaning.

"IT'S JUST NOT AS DIRECT AS WE'D LIKE IT"

Another letter I received from a reader leads to the same conclusion. It was written by the curator of a private art collection—a woman who was dependent on three young men to install works of art for exhibition according to her vision. In explaining how she learned to work with these men, she wrote:

> Usually when I get really upset I just walk away, shed a few tears alone and then return to continue as though nothing happened. I've come to realize that they admire me for this. I never flog them with my tears, but they respect that they've gone too far and we usually end up compromising in a satisfactory way. That I can let go of the disagreement is a marvel

to them—women usually don't let it go. We fight, we return to work, joking and enjoying each other's company. I've learned to validate my own anger—and the fact that they tease me afterwards is an acknowledgment that they validate it too.

They're actually quite sensitive and endearing fellows—as long as I don't make them *talk* about their feelings. If I try to do that, they get quite annoyed. So we don't talk about *anybody's* feelings, but, if I listen carefully, they tell me things about themselves (and me!) in little bits of conversation. They really pay attention to me—they're all very sensitive to my moods and safety. But, to look at them, you'd think they didn't know I was alive.

Men, I think, are more subtle than women and I really appreciate this difference. Women need to learn to listen to what men say—because it really is there, it's just not as direct as we'd like it to be.

This woman's insights are a revelation in many ways. She knows the men she works with have registered and responded to her anger not because they say so but because they tease her—an indirect way of acknowledging that they've gone too far if they've driven her to tears. She sees them as sensitive not because they say they care about her but because they act as if they do, by compromising, allowing for her moods, and watching out for her safety. She concludes that they are simply more indirect than women. (The impression that their signals are "subtle" seems typical of the impression made by an unfamiliar signaling system; it's subtle because its meaning is not evident.)

The suggestion that men are more indirect than women must come as a surprise to many. But we are all indirect, meaning more than we put into words and deriving meaning from others that they never actually say. It's a matter of where, when, and how we each tend to be indirect and look for hidden meanings. Most studies finding women to be more indirect are about getting others to do things. That too can be common among men—as the cases of the military officer and the manager I called Sid demonstrated. But the situations in which men are most often found to be indirect have to do with the expression of weakness, problems, and errors, and of emotions other than anger.

Just that kind of indirectness was observed by linguist Nancy Ainsworth-Vaughn in a study of doctors talking to patients. As an example of a doctor who changes topics without getting the patient's explicit verbal agreement, Ainsworth-Vaughn presents an exchange she taped in which a patient expressed such extreme emotional distress that she wondered aloud whether life was worth living. The doctor responded by asking about an appointment with a therapist:

> [Patient has reported severe side effects from medication for lowering cholesterol, and physician has replied that the medication prevents an early death.]

> Doctor: And if we're going to (treat) your cholesterol if you decide that you want to do that, ahh, together with me, then like I said, there's not a whole lot of other options in terms of medications for your cholesterol.
> Patient: Yeah, so you prolong your life for what, you know?
> Doctor: (3-second pause) Do you have an appointment to see a therapist soon?

On the surface, the doctor's response had no direct relation to what the patient had just said. He made no explicit reference to her feelings or to the value of life. Instead, he seemed to change the subject, but what he changed it to was her seeing a therapist—someone who could, presumably, deal with her feelings that life wasn't worth living.

Parallel to the assumption that men tend to be more direct than women is the belief that men focus more on information, whereas women focus more on interaction—another type of indirectness. But this too depends on the activity and the situation.

Linguist Joanne Winter compared two political interviewers, one male and one female, on Australian television and concluded that the woman was more focused on information, asking relatively unbiased questions without expressing her own opinions, while the man was more focused on the interaction: He voiced his own opposing views, was more emotional, and turned the interview into a competitive conflict in which he was a full participant. I offer this example not to imply that all interviewers function in this way, but to show that at least one study found the woman to be more focused on information than the man, not less.

THE DANGERS OF INDIRECTNESS:
COMING IN FOR A LANDING—OR A CRASH

On January 13, 1982, a freezing-cold, snowy day in Washington, D.C., Air Florida Flight 90 took off from National Airport, but it could not get the lift it needed to keep climbing. Down, down it went, until it crashed into a bridge linking the District to the state of Virginia and plunged into the Potomac. Of the seventy-four people on board, all but five perished, many floundering and drowning in the icy water while horror-stricken bystanders watched helplessly from the river's edge, and thousands more watched, aghast, on their television screens. Experts later concluded that the plane had waited too long after de-icing to take off. Fresh buildup of ice on the wings and engine brought the plane down. How could the pilot and co-pilot have made such a blunder? Didn't at least one of them realize it was dangerous to take off under these conditions?

In accordance with airline regulations, all conversations that take place in the cockpits of planes are automatically recorded. If a flight proceeds without mishap, the tape is erased, but if the plane crashes, the heavily armored "black box" containing the tapes can be recovered to help analysts figure out what happened before the crash. Linguist Charlotte Linde has studied the "black box" recordings of cockpit conversations that preceded crashes as well as tape recordings of the conversations that took place among crews during flight simulations in which problems were presented. Among the black-box conversations she studied was the one between the pilot and co-pilot just before the Air Florida crash. The pilot, it turned out, had little experience flying in icy weather. The co-pilot had a bit more, and it became heartbreakingly clear on analysis that he had tried to warn the pilot, but he did so indirectly.

The co-pilot repeatedly called attention to the bad weather and to ice building up on other planes:

> Co-pilot: Look how the ice is just hanging on his, ah, back, back there, see that?
> Captain: Side there.
> . . .
> Co-pilot: See all those icicles on the back there and everything?
> Captain: Yeah.

He expressed concern early on about the long waiting time between de-icing:

> Co-pilot: Boy, this is a, this is a losing battle here on trying to de-ice those things, it (gives) you a false feeling of security, that's all that does.

Shortly after they were given clearance to take off, he again expressed concern:

> Co-pilot: Let's check these tops again since we been setting here awhile.
> Captain: I think we get to go here in a minute.

When they were about to take off, the co-pilot called attention to the engine instrument readings, which were not normal:

> Co-pilot: That don't seem right, does it? (3-second pause). Ah, that's not right. (2-second pause) (Well) ...

Captain: Yes, it is, there's eighty.
Co-pilot: Naw, I don't think that's right. (7-second pause)
Ah, maybe it is.
Captain: Hundred and twenty.
Co-pilot: I don't know.

The takeoff proceeded, and thirty-seven seconds later the pilot and co-pilot exchanged their last words:

Co-pilot: Larry, we're going down, Larry.
Captain: I know it.
((Sound of impact))

The co-pilot repeatedly called the pilot's attention to dangerous conditions but did not directly suggest that they abort the takeoff. In Linde's judgment, he was expressing his concern indirectly, and the captain did not pick up the hints—with unspeakably tragic results.

That the co-pilot was trying to warn the captain indirectly is supported by evidence from another airline accident—a more minor one—investigated by Linde that also involved the unsuccessful use of indirectness. On July 9, 1978, Allegheny Airlines Flight 453 was landing at Monroe County Airport in Rochester, New York, when it overran the runway by 728 feet. Fortunately, everyone survived. This meant that the pilot and co-pilot could be interviewed. It turned out that the plane was flying too fast for a safe landing. The pilot should have realized this and flown around a second time, decreasing his speed before attempting to land. The captain said he simply had not been aware that he was going too fast. But the co-pilot told interviewers that he "tried to warn the captain in subtle ways, like mentioning the possibility of a tailwind and the slowness of flap extension." His exact words were recorded in the black box:

Co-pilot: Yeah, it looks like you got a tailwind here.
Pilot: Yeah.
? Yeah it moves awfully # slow.

Co-pilot: Yeah the # flaps are slower than a #.
Pilot: We'll make it, gonna have to add power.
Co-pilot: I know.

The co-pilot thought the captain would understand that if there was a tailwind, it would result in the plane going too fast, and if the flaps were slow, they would be inadequate to break the speed sufficiently for a safe landing. He thought the captain would then correct for the error by not trying to land. But the captain said he didn't interpret the co-pilot's remarks to mean they were going too fast.

Linde believes it is not a coincidence that the people being indirect in these conversations were the co-pilots. (But then if a pilot perceives danger, he doesn't have to worry about how he is going to communicate it; he just acts on his perceptions.) In her analyses of flight-crew conversations, she found it was typical for the speech of subordinates to be more mitigated, although requests were less mitigated in problem flight conditions. She also found that topics broached in a mitigated way were more likely to fail, and that captains were more likely to ignore hints from their crew members than the other way around.

These findings are evidence that not only can indirectness be sincerely misunderstood, but it is also easier to be deliberately ignored. In the Air Florida case, it is doubtful that the captain did not realize what the co-pilot was suggesting when he said, "Let's check these tops again since we been setting here awhile" (though it seems safe to assume he did not realize the gravity of the co-pilot's concern). But the indirectness of the co-pilot's phrasing certainly made it easier for the pilot to ignore it. In this sense, the captain's response, "I think we get to go here in a minute," was an indirect way of saying, "I'd rather not." In view of these patterns, flight crews of some airlines are now given coaching to express their concerns, even to superiors, in more direct ways.

INDIRECTNESS TRAINING

The conclusion that people should learn to express themselves more directly has a ring of truth to it—especially for Americans. But direct communication is not necessarily always preferable. If more direct expression is better communication, then the most direct-speaking crews should be the best ones. Linde was surprised at first to find in her research that crews that used the most indirect speech might be the best crews. As part of the study of talk among cockpit crews in flight simulations, retired but still active pilots observed and rated the performances of the simulation crews. The crews they judged top in performance had a higher rate of mitigation than crews they judged to be poor.

This finding seems at odds with the role played by indirectness in the examples of crashes that we just saw. Linde concluded that since every utterance functions on two levels—the propositional (what it says) and the relational (what it implies about the speakers' relationships)—crews that attend to the relational level will be better crews. A similar explanation was suggested by sociolinguist Kunihiko Harada. Harada believes that the secret of successful communication lies not in teaching subordinates to be more direct, but in teaching higher-ups to be more sensitive to indirect meaning. In other words, the accidents resulted not only because the co-pilots tried to alert the captains to danger indirectly but also because the captains were not attuned to the co-pilots' hints. In this view, what made for successful performance among the best crews might have been the ability—or willingness—of listeners to pick up on hints, just as members of families or long-standing couples come to understand each other's meaning without anyone being particularly explicit. It is not surprising that a Japanese sociolinguist came up with this explanation; what he described is the Japanese system, by which good communication is believed to take place when meaning is gleaned without being stated directly—or at all.

Whereas Americans believe, "The squeaky wheel gets the grease" (so it's best to speak up), the Japanese say, "The nail that sticks out gets hammered back in" (so it's best to remain silent if you don't want to be hit on the head). Many Japanese scholars writing in English have tried to explain to bewildered Americans the ethics of a culture in which greater value is placed on silence than on speech, and ideas are believed to be best communicated without being explicitly stated. Key concepts in Japanese give a flavor of the attitudes toward language that they reveal—and set in relief the strategies that Americans encounter at work when talking to other Americans.

Japanese anthropologist Takie Sugiyama Lebra explains that one of the most basic values in Japanese culture is *omoiyari,* which she translates as "empathy." Because of *omoiyari,* it should not be necessary to state one's meaning explicitly; people should be able to sense each other's meaning intuitively. Lebra explains that it is typical for a Japanese speaker to let sentences trail off rather than complete them because expressing ideas before knowing how they will be received seems intrusive. Related to this is *enryo,* the self-restraint required to avoid disagreeing with opinions that the majority seem to hold. In stark contrast to Americans' assumptions that directness is best, Lebra explains that the Japanese hold in high regard those who communicate indirectly, implicitly, subtly, and even nonverbally, trusting the listener's empathy to fill in their meaning. They "believe that only an insensitive uncouth person needs a direct, verbal, complete message."

Another concept in Japanese communication is *sassuru,* which refers to the highly praised ability to anticipate another person's message intuitively. *Sasshi,* the anticipation of another's message through insightful guesswork, is considered an indication of maturity.

Considering the value placed on direct communication by Americans in general, and especially by American business people, it is easy to imagine that many American readers may scoff at such conversational habits. But the success of Japanese businesses makes it impossible to continue to maintain that there is anything inherently inefficient about such conversational rituals.

MOTHER POWER

Before returning to a more direct discussion of how Americans use indirectness at work, I want to explore one more aspect of Japanese communication that sheds light on American assumptions about power. It comes from the extremely powerful role of a mother talking to a small child.

Linguist Patricia Clancy tape-recorded talk between three Japanese mothers and their two-year-old children. She noticed that these mothers rarely denied their children's requests with flat-out no's. Instead, they might avoid or delay, ignore the request, promise to do it later, try to distract the child, suggest something else, or simply ask questions about the request. They often explained why they could not or would not do what the children asked. For example, when one child told his mother to draw a truck with a siren on it, she asked him, "Does it have that kind of thing?" and did not comply. When he wanted candy, she simply asked, "Didn't you eat a lot of candy this morning?" and left it at that. To get their children to stop doing something, the mothers rarely said "Don't," but instead appealed to what others might think or how others might feel. When a child pretended to eat a toy dish, her mother said, "Isn't it strange to do that kind of thing, if you eat a plate? No one eats plates, do they? Who eats plates?" Another time, the mother tried to get the child to stop misbehaving by attributing disapproval to the researcher, whom she referred to (as is customary in Japanese) as "older sister": "Older sister is saying, 'I'm surprised. I'm surprised at Maho.'" One mother even made an appeal to the feelings of fruit to convince her child to stop dropping apples on the floor: "If you do that kind of thing, Mr. Apple says, 'Ouch!'"

Clancy gives the following explanation for why Japanese mothers do not say no directly to their small children:

Why do Japanese mothers bother to give reasons for refusing requests when, at the age of 2 years, the children do not seem to understand or to care what the reasons might be? In addition to their more general wish to avoid a direct refusal, an important factor is probably the mothers' wish to maintain their status as rational adults in going against their children's wishes. Simply refusing requests with *Iya* "No/I don't want to," as the children usually did, would bring a mother down to the same level as her 2-year-old, making her sound selfish and childish. It would also reduce the exchange to a battle of wills, bringing the mother into direct conflict with her child. In contrast, giving reasons for her refusal puts the mother in a superior position and helps mitigate the conflict.

The contrast is stunning. Many Americans believe that talking indirectly shows insecurity and powerlessness. In this context, Japanese mothers assume that speaking directly means losing status, and speaking indirectly (giving reasons instead of just saying no) means gaining status. Why does an American mother feel more authoritative when she says no and adds "Because I said so," while a Japanese mother feels she is maintaining her status when she refrains from saying no and gives reasons?

The explanation is, in a way, circular. Clancy, like many other analysts of Japanese style, explains that Japanese norms for speaking prescribe that conflict should be avoided, harmony should be maintained, and almost no one says no in public. She cites a Japanese writer named Keiko Ueda who wrote an article called "Sixteen Ways to Avoid Saying 'No' in Japan." (Clancy notes that some of these include "silence; ambiguity; expressions of apology, regret, and doubt; and even lying and equivocation. Ueda's subjects reported using direct no at home, but very rarely in public.")

As a result, saying no is something associated with children who have not yet learned the norm. If a Japanese mother spoke that way, she would feel she was lowering herself to her child's level precisely because that way of speaking is associated with Japanese children. As another scholar, Patricia Wetzel, put it, "assertion of dominance," "making direct declarations of fact and opinion," and other behaviors that Americans associate with authority "contrast with what it means to be a mature adult" in Japan, where they "are much more likely to be viewed as immature or childish behavior." Because American norms for talk are different, it is common, and therefore expected, for American parents to "just say no." That's why an American mother feels authoritative when she talks that way: because it fits her image of how an authoritative adult talks to a child.

The point of this contrast is that ways of speaking do not *in and of themselves* communicate psychological states like authority, security, or confidence. We perceive them to connote those states because we associate certain ways of speaking with people we assume feel those emotions. Because Japanese adults learn to be indirect, they associate indirectness with maturity and power. Because middle-class European-American women are more likely to give orders and make requests in an indirect way, we associate indirectness with powerlessness and insecurity—emotions that women in our society are expected to have. And the situation is reinforced by the negative response people are likely to get if they do not speak in expected ways. As we will see in later chapters, women who do give direct commands are often viewed negatively.

THE USES OF INDIRECTNESS

The Japanese communication system sheds light on the benefits of indirectness that may not be immediately apparent to Americans, who are inclined to see it as pointlessly confusing—so much so that they wonder, Why bother with it at all? The reason is that those who expect indirectness will be offended by talk in any other mode. The secretary to the university president who appeared in my first example told me that she is very happy working for this president—precisely because she speaks to her in what the secretary regards as a respectful way.

An indirect/polite way of speaking, like any way of speaking, works well when used with those who understand its ritual nature and are accustomed to it. I saw indirectness working well among women and men who preferred this style, again and again. Here is just one example.

While spending time in a small community-outreach center, I was with Sally, the manager of support services, in her office. Our conversation was interrupted by a telephone call, which she answered on the speaker phone. It was Marian, the administrative assistant to the department's director, whose job included answering calls coming in to the agency. The conversation went like this:

> Marian: Sal, are you busy?
> Sally: No.
> Marian: What're you doing?
> Sally: Just talking to Deborah Tannen. Do you need me to cover the phone?
> Marian: Yes, I have to go to the accounting office.
> Sally: Okay, I'll be right there.

The indirect question clued Sally in that she should offer to help, so her colleague didn't need to ask. By the same token, Marian did not take at face value Sally's reply "No" to her question "Are you busy?" Obviously, Sally was doing *something* when Marian called. Even though Sally had answered that she wasn't busy, Marian asked what exactly she was doing before pursuing her request. By not having to ask directly, Marian did not need to risk being turned down or appearing demanding, and Sally could feel that she was volunteering rather than being *asked* to cover the phones—something that, after all, was not part of her job (but not unusual in a small business).

I hear myself giving instructions to my assistants without actually issuing orders: "Maybe it would be a good idea to . . ."; "It would be great if you could . . ." all the while knowing that I expect them to do what I've asked right away. If I discover several days later that something hasn't been done, I'm annoyed. This rarely creates problems, though, because the people who work for me know that there is only one reason I mention tasks—because I want them done. I *like* giving instructions in this way; it appeals to my sense of what it means to be a good person, which in my mind (as in many other women's), requires being "nice," taking others' feelings into account. And I have been told by many of my assistants (all women) that they appreciate it too. What I don't like is when the tasks don't get done. But I have never been told that the reason was that my directions were not clear.

"LET'S BE HONEST ABOUT IT"

Another common misjudgment is that being indirect is somehow less than honest. This was the opinion of a young man working in an office as a general assistant who was asked to organize the recently relocated office library. All the books were still packed in boxes in a closet. He took out the boxes, spread them on the floor in front of the library shelves, then set about the task by emptying each box and stacking its contents into piles on the floor before placing them in the right order on the shelves. The secretary commented that the boxes and stacks of books on the floor were unsightly. He agreed and diligently kept working. Later, his boss came in and said, "You really should put all the books on the shelf first and then organize them from within." The secretary then added her voice: "That's what I *told* him." The young man didn't mind being told to do the job in a different way, but he was incensed by the secretary's jumping on the bandwagon and claiming to have told him something she hadn't. He didn't realize that she thought she *had* told him—by pointing out that the way he was doing it was making a mess.

The problem in this instance was not that the secretary communicated indirectly, but that she communicated indirectly to someone who did not share her style. Yet in our culture, the burden seems to rest on those who are indirect. I rarely hear someone question their tendency to be direct ("What's wrong with me? Why do I say what I mean?"), but I often hear people—especially women—question themselves for being indirect ("Why do I do that? Why do I ask 'Are you hungry?' when *I* want to go for lunch?"). Distrust of indirectness is so pervasive that it has affected psychological treatment. A gay man told me that when he was an adolescent, he was in treatment with a psychotherapist who attributed homosexuality to indirectness. "I can always tell homosexuals when I pass them in the street," this fully credentialed psychologist told him. "They won't look you in the eye." He advised his young patient that if he would only learn to be more direct, he would stop having homosexual feelings. In an odd sort of way, I wonder whether the psychologist might have taken this stance because he associated indirectness with women. In any case, this is not as isolated an example as one might hope. Following a talk I gave at a university, a psychologist said that when he counsels women students, he often tells them that their indirectness evinces insecurity, and he teaches them to be more direct.

Even if they are not in therapy, many people—especially but not only women—feel that their styles are wrong and reveal deep-seated psychological problems. Two things must be said. First, it is not the case that women are always more indirect, as I've just shown. Second, there is nothing wrong with indirectness as a strategy when it is shared. When it's not shared, however, trouble can result—not from the indirectness, but from the difference in styles.

CROSSING STATE LINES

I found myself falling into just such a cross-cultural crack while discussing a lecture I was scheduled to give. I was talking on the telephone to a woman I'll call Loraine, the personal assistant to the

CEO of the company I was planning to visit. In the midst of our conversation, she said to her secretary, without making an effort to muzzle the phone, "Tell him I'm talking to Deborah Tannen." Then she said to me, "That's the CEO." I was confused. I thought that if her boss wanted to talk to her, she should excuse herself from the conversation with me and talk to him. I wouldn't have minded, since I had plenty of other things to do at my desk. But she gave me no overt indication that she wanted to end our conversation. I was reminded of how my agent often calls out, in the midst of a phone conversation, "Tell him I'll call him back in a few minutes." Although this is not ostensibly addressed to me, it lets me know she has another call and would like to finish with me in a few minutes.

I wasn't sure how Loraine wanted to handle this. So I asked, "Should I wait?" She said, "Well, I have to talk to him about a few things." This still didn't tell me whether she wanted me to hold on, hang up, or finish quickly. In the absence of a clear signal to end the conversation, I continued it, but Loraine was obviously preoccupied until she finally blurted out, "He doesn't like to wait. I'd better talk to him," and I said immediately, "Of course. Call me back if there are any questions," and hung up. It was only then that I realized I should have volunteered to get off the phone. Loraine probably thought I was rude not to; had I not known about conversational style, I would have thought her odd, if not manipulative, because she didn't simply say, "I'm sorry, I have an important call I have to take; may I call you back later?"

Though we were both women, both white, and both middle class, we had different senses of conversational politeness. She thought it would be rude to tell me to get off the phone, so she gave me a clue and expected me to offer to get off. I knew something was up, but I expected a direct indication of what she wanted— which she could not give me, since she felt it would be rude. Our different conversational expectations probably had less to do with gender than with our geographic backgrounds—mine from New York City, hers from Minnesota, together with the fact that we didn't know each other well.

Habits regarding indirectness vary greatly with ethnic and geographic background. In my own research, I explored how Greeks and Americans interpreted a conversation. I found that Greeks— both men and women—were far more likely to interpret a question as an indirect way of making a request. (For example, someone who asked, "Do you want to have a meeting about this?" would be heard to mean, "I want to have a meeting.") And Greek-Americans, who seem on the surface to be indistinguishable from other Americans, fell somewhere in the middle: less likely than Greeks but more likely than the other Americans in my study to take questions as hints.

"DON'T LOOK AT ME—I DIDN'T SAY IT"

Like any conversational strategy, indirectness can be used for negative as well as positive ends. An academic colleague told me he gave a talk presenting material so new, he was uncertain of his ability to speak about it coherently. After the talk, a woman came up to him and said, "I'm one of your greatest fans. I keep coming back to hear you again because I feel I learn so much from you, even though I've heard you give the same talk so many times." Like a shot from a gun with a silencer, the comment seemed to pass as a compliment, and yet underneath there was a bullet whizzing: "All your talks are the same; you just say the same thing over and over."

Another colleague told me a similar experience. One day a graduate student in her program came into her class early and began a conversation. "I left your article out on the dining-room table," she said, "and my husband read it." "Oh, that's nice," my colleague responded, beginning to puff up just a bit as she prepared herself for a compliment. The student went on: "He thinks you're crazy." My colleague was hurt by this secondhand insult (which is why she told me about it), but I suspected that the remark had little to do with her work and everything to do with the student's relationship with her husband. It turns out that her husband did not approve of his wife returning to school to get a graduate degree, so scoffing at her professor's work—saying she's crazy—was simply one more way to imply that his wife is crazy to pursue graduate studies.

But why did the student repeat the remark to her professor? Perhaps she was laying the burden of her husband's objections at the feet of someone she saw as stronger than she, someone in a better position to fight her battle. My colleague, however, simply felt she was being attacked—indirectly. The indirectness can make such swipes more difficult to deal with, because they sneak up on you, are harder to pinpoint, and allow the critic to appear as a neutral conduit of information—which is just the reason they are so common and so handy.

INDIRECT AND PROUD OF IT

Robin Lakoff, one of the first linguists to write about indirectness, identified two benefits of not saying exactly what you mean in so many words. One is defensiveness; the other is rapport. Defensiveness refers to the preference not to go on record with an idea in order to be able to disclaim, rescind, or modify it if it does not meet with a positive response. The rapport benefit of indirectness results from the pleasant experience of getting your way not because you demanded it but because the other person wanted the same thing. Assuming that only the powerless use indirectness reflects its defensive payoff but ignores the payoff in rapport.

A woman who owns a bookstore had to have a talk with the store manager. She had told him to do something; he had agreed to do it; and yet, days later, it hadn't been done. When they sat down to talk about it, they traced what she saw as his recalcitrance to a difference in conversational styles. The owner had said, "The bookkeeper needs help with the billing. What would you think about helping her out?" He'd said, "Okay," by which he meant, "Okay, I'll think about helping her out." He thought about it and came to the conclusion that he had too many other important things to do and couldn't spare the time to help the bookkeeper with the billing. The owner felt she had told him what to do in a considerate way, but he hadn't heard her question as an order at all. He thought he had been given an option and was within his rights to choose not to do it. Some months later, I asked the bookstore owner how things were going with the manager. She answered, "Fine. We don't have any more problems." I asked, "Have you changed the way you tell him to do things?" "No," she said. "Now he understands how I mean what I say."

Because she was the boss, the owner did not have to alter her own style. Also, the ease with which the manager learned to understand how she meant what she said is evidence that there is nothing inherently incomprehensible about indirect communication. In this instance, as with all the elements of conversational style, flexibility is the key to success—along with mutual respect.

FOUR

Marked: Women in the Workplace

Some years ago I was at a small working conference of four women and eight men. Instead of concentrating on the discussion, I found myself looking at the three other women at the table, thinking how each had a different style and how each style was coherent.

One woman had dark brown hair in a classic style that was a cross between Cleopatra and Plain Jane. The severity of her straight hair was softened by wavy bangs and ends that turned under. Because she was beautiful, the effect was more Cleopatra than plain.

The second woman was older, full of dignity and composure. Her hair was cut in a fashionable style that left her with only one eye, thanks to a side part that let a curtain of hair fall across half her face. As she looked down to read her prepared paper, the hair robbed her of binocular vision and created a barrier between her and the listeners.

The third woman's hair was wild, a frosted blond avalanche falling over and beyond her shoulders. When she spoke, she frequently tossed her head, thus calling attention to her hair and away from her lecture.

Then there was makeup. The first woman wore facial cover that made her skin smooth and pale, a black line under each eye, and mascara that darkened her already dark lashes. The second wore only a light gloss on her lips and a hint of shadow on her eyes. The third had blue bands under her eyes, dark blue shadow, mascara, bright red lipstick, and rouge; her fingernails also flashed red.

I considered the clothes each woman had worn on the three days of the conference: In the first case, man-tailored suits in primary colors with solid-color blouses. In the second, casual but stylish black T-shirt, a floppy collarless jacket and baggy slacks or skirt in neutral colors. The third wore a sexy jumpsuit; tight sleeveless jersey and tight yellow slacks; a dress with gaping armholes and an indulged tendency to fall off one shoulder.

Shoes? The first woman wore string sandals with medium heels; the second, sensible, comfortable walking shoes; the third, pumps with spike heels. You can fill in the jewelry, scarves, shawls, sweaters—or lack of them.

As I amused myself finding patterns and coherence in these styles and choices, I suddenly wondered why I was scrutinizing only the women. I scanned the table to get a fix on the styles of the eight men. And then I knew why I wasn't studying them. The men's styles were unmarked.

The term "marked" is a staple of linguistic theory. It refers to the way language alters the base meaning of a word by adding something—a little linguistic addition that has no meaning on its own. The unmarked form of a word carries the meaning that goes without saying, what you think of when you're not thinking anything special.

The unmarked tense of verbs in English is the present—for example, *visit*. To indicate past, you have to mark the verb for "past" by adding *ed* to yield *visited*. For future, you add a word: *will visit*. Nouns are presumed to be singular until marked for plural. To convey the idea of more than one, we typically add something, usually *s* or *es*. More than one *visit* becomes *visits*, and one *dish* becomes two *dishes*, thanks to the plural marking.

The unmarked forms of most English words also convey "male." Being male is the unmarked case. We have endings, such as *ess* and *ette*, to mark words as female. Unfortunately, marking words for female also, by association, tends to mark them for frivolousness. Would you feel safe entrusting your life to a doctorette? This is why many poets and actors who happen to be female object to the marked forms "poetess" and "actress." Alfre Woodard, an Oscar nominee for Best Supporting Actress, says she identifies herself as an actor because "actresses worry about eyelashes and cellulite, and women who are actors worry about the characters we are playing." Any marked form can pick up extra meaning beyond what the marking is intended to denote. The extra meanings carried by gender markers reflect the traditional associations with the female gender: not quite serious, often sexual.

I was able to identify the styles and types of the women at the conference because each of us had to make decisions about hair, clothing, makeup and accessories, and each of those decisions carried meaning. Every style available to us was marked. Of course, the men in our group had to make decisions too, but their choices carried far less meaning. The men could have chosen styles that were marked, but they didn't have to, and in this group, none did. Unlike the women, they had the option of being unmarked.

I took account of the men's clothes. There could have been a cowboy shirt with string tie or a three-piece suit or a necklaced hippie in jeans. But there wasn't. All eight men wore brown or blue slacks and standard-style shirts of light colors.

No man wore sandals or boots; their shoes were dark, closed, comfortable, and flat. In short, unmarked.

Although no man wore makeup, you couldn't say the men

didn't wear makeup in the sense that you could say a woman didn't wear makeup. For men, no makeup is unmarked.

I asked myself what style we women could have adopted that would have been unmarked, like the men's. The answer was: none. There is no unmarked woman.

There is no woman's hairstyle that could be called "standard," that says nothing about her. The range of women's hairstyles is staggering, but if a woman's hair has no particular style, this in itself is taken as a statement that she doesn't care how she looks—an eloquent message that can disqualify a woman for many positions.

Women have to choose between shoes that are comfortable and shoes that are deemed attractive. When our group had to make an unexpected trek, the woman who wore flat laced shoes arrived first. The last to arrive was the woman with spike heels, her shoes in her hand and a handful of men around her.

If a woman's clothes are tight or revealing (in other words, sexy), it sends a message—an intended one of wanting to be attractive but also a possibly unintended one of availability. But if her clothes are not sexy, that too sends a message, lent meaning by the knowledge that they could have been. In her book *Women Lawyers,* Mona Harrington quotes a woman who, despite being a partner in her firm, found herself slipping into this fault line when she got an unexpected call to go to court right away. As she headed out the door, a young (male) associate said to her, "Hadn't you better button your blouse?" She was caught completely off guard. "My blouse wasn't buttoned unusually low," the woman told Harrington. "And this was not a conservative guy. But he thought one more button was necessary for court." And here's the rub: "I started wondering if my authority was being undermined by one button."

A woman wearing bright colors calls attention to herself, but if she avoids bright colors, she has (as my choice of verb in this sentence suggests) avoided something. Heavy makeup calls attention to the wearer as someone who wants to be attractive. Light makeup tries to be attractive without being alluring. There are thousands of products from which makeup must be chosen and myriad ways of applying them. Yet no makeup at all is anything but unmarked. Some men even see it as a hostile refusal to please them. Women who ordinarily do not wear makeup can be surprised by the transforming effect of putting it on. In a book titled *Face Value,* my colleague Robin Lakoff noted the increased attention she got from men when she went forth from a television station still professionally made-up.

Women can't even fill out a form without telling stories about themselves. Most application forms now give four choices for titles. Men have one to choose—"Mr."—so their choice carries no meaning other than to say they are male. But women must choose among three, each of them marked. A woman who checks the box for "Mrs." or "Miss" communicates not only whether she has been married but also that she has conservative tastes in forms of address, and probably other conservative values as well. Checking "Ms." declines to let on about marriage (whereas "Mr." declines nothing since nothing was asked), but it also marks the woman who checks it on her form as either liberated or rebellious, depending on the attitudes and assumptions of the one making the judgment.

I sometimes try to duck these variously marked choices by giving my title as "Dr."—and thereby risk marking myself as either uppity (hence sarcastic responses like "Excuse *me!*") or an overachiever (hence reactions of congratulatory surprise, like "Good for you!").

All married women's surnames are marked. If a woman takes her husband's name, she announces to the world that she is married and also that she is traditional in her values, according to some observers. To others it will indicate that she is less herself, more identified by her husband's identity. If she does not take her husband's name, this too is marked, seen as worthy of comment: She has *done* something; she has "kept her own name." Though a man can do exactly the same thing—and usually does—he is never said to have "kept his own name," because it never occurs to anyone that he might have given it up. For him, but not for her, using his own name is unmarked.

A married woman who wants to have her cake and eat it too

may use her surname plus his. But this too announces that she is or has been married and often results in a tongue-tying string that makes life miserable for anyone who needs to alphabetize it. In a list (Harvey O'Donovan, Jonathon Feldman, Stephanie Woodbury McGillicutty), the woman's multiple name stands out. It is marked.

Pronouns conspire in this pattern as well. Grammar books tell us that "he" means "he or she" and that "she" is used only if a referent is specifically female. But this touting of "he" as the sex-indefinite pronoun is an innovation introduced into English by grammarians in the eighteenth and nineteenth centuries, according to Peter Mühlhäusler and Rom Harré in their book *Pronouns and People*. From at least about the year 1500, the correct sex-indefinite pronoun was "they," as it still is in casual spoken English. In other words, the female was declared by grammarians to be the marked case.

Looking at the men and women sitting around the conference table, I was amazed at how different our worlds were. Though men have to make choices too, and men's clothing styles may be less neutral now than they once were, nonetheless the parameters within which men must choose when dressing for work—the cut, fabric, or shade of jackets, shirts, and pants, and even the one area in which they are able to go a little wild, ties—are much narrower than the riotous range of colors and styles from which women must choose. For women, decisions about whether to wear a skirt, slacks, or a dress is only the start; the length of skirts can range from just above the floor to just below the hips, and the array of colors to choose from would make a rainbow look drab. But even this contrast in the range from which men and women must choose is irrelevant to the crucial point: A man can choose a style that will not attract attention or subject him to any particular interpretation, but a woman can't. Whatever she wears, whatever she calls herself, however she talks, will be fodder for interpretation about her character and competence. In a setting where most of the players are men, there is no unmarked woman.

This does not mean that men have complete freedom when it

comes to dress. Quite the contrary—they have much less freedom than women have to express their personalities in their choice of fabrics, colors, styles, and jewelry. But the one freedom they have that women don't is the point of this discussion—the freedom to be unmarked.

That clothing is a metaphor for women's being marked was noticed by David Finkel, a journalist who wrote an article about women in Congress for *The Washington Post Magazine*. He used the contrast between women's and men's dress to open his article by describing the members coming through the doors to the floor of the U.S. House of Representatives:

> So many men, so many suits. Dark suits. Solid suits. Blue suits that look gray, gray suits that look blue. There's Tom Foley—he's in one, and Bob Michel, and Steny Hoyer, and Fred Grandy, and Dick Durbin, and dozens, make that hundreds, more.
>
> So many suits, so many white shirts. And dark ties. And five o'clock shadows. And short haircuts. And loosening jowls. And big, visible ears.
>
> So many, many men.
>
> . . .
>
> And still the members continue to pour through the doors—gray, grayer, grayest—until the moment when, emerging into this humidor, comes a surprise:
>
> The color red.
>
> It is Susan Molinari, a first-termer from New York . . .
>
> Now, turquoise. It is Barbara Boxer . . .
>
> Now, paisley. It is Jill Long . . .

Embroidering his color-of-clothing metaphor, Finkel, whose article appeared in May 1992, concluded, "Of the 435 members of the House of Representatives, 29 are women, which means that if Congress is a gray flannel suit, the women of Congress are no more than a handful of spots on the lapel."

WHEN IS SEXISM REALISM?

If women are marked in our culture, their very presence in professional roles is, more often than not, marked. Many work settings, just like families, come with ready-made roles prescribed by gender, and the ones women are expected to fill are typically support roles. It was not long ago when medical offices and hospitals were peopled by men who were doctors and orderlies and women who were nurses and clerical workers, just as most offices were composed of men who ran the business and women who served them as receptionists, clerks, and secretaries. All members of Congress were men, and women found in the Capitol Building were aides and staff members. When a woman or man enters a setting in an atypical role, that expectation is always a backdrop to the scene.

All the freshmen women in Congress have had to contend with being mistaken for staff, even though they wear pins on their lapels identifying them as members. For her book *A Woman's Place,* Congresswoman Marjorie Margolies-Mezvinsky interviewed her female colleagues about their experiences. One congresswoman approached a security checkpoint with two congressmen when a guard stopped only her and told her to go through the metal detector. When Congresswoman Maria Cantwell needed to get into her office after hours, the guard wanted to know which member she worked for. But her press secretary, Larry West, has gone through the gate unthinkingly without being stopped. When Congresswoman Lynn Schenk attended a reception with a male aide, the host graciously held out his hand to the aide and said, "Oh, Congressman Schenk."

You don't have to be in Congress to have experiences like that. A woman who owned her own business found that if she took any man along on business trips, regardless of whether he was her vice president or her assistant, people she met tended to address themselves to him, certain that he must be the one with power and she his helper. A double-bass player had a similar experience when she arrived for an audition with a male accompanist. The people who greeted them assumed she was the accompanist. A woman who heads a research firm and holds a doctorate finds she is frequently addressed as "Mrs.," while her assistant, who holds only a master's degree, is addressed as "Dr."

One evening after hours, I was working in my office at Georgetown University. Faculty offices in my building are lined up on both sides of a corridor, with cubicles in the corridor for secretaries and graduate-student assistants. Outside each office is a nameplate with the professor's title and last name. The quiet of the after-hours corridor was interrupted when a woman came to my door and asked if she could use my phone. I was surprised but glad to oblige, and explained that she had to dial "9." She made the call, thanked me, and left. A few minutes later, she reappeared and asked if I had any correction fluid. Again surprised, but still happy to be of help, I looked in my desk drawer but had to disappoint her: Since my typewriter was self-correcting, I had none. My patience began to waver, but my puzzlement was banished when the woman bounded into my office for the third and final time to ask if I was Dr. Murphy's secretary, in which case she would like to leave with me the paper she was turning in to him.

I doubt this woman would have imposed on my time and space to use my telephone and borrow correction fluid if she had known I was a professor, even though I would not have minded had she done so. At least she would probably have been more deferential in intruding. And the experience certainly gave me a taste of how hard it must be for receptionists to get any work done, as everyone regards them as perpetually interruptible. But what amused and amazed me was that my being female had overridden so many clues to my position: My office was along the wall, it was fully enclosed like all faculty offices, my name and title were on the door, and I was working after five, the hour when offices close and secretaries go home. But all these clues were nothing next to the master clue of gender: In the university environment, she expected that professors were men and women were secretaries. Statistics were on her side: Of the eighteen members of my department at the time, sixteen were men; of the five members of Dr. Murphy's department, four were men. So she was simply trusting the world to be as she knew it was.

It is not particularly ironic or surprising that the student who mistook me for a secretary was female. Women are no less prone to assume that people will adhere to the norm than are men. And this includes women who themselves are exceptions. A woman physician who works in a specialty in which few of her colleagues are female told me of her annoyance when she telephones a colleague, identifies herself as "Dr. Jones calling for Dr. Smith," and is told by Dr. Smith's receptionist, "I'll go get Dr. Smith while you put Dr. Jones on the line." But this same woman catches herself referring to her patients' general practitioners as "he," even though she ought to know better than anyone that a physician could be a woman.

Children seem to pick up norms as surely as adults do. A woman who was not only a doctor but a professor at a medical school was surprised when her five-year-old said to her, "You're not a doctor, Mommy. You're a nurse." Intent on impressing her daughter, she said, "Yes, I am a doctor. In fact, I teach other doctors how to be doctors." The little girl thought about this as she incorporated the knowledge into her worldview. "Oh," she said. "But you only teach women doctors." (Conversely, male nurses must deal with being mistaken for doctors, and men who work as assistants must deal with being mistaken for their boss.)

Another of my favorite stories in this mode is about my colleague who made a plane reservation for herself and replied to the question "Is that Mrs. or Miss?" by giving her title: "It's Dr." So the agent asked, "Will the doctor be needing a rental car when he arrives?" Her attempt to reframe her answer to avoid revealing her marital status resulted in the agent reframing her as a secretary.

I relate these stories not to argue that sexism is rampant and that we should all try to bear in mind that roles are changing, although I believe these statements to be true. I am inclined to be indulgent of such errors, even though I am made uncomfortable when they happen to me, because I myself have been guilty of them. I recall an occasion when I gave a talk to a gathering of

women physicians, and then signed books. The woman who organized the signing told me to save one book because she had met a
doctor in the elevator who couldn't make it to the talk but asked to
have a book signed nonetheless. I was pleased to oblige and asked,
pen poised, to whom I should sign the book—and was surprised
when I heard a woman's name. Even though I had just spent the
evening with a room full of doctors who were all women, in my
mind "a doctor" had called up the image of a man.

So long as women are a minority of professional ranks, we
cannot be surprised if people assume the world is as it is. I mention
these stories to give a sense of what the world is like for people who
are exceptions to expectations—every moment they live in the unexpected role, they must struggle against others' assumptions that
do not apply to them, much like gay men and lesbians with regard
to their sexual orientation, and, as Ellis Cose documents in his
book *The Rage of a Privileged Class,* much like middle-class black
professionals in most American settings.

One particular burden of this pattern for a woman in a position of authority is that she must deal with incursions on her time,
as others make automatic assumptions that her time is more ex-
pendable, although she also may benefit from hearing more information because people find her "approachable." There is a sense in
which every woman is seen as a receptionist—available to give information and help, perennially interruptible. A woman surgeon
complained that although she has very good relations with the
nurses in her hospital, they simply do not wait on her the way they
wait on her male colleagues. (The very fact that I must say "woman
surgeon" and "male nurse" reflects this dilemma: All surgeons are
presumed male, all nurses presumed female, unless proven otherwise. In other words, the unmarked surgeon is male, the unmarked
nurse female.)

EXPECT THE EXPECTED

We approach new perceptions by measuring them against our past experience. This is a necessary process that makes it possible for us to get through life without regarding each incoming perception as brand-new. It works very well when the world we encounter is behaving as the world has done in the past but leads us astray when the world is new. And right now, we are all learning to deal with a world that is changing much faster than our expectations can keep up with.

A man was walking by a construction site in a large, busy city, absentmindedly surveying the scene, when his eyes met a surprise: The person sitting way up in the cab of a huge derrick, calmly making the crane grab mouthfuls of dirt, was a woman. He cheerfully called out to her, "Hey Mama, what's for supper?" It seemed to him a clever joke, and of course it was fleeting and not particularly well thought out, but in a wink he had reminded her that she was out of her place—which was in the kitchen.

If someone walks into a hospital and expects the doctors to be men and the nurses to be women—which means, by implication, that the women in white coats will be nurses and the men in white coats will be doctors—it will still be true most of the time. But it is not *always* true, and that is a problem for the women who are doctors and the men who are nurses and the patients who need to know which is which. When our expectations are not met, we call it sexism—responding to old patterns of gender that no longer apply, or no longer apply in all instances.

We are no less likely to respond to others according to expectations that we ourselves do not fit. I recall meeting a journalist years ago who had taken an interest in an article I had written about New York Jewish conversational style—an article in which I had identified myself as a native speaker of that style. As I waited for him outside the appointed restaurant, I saw him approach (I knew who he was because I had heard him give a talk) and saw his eyes run unseeing over me, as he looked for Deborah Tannen. When I identified myself, he said he didn't expect me to be blond, since he was looking for a fellow Jew—and then he laughed, because of all the times he himself had been told he didn't look like what people expected, because he too is a blond Jew.

What I am getting at is that there is no point in blaming those who expect the world to continue as it has been in the past, but we should not let anyone off the hook either—including ourselves. We must continually remind ourselves that the world is changing, and women and men no longer can be depended upon to stay in the narrowly prescribed roles we were consigned to in the past. But we must also be on guard for signs that such expectations are getting in our way. One of the major ways that expectations impede us is in the strong associations we have of how women and men should speak and behave. With women entering situations that were previously all male, where established norms for behavior are based on the ways men behaved in those roles, expectations must give way—either expectations for how someone in that role should behave, or expectations of the women who move into those roles. Which will it be? Will women change their ways of talking to fit existing norms, or will they change the norms—establish new expectations for the roles they come to fill?

"YOUR STYLE OR MINE?"

There is a mountain of research attesting that when females and males get together in groups, the females are more likely to change their styles to adapt to the presence of males—whether they are adults or children. Psychologist Eleanor Maccoby cites studies by Linda Carli and by Judith Hall and Karen Braunwald showing that when women are with men, they become more like men: They raise their voices, interrupt, and otherwise become more assertive. But, Maccoby continues,

> there is also evidence that they carry over some of their well-practiced female-style behaviors, sometimes in exaggerated form. Women may wait for a turn to speak that does not

come, and thus they may end up talking less than they would in a women's group. They smile more than the men do, agree more often with what others have said, and give nonverbal signals of attentiveness to what others—perhaps especially the men—are saying (Duncan and Fiske 1977). In some writings this female behavior has been referred to as "silent applause."

Psychologist Campbell Leaper observed girls' tendency to adapt to boys' styles in his study of 138 children playing in pairs at the ages of five and seven. Although "collaborative" speech accounted for the majority of all the children's speech, whether or not they were talking to other children of the same sex, there were nonetheless differences in degree. He found collaborative and cooperative exchanges to be more frequent when girls played with girls, and controlling and domineering exchanges more frequent when boys played with boys, especially when the children were older. Boys were less likely than girls to adopt strategies typical of the other sex when they played co-ed. When girls played with boys, they used more controlling speech than when they played with girls. Leaper suspects this occurred because the boys tended to ignore the girls' polite speech. Again, we get a glimpse of the ritual nature of conversation. The girls' strategies worked best when used with other girls who shared the same strategies. When they used these strategies with boys, they didn't work as well, so the girls had to adapt to the boys' style to get results.

The tendency of women to adapt their styles to men's has been found even on the most small-scale and personal level. Donna Johnson and Duane Roen examined peer-review letters written by graduate students to fellow students whose term papers they had evaluated. The results showed that women students used slightly more positive evaluation terms, such as "interesting" and "helpful," than the men, but the most striking finding was that the women offered positive evaluation terms far more frequently *to other women* than they did to men, whereas the men offered only slightly more such terms to women than to other men. In other words, the women adjusted more in response to whether they were addressing another woman or a man. (An indirect result of this pattern was that men received the least praise, whether they were talking to other men or to women.)

"WHY CAN'T A WOMAN BE MORE LIKE A MAN?"

There are many ways that women entering the world of work are entering "the men's house," to use the phrase coined by Captain Carol Barkalow as the title of her book about her military career. The very language spoken is often based on metaphors from sports or from the military, terms that are just idioms to many women, not references to worlds they have either inhabited or observed with much alacrity. Such expressions as "stick to your guns," "under the gun," "calling the shots," "an uphill battle," "a level playing field," "a judgment call," "start the ball rolling," "a curve-ball," "the ball's in their court," "batting a thousand," "struck out," "getting flak," "the whole nine yards," "in the ballpark," and "deep-six it" are part of our everyday vocabulary. (The list could go on and on.) Author Mark Richard recalls that when he was a struggling writer living in Virginia Beach, the fiction editor of a national magazine told him, "You want to play hardball fiction? You've got to come to New York."

In some cases, women (or men) not very familiar with sports may know how an expression is used without knowing its source. In others, a lack of familiarity with sports can lead to a failure of comprehension. A woman was told by her lawyer that according to a contract they were negotiating, "they can't sell you to Buffalo." She had to ask what he meant by that.

This is an area in which, it seems, women are already beginning to do things their own way, using metaphors from cooking, birthing, and sewing along with those from war and sports. For example, a woman discussing her plans for a company that would produce a series of videotapes said, "I'd like to be able to pop them out—not like breadsticks, but like babies." The 1994 Poet Laureate of the United States, Rita Dove, compared a poem to a bouillon cube, because it's concentrated, portable, and useful. A woman described an editorial project she was working on as being like needlepoint, in the sense that it required close attention to detail.

Although there is evidence that women do adapt their styles to those of men when they find themselves in interaction with men, they rarely adopt men's styles whole-hog. And it is well that they don't, because men and women who model their behavior on someone of the other gender often get a very different reaction than their role models get. In a workplace situation, it is frequently a man who has been the model, while a woman who tries to behave like him is distressed to find that the reaction she gets is very different.

A dramatic example of this phenomenon happened to Captain Carol Barkalow. One of the first women to attend West Point, Captain Barkalow rose to the position of company commander at Fort Lee in Virginia. In her attempt to make herself more like a male commanding officer, she took up bodybuilding. What better way to challenge the unfair assumption that women are not as strong as men, not strong enough to lead their unit? She did so well that she won second place in a bodybuilding competition.

Two months before Captain Barkalow was to take her command, news of her triumph was published in the post newspaper, along with the standard championship photograph in which she posed standing beside her trophy, clad in a bikini designed to show off the muscles she had worked so hard to develop. And this photograph very nearly cost her the command and her career. In the words of the brigade commander, "She had become the masturbatory fantasy of every goddamned male noncommissioned officer in the company." Her attempt to enhance her image in a male domain—the strength of her muscles—was interpreted sexually because a photograph of a woman posing in a bikini, even though the pose she struck was designed to look powerful rather than seductive, brought to mind an image not of fitness and strength but of a pinup. This is a particularly dramatic example of what Captain

Barkalow learned during her years in the military, as she explains in her book: She could not be an officer in the same way that men were; she had to find her own way, a way that fulfilled the requirements of her job as a military officer without violating too many expectations for how a woman should be.

CHANGE OTHERS BY ADAPTING YOUR STYLE

In talking to women physicians, I heard two different and conflicting themes repeated. From some, I heard that nurses were a problem. They simply did not give the women physicians the same respect they gave to male doctors; they would not do for them what they do for the men. From others, I heard that nurses were their best allies. The nurses they worked with would do anything for them, and more than once saved their skins. Which was the truth about how nurses, who are almost all women, tend to treat women doctors?

A possible explanation was offered by a prominent surgeon who was one of the few women in her specialty. She explained that when she first became a surgeon, she modeled her behavior on that of the male surgeons who had been her teachers. Having seen that the operating room functioned like the military, with the surgeon the captain, she tried barking orders like the other surgeons. But she found it didn't work. No one would take orders from her. So she had to change her style, finding ways of being firm that did not sound as authoritarian. And this, she believes, explains the different experiences women physicians reported having with nurses. If you try to be authoritarian, like many of your male colleagues are, it won't work with most nurses, but if you ally yourself with them and respect them as professional colleagues, they will be your best allies.

This seemed to offer a possible solution to the puzzle: Different women doctors may have different impressions of how nurses treat women doctors because of the different ways they treat nurses. It is interesting to note that men as doctors can choose whether or not they wish to adopt an authoritarian or even an imperious style without suffering a loss of service from nurses, but women doctors cannot. It is also instructive to consider the role that women play in ensuring that other women adhere to the norms for female interaction, just as men exert pressure on other men to behave according to norms for male interaction.

Indeed, there is ample evidence that women tend to speak differently from men, not in an absolutely predictable pattern but as a matter of degree. Allowing for the exceptions of individuals, and the great range of personal and cultural styles, there is nonetheless evidence (for example in the work of Candace West and of Nancy Ainsworth-Vaughn) that women physicians tend to talk differently to their patients than male doctors do, and that women lawyers tend to operate differently from men. But many are not aware that they are doing things differently, and those who are aware of it may be reluctant to admit it, since deviating from accepted norms always carries a price.

Linguist Barbara Johnstone interviewed four prominent and successful Texas women, because she was interested in how they thought their being women affected their public-speaking styles. But when Johnstone interviewed them, all four denied that their being female affected their ways of speaking. For example, an attorney said, ". . . people have told me that they think that I'm successful in the courtroom because I can identify with the jury, that the juries like me. And I haven't ever figured out why, except that . . . I try to smile, and I try to just be myself. And I don't put on any airs." Although I do not doubt that this attorney is indeed just being herself, it is nonetheless well documented that women tend to smile more than men. And placing value on not putting on airs sounds quite a bit like the assumption that a person should not flaunt her authority that typifies the way many women talk about management. (I offer evidence of this in Chapter Six.) Interestingly, all four women Johnstone interviewed spoke with pride of how their styles were influenced by their being Texan.

Mona Harrington writes of three women who left large law

firms to start their own "alternative" firm specializing in commercial litigation. They determined to do things differently from the ways things were done in the large firms where they had worked before—both in managing their relationships with each other and in doing work for their clients.

In terms of interoffice relations, in the women's firm all partners make decisions together at meetings, have offices equal in size, and divide money earned equally among them, regardless of who brought in the client or who worked on the case. In terms of their working styles, the women told Harrington that they represent clients not by being as aggressive and confrontational as possible, but by listening, observing, and better "reading" opponents. One pointed out that in taking depositions, they get better results by adopting a "quiet, sympathetic approach," charming witnesses into forgetting that the attorney deposing them is their adversary, than by grilling witnesses and attacking them.

Yet when interviewed by the press about their approach, these same women do not mention their different styles, not even to explain how well they work. Just the opposite, they stress that they are "tough" litigators and seasoned veterans of traditionally contentious legal settings. The reason, they explained to Harrington, is that if they told the truth about their styles, they would be dismissed as soft and weak. Their conclusion has been that you can't talk about it; you have to just *be* it, and get a reputation based on results.

A BRAID IS A STRONGER ROPE

Although I describe patterns of women's and men's typical (not universal) styles, and show that styles expected of women can work against them in work settings, I would not advise women to adopt men's styles to succeed—although in some cases, in some ways, this might work. In general, that advice is no more practical than advising women to go to work dressed in men's clothes. Instead, I would argue for flexibility and mutual understanding. The frustration of both genders will be reduced, and companies as well as individuals will benefit, if women and men (like Easterners and Southerners, old and young, and people of different classes and ethnic backgrounds) understand each other's styles. Once you understand what is happening to you, you can experiment on your own, trying new ways of behaving to solve your problems. Of course, all problems will not summarily disappear, but the sense of puzzlement and lack of control will at least subside.

Another reason it would be a mistake for women to try to behave like men is that businesses need to communicate with clients of different sorts, including more and more women. For instance, newspapers need to appeal to women as readers in order to sell newspapers, so it would do them no good to hire a slew of women who are just like men. I sometimes give the example of a woman who worked at an appraisal firm. One of her colleagues told her he had just gotten a very strange call from a client. After identifying herself, the client simply told him that she would be going on vacation that week and hung up, without giving him any comprehensible reason for her call. The woman who told me this said she was pretty sure she understood what this was about and called the client back to apologize for the slight delay in the appraisal she had ordered and reassure her that it would be ready when she returned from her vacation.

The appraiser also told me that she had been nonplussed by a client who called her up and began angrily berating her because his appraisal was late. Taken aback by the verbal assault, which seemed to her unacceptable in the context of a business relationship, she had become tongue-tied and unable to give him the assurances she had just given the other client, so she had her colleague call the man back and deal with him. This example shows how pointless it would be to ask which appraiser's style was "best." Each one was best at dealing with certain clients. Rather than trying to determine which style is best and hire a staff with uniform styles, the company clearly is benefiting from having a range of styles among its sales staff.

Nobody Nowhere was the first book by Donna Williams, the remarkable woman with autism, in which she describes her experience as a child and young adult, explaining what autism feels like from the inside and how she was able to function within its constraints. Among the effects of autism is increased sensitivity to all incoming sensory information, and an inability to process this information in a coherent way. In her second book, *Somebody Somewhere*, Williams recounts her continuing efforts to make contact with the world outside, including the events surrounding the publication of her first book. When an agent went in search of a publisher for *Nobody Nowhere*, he found not one but two major companies that wanted to publish the book, so the author had to choose between them. Williams's description of her meetings with the two publishers' emissaries is instructive. She met them in the home of her landlords, a couple named Mr. and Mrs. Miller.

Tall and square, the first one resembled an insurance salesman. As he entered the Millers' place, he handed me an advertising catalogue for his company. I examined the picture of the ocean on the cover. What am I meant to do with this? I wondered.

. . .

He spoke confidently. Yet he was too self-assured and his ego dwarfed mine by comparison. . . . He took Mr. Miller aside to discuss the deal. I realized he considered me more as an oddity with some intelligent bits rather than an equal human being. I smiled to myself. One down, one to go.

The next publisher had bright red hair and looked like the children's storybook character Holly Hobbie. She had a whisper of a voice to match. She was stiff as a board and shook like a sparrow confronted by a cat. I liked her even though her anxiety made me feel I was a psychopath. She was not at all self-assured, so there was enough social space to find myself present in her company. It is hard to make a decision when your body and voice are present but your sense of self is absent. Holly Hobbie made it easier.

She was about to go. I remembered the other guy with the company advertising catalogue. "Do you have anything to give me?" I asked. "Yes," she replied, producing three glossy picture books of landscapes of the Australian outback and tales of childhood and the plight of Australian Aborigines. This woman knew she was taking a person on board, not just a meal ticket. I decided to work with her. The book was on the road to publication.

Imagine a publishing executive making a decision about which of two individuals to hire: One is extremely confident and self-assured; the other is so lacking in confidence that when faced with an atypical author, she shakes visibly. The first is straightforward; the second speaks in a whisper. The first goes to a business meeting ready to talk deals with someone capable of understanding what he's talking about; the second comes armed with picture books. But the confident, self-assured, straight-talking publisher lost the book that turned out to be an international best-seller, and the quaking, whispering, picture-book-bearing publisher landed it.

Donna Williams is an unusual author. But there are many authors, or clients in other businesses, who would be more comfortable with a less assured style that does not overwhelm them. And there are many women who would be put off by someone who addresses himself to their landlord—or any man who happens to be present—rather than to her. Companies that have a uniform model of a "good"-style employee will end up with a staff equipped to perform well when talking to individuals with some styles but not others. The company that is able to accommodate employees with a range of styles will have far more flexibility in dealing with customers whose styles also cover a range.

Not only customers, but the employees within a company, no longer come from the same mold. Bringing together people of different ethnic and class backgrounds, from different parts of the country and the world, all with their own personalities, inevitably results in a mix of conversational styles within the organization as well. Making the workplace more amenable to people with a range of styles will benefit not only women but everyone; not all men have the same style, and not all men have styles that are rewarded in traditional business environments. If more people's styles are accommodated, more talents and ideas will be available to the company.

WILL TALK ABOUT GENDER DIFFERENCES POLARIZE?

Some people fear that putting people into two categories by talking about "women" and "men" can drive a wedge between us, polarizing us even more. This is a serious concern. I know of at least one instance in which that is exactly what happened. A female executive at a large accounting firm was so well thought of by her firm that they sent her to a weeklong executive-training seminar at the company's expense. Not surprisingly, considering the small number of women at her level, she was the only woman at the seminar, which was composed of high-ranking executives from a variety of the corporation's wide-ranging divisions. This did not surprise or faze her, since she was used to being the only woman among men.

All went well for the first three days of the seminar. But on the fourth, the leaders turned their attention to issues of gender. Suddenly, everyone who had been looking at her as "one of us" began to look at her differently—as a woman, "one of them." She was repeatedly singled out and asked to relate her experiences and impressions, something she did not feel she could do honestly, since she had no reason to believe they would understand or accept what she was talking about. When they said confidently that they were sure there was no discrimination against women in their company, that if women did not get promoted it was simply because they didn't merit promotion, she did not feel she could object. Worst of all, she had to listen to one after another of her colleagues express what she found to be offensive opinions about women's abilities. By the end of the day, she was so demoralized that she was questioning whether she wanted to continue to work for this company at all. Whereas she had started out feeling completely comfortable, not thinking of herself as different from the men, the discussion of gender issues made her acutely aware of how different she was and convinced her she could never again fit comfortably into this group.

The group in which this occurred was made up of people from far-flung offices, not many of whom were from her own home office. As a result, she was able eventually to get past the experience, and it did not poison her day-to-day relationships at work. If a similar workshop had been held among her daily co-workers, it could have been much more destructive. And the saddest part is that the unfortunate outcome resulted from a program designed to help. As anthropologist Gregory Bateson explained in his work on cybernetics, any time people interfere with a system to change it, they risk making things worse, because they don't understand all the elements in the system and how they interrelate.

But the alternative, doing nothing, is not a viable one, because the situation as it is will have to change. In the case of women in the workplace, the situation is changing, whether we talk about it or not. And the hope that all we had to do was open the doors and let women in has simply not been borne out. Twenty years after women began receiving MBAs and entering businesses where they had not been before, they still make up only a small percentage of higher-level executives. The "pipeline" argument has simply not panned out. Years after women entered the pipeline, they just aren't coming through the other end in proportion to their numbers going in. Instead, more and more women are leaving the corporate world, in greater numbers than men, either to start their own businesses, to be independent contractors, or to do other things entirely. (For example, a 1993 survey of those who received MBAs from Stanford University over the preceding ten-year period found that 22% of the women, as compared to 8% of the men, had left large corporations to start their own businesses.) Some of this may be a privilege that men too would take advantage of if they had the chance. But a lot of women are seeking alternatives simply because they tire of feeling like strangers in a strange land when they go to work each day. In a word, they tire of being marked.

Simply opening the doors and letting in women, or any individuals whose styles do not conform to those already in place, is not enough. As the experience of the executive at the training seminar showed, neither are localized efforts at diversity training, though surely these can help if they are done well. Finally, we can't just tell individuals that they should simply talk one way or another, as if ways of talking were hats you can put on when you enter an office and take off when you leave. For one thing, if you try to adopt a style that does not come naturally to you, you leave behind your intuitions and may well behave in ways inappropriate in any style or betray the discomfort you actually feel. Most important, we do not regard the way we talk—how we say what we mean, how we show consideration or frustration to others—as superficial, masks to be donned and doffed at will. Comprehensive training and awareness are needed, until everyone is working to make the workplace a world where differing styles are understood and appreciated.

FIVE

The Glass Ceiling

A man who heads up a large division of a multinational corporation was presiding at a meeting devoted to assessing performance and deciding who would be promoted into the ranks of management. One after another, each senior manager got up, went down the list of individuals in his group and evaluated them, explaining whether or not they were promotable, and why. Though there were significant numbers of women in every group, not a single person singled out for advancement was female. One after another, every senior manager pronounced every woman in his group not ready for promotion because she lacked the necessary confidence. The division head began to doubt his ears. How could it be that *all* the talented women in the division suffered from a lack of confidence?

The situation described by this manager seemed to me to hold a clue to one described by a top executive at another multinational corporation who contacted me for help: "We started full of hope but we've reached an impasse. We are very successful at recruiting top women—they're creative, motivated, with fabulous credentials. They look just as good as the men when we hire them, if not better. But they don't get promoted. Years into our affirmative-action program, we still don't have any women in top management." The women who had been hired either were stuck at the level of middle management or had left the company or the field. He was describing what is sometimes referred to as the glass ceiling: an invisible barrier that seems to keep women from rising to the top. The problem is considered so widespread and serious that a Glass Ceiling Commission was created as part of the Civil Rights Act of 1991, chaired by the secretary of labor.

Many earnest executives sincerely believe that there is no glass ceiling but only a pipeline problem: When women have been in the pipeline long enough to work their way up, some will reach positions at the top. But the longer this situation prevails, the less tenable the pipeline theory becomes. According to a 1991 report by the United States Department of Labor, progress has been extremely slow. During the ten-year period from 1979 to 1989, the representation of women and minorities in the top executive positions of the one thousand largest American corporations rose from 3% to 5%. Another 1991 survey based on 94 randomly selected Fortune 1000–sized companies found women comprised 37% of employees, 17% of managers, but only 6½% of executive-level managers.

The temptation is to see the cause of the glass ceiling as "sexism," and surely there is truth in this characterization. But "sexism" tells us where we are without telling us how we got there, and without providing help in getting out. I do not doubt that there are men (as well as women) who do not wish to see women advance. It may be that the presence of women in their work lives is a complication they did not bargain for when they chose their life's work. They may see every woman who fills a job in their field as taking that job from a man (rather than seeing half the men in their field as taking jobs that should have gone to qualified women). They may even feel that women do not belong in positions of authority, certainly not in authority over them. But not all men fit this description. There are many men who sincerely want to see women advance and are trying to do something about it.

The executive I just quoted was one of many men who have written to me in hopes of remedying the situation. There are enough men (and women) who sincerely wish to be fair, even to actively promote women, to make one wonder why they are not having more success in ensuring that women advance in their organizations. The men who contacted me did so because, in reading *You Just Don't Understand,* they thought they were seeing a potential partial explanation for what was going on: that the differences in women's and men's ways of talking work against women.

"CAN SHE DO THE JOB?"

In all the companies I observed, I met women who did not seem to be getting full credit for the jobs they were doing. This can be tricky to describe, especially when women were getting a lot of recognition or had achieved a high level of acceptance. It seemed like bad form for them to complain, and (perhaps for this reason) few did. But they were often aware of an imbalance. A physician working in a university context who was highly respected in her field did not doubt that had she been a man, she would have been head of a department long ago. A woman who headed a major division of her company, and who did work comparable to that of six men who headed the other six divisions, had the title "director," whereas the men were vice presidents. Another woman was doing work parallel to the jobs of several other men who reported to a particular vice president, but on paper she reported to someone else who reported to him. In a company, your prestige is partly determined by the status of the person to whom you report, and there may be very real repercussions in terms of what meetings you attend and what information you get, so the intermediate boss lessened her clout, as well as the impression of it.

In all the companies I visited, I observed what happened at lunchtime. I saw women who ate lunch in their offices and women who skipped lunch to run or exercise in the gym and women who ate in groups with other women or with men. I observed men who ate alone or with colleagues and a few who went home to have lunch with their wives. I observed young men who made a point of having lunch with their bosses, and men at high levels of management who ate lunch with the big boss. I rarely noticed women who sought out the highest-level person they could eat lunch with.

Early on, I became aware of an irony. On one hand, it was from men that I heard that if women weren't promoted, they simply weren't up to snuff, whereas women everywhere agreed that something outside themselves prevents women from advancing. But on the other hand, it was women, more often than men, who seemed to feel that all that was necessary for success was to do a great job, that superior performance would be recognized and rewarded. Yet looking around, I could see that much more seemed to go into getting recognized and rewarded, and I saw men more often than women behaving in these ways.

In addition to doing excellent work, you must make sure that your work is recognized. This may consist of making a point to tell your boss, or your boss's boss, what you have done—either orally, or by sending reports or copies of pertinent correspondence. If a group meets, the person who is the first to report the group's results may get the most credit for them, whether or not that person was the source of the ideas in the first place. When lunchtime comes, the one who eats lunch with the boss may be doing more to get ahead than the one who stays in the office, eating a sandwich and working. Doing brilliantly at a project that no one knows about will do little good in terms of personal advancement; doing well at a high-profile project, or one that puts you into contact with someone in power who will thereby gain firsthand knowledge of your skill, may make the big difference when that person speaks up at a meeting at which promotions are decided. All of these dynamics could be derisively dismissed as "office politics," but they are simply a matter of human nature. How *are* the bosses to know who's done what? It is understandable (though not necessarily admirable) if they notice what appears before them and fail to notice what they would have to rout around to see. Put another way, influence flows along lines of affiliation and contact.

THE GLASS CEILING AS A WALL OF WORDS

Here is a brief explanation of how conversational-style differences play a role in installing a glass ceiling. When decisions are made about promotion to management positions, the qualities sought are a high level of competence, decisiveness, and ability to lead. If it is men, or mostly men, who are making the decisions about promotions—as it usually is—they are likely to misinterpret women's ways of talking as showing indecisiveness, inability to assume authority, and even incompetence. All the conversational-style differences discussed thus far can work against women who use them in an office setting. For example, a woman who feels it is crucial to preserve the appearance of consensus when making decisions because she feels anything else would appear bossy and arrogant begins by asking those around her for their opinions. This can be interpreted by her bosses as evidence that she doesn't know what she thinks should be done, that she is trying to get others to make decisions for her.

Again and again, I heard from women who knew they were doing a superior job and knew that their immediate co-workers knew it but the higher-ups did not. Either these women did not seem to be doing what was necessary to get recognition outside their immediate circle, or their superiors were not doing what was necessary to discern their achievements and communicate these upward. The kinds of things they were doing, like quietly coming up with the ideas that influenced their groups and helping those around them to do their best, were not easily observed in the way that giving an impressive presentation is evident to all.

136

Even so small a linguistic strategy as the choice of pronouns can have the effect of making one's contributions more or less salient. It is not uncommon for many men to say "I" in situations where many women would say "we." One man told me, "I'm hiring a new manager; I'm going to put him in charge of my marketing division," as if he owned the corporation he worked for and was going to pay the manager's salary himself. Another talked about the work produced by all the members of his group in the same way: "This is what I've come up with on the Lakehill deal." In stark contrast, I heard a woman talking about what "we" had done, but on questioning discovered that it was really she alone who had done the work. By talking in ways that seemed to her appropriate to avoid sounding arrogant, she was inadvertently camouflaging her achievements and lessening the chances they would be recognized.

DOING WHAT COMES UNOBTRUSIVELY

Sociolinguist Shari Kendall spent two days shadowing the technical director for a news/talk show at a local radio station. The woman, Carol, was responsible for making sure all the technical aspects of the show went smoothly, and she did her job very well. The following incident, presented and analyzed by Kendall, reveals both why Carol was so good at her job and why her excellence was likely to go unrecognized.

Carol knew she had a challenge on her hands: the "board op," the technician who sits at the soundboard (the radio show's control tower), was out sick, and Harold, the man filling in, was very, very nervous. He had to get all the right prerecorded bits of music and talk onto the air at the right time, make sure that callers got on just when the host wanted to talk to them, and generally throw switches in the right direction at the right moment—switches chosen from a dizzying array that made up the soundboard. Though Harold had a thorough technical knowledge of the equipment, he was unfamiliar with the routines of this show and inexperienced in this role. He was so nervous, he was shaking. For her part, Carol knew that if Harold fouled up, she would be blamed. She also knew that it is hard to throw a switch in the right direction with split-second timing when your hands are shaking. So, in addition to making sure he knew all the routines, she had to help Harold relax, which meant she had to make him feel competent and up to the job.

First Carol made sure that she gave Harold the information he needed to run the show and cautioned him about potential errors, all in a way that did not make him feel incompetent. Kendall points out that Carol gave Harold information phrased so as to imply it was not general technical knowledge (which he should have) but information particular to this show (which he could not be expected to have). For example, instead of saying, "Don't forget that tapes have a one-second lead-in," she said, "On this show everything has that one-second dead roll." Rather than saying, "Don't mix up the tapes; make sure you get them on in the right order," she said, "The only thing that people usually have trouble with is that they end up playing the promos and cassette tags and stuff in the wrong order." She avoided giving direct orders by saying, for example, "Probably we will want to re-cue the switch" when obviously it was he who had to re-cue the switch. In other words, Carol managed to apprise Harold of what he had to do without giving the impression she thought he was in danger of getting it wrong, and without framing him as potentially incompetent.

When she had done all she could to ensure that Harold knew what he had to do, Carol did not consider her job finished. She still wanted to make sure he felt calm and in control. She could have done this directly, by reassuring him: "Now, look, you're a techie—you know a lot about this equipment; you'll do just fine," but when you think about it, that sounds condescending. Reassuring him would position her as superior and him as a novice needing reassurance. So she built up his confidence indirectly by framing him as an expert in an area in which he knew he was competent. She picked up his copy of *Mac Weekly* and engaged him in conversation about computers. He took this opportunity to give her information about purchasing used Macs. Kendall, who was in the room observing, noticed that Harold sat back, put his feet up, and visibly relaxed during this conversation. Right before her eyes, he was transformed from the nervous novice to the self-assured teacher. As I pictured this scene in my mind, it was as if someone had inserted a tube in his foot and blown him back up. Carol remained with Harold throughout the show, and when it proceeded without requiring anything of him, she again asked him questions about computers. She later told Kendall that she sometimes keeps technicians talking during periods when they're not working the soundboard to reduce tension and prevent errors.

Carol's efforts paid off. The self-confidence she inspired in Harold carried him through the show, which went without a hitch—a success that no one would know was due in part to Carol. Quite the contrary, imagine the impression their supervisor might have gotten had he come into the studio shortly before airtime and found Harold with his feet up, answering Carol's questions about computers. It is likely he would have thought, even if he didn't think it through, that Harold was very much in command of the situation, and Carol was a rather underqualified technical supervisor who needs technical advice from her pinch-hitting board op. How different this impression would have been had she been less competent—say, if she had rushed into the studio at the last moment, rather than early, and had been busily giving direct orders to the board op right up to airtime. Now that would have created an image of firm control, even as it would have rattled Harold and caused him to make errors.

In two other conversations Kendall analyzed (conversations I will present in detail in the next chapter), Carol was working with a colleague named Ron, the manager of another control room. It was Carol's job to see that all went smoothly with the technical aspects of her show; it was Ron's to see that everything went well with all shows. In this instance, Carol foresaw a potential problem with the telephone hookup to be used when her show went on the road the following week. Ron, however, had not foreseen any problem. Kendall shows that Carol managed to call the potential problem to Ron's attention and to enlist his aid in heading it off. This show too went off without a hitch.

The proof of the pudding is in the eating. Carol had a low rate of technical errors on her watch. But the proof of her competence was invisible: the *absence* of errors. How do you get your bosses to see something that did not happen? Carol herself expressed concern that her excellent work and job skills might not be recognized when new appointments were made.

This example is hauntingly similar to one described by journalist Sharon Barnes, who tells of an office that had to switch from manual to computer operations. Barnes contrasts the way two managers, a man and a woman, handled the switch. The woman foresaw the need for computerization and gradually hired secretaries with computer experience, so the transfer to computerization took place without a ripple. The man did not prepare, so when the time came to switch to computers, his staff was in revolt. He mollified them by catering a lunch at which a consultant taught them what they needed to know. His troubleshooting was rewarded with a letter of commendation and a bonus. Barnes calls this "the white knight methode"—letting problems happen and then ostentatiously solving them. This attracts attention, whereas making sure the problems don't arise in the first place is likely to go unnoticed—and unrewarded. According to Barnes, the white knight methode is more common among men, the problem-preventing method more common among women.

Here is another example of a woman getting others to do their best at the risk of her own credibility. It comes from the curator of a private art collection I referred to in Chapter Three. The young men who were responsible for constructing the art installations were generally competent with tools, but they were artists, not construction workers, so they did not always know how to execute what she wanted. Her job was complicated by the fact that they would not tell her when they didn't know how to do something. She noticed that one of the three had more knowledge and skill than the other two. He often set about doing a job while the others stood by—not asking, but not working either. She figured out that if *she* asked for an explanation, the other two, hearing the explanation they needed, would start working. In her own words, she got the information out by taking the stance "I'm just a girl who doesn't understand." Like Carol, she framed herself as ignorant in order to get the job done. In this situation, the curator was the boss. There was no one over her to observe the interaction, miss her intent, and conclude that she was underqualified. The knowledgeable man *did* once explode, "Every time we do something, you ask the same stupid questions!" She simply walked away and explained later—in private—what she was doing and why; he immediately understood and apologized.

This corrective was simple enough, but not likely to happen with a boss who might well say nothing but form his opinion and keep his counsel. Once again, there is no harm in assuming the ritual appearance of incompetence so long as everyone knows that it is ritual. When it is taken literally, and when only one person in an interaction is using that style, the strategic use of an appearance of incompetence can be mistaken for the real thing.

SOFTENING THE BLOWS

In these examples, women adjusted their ways of speaking to make sure the job got done. In a study I conducted, together with a colleague, of doctor-patient communication, I observed a pediatrician who spoke in a seemingly unsure way in order to buffer the emotional impact of what she was saying. Because her work involved not only examining her young patients and consulting with their parents but also reporting to other clinical staff, we had an unusual opportunity to hear her talking about the same information under different circumstances, where she made a very different impression.

My colleague Cynthia Wallat and I analyzed videotapes of the pediatrician talking in several different contexts about a child with cerebral palsy who had recently been diagnosed as having an arte-riovenous malformation in her brain. In one of the videotapes, the doctor was examining the child in the presence of the mother. She pointed out that hemangiomas, visible as red marks on the child's face, were basically the same type of malady as the arteriovenous malformation in the brain. This gave the mother an opportunity to express a concern, and the doctor responded to the indirect ques-tion by providing an explanation:

> Mother: I've often wondered about how dangerous they—they are to her right now.
> Doctor: Well, um, the only danger would be from bleeding. *From* them. If there was any rupture, or anything like that. Which *can* happen. ... um, That would be the danger. *For* that. But they're ... mm ... *not* going to be something that will get worse as time goes on.
> Mother: Oh, I see.
> Doctor: But they're just *there*. Okay?

The doctor seemed rather insecure in this excerpt. Her talk was full of hesitations ("Well," "um," pauses). She uttered extra verbiage that didn't add meaning ("or anything like that," "which *can* hap-pen"). She added phrases after her sentences were done ("the only danger would be from bleeding. *From* them." "That would be the danger. *For* that.") Emphasis seemed to fall in odd places.

But the doctor's hesitance and circumlocution in this setting contrasts sharply with her fluency and assurance when she talked about the same condition in a meeting with her peers. There she articulated part of the reason for her lack of fluency in speaking to the mother: She did not know how much information the parents already possessed about the danger of the child's condition, and she was hesitant not about the information she was imparting but about the effect it might have on the mother:

> uh, I'm not sure how much counseling has been *done, with* these parents, around the issue ... of the a-v malformation.

Mother asked me questions, about the operability, inoperabil-
ity of it, um, which I was not able to answer. She was told it
was inoperable, and I had to say, "Well, yes, some of them are
and some of them aren't." And I think that this is a—a—an
important point. Because I don't know whether the possibility
of sudden death, intracranial hemorrhage, if any of this has
ever been dis*cuss*ed with these parents.

The physician, who showed so much hesitation and repetition in
explaining the danger of the a-v malformation in the child's brain
to the mother, expressed the same information in the staff meeting
strongly and directly: There is a possibility of "sudden death, intracranial hemorrhage." When my colleague and I talked to the doctor, we were not surprised to learn that in speaking to the mother,
she had been considering the emotional impact of telling a mother
that her child might die suddenly because the a-v malformations
could cause a hemorrhage in the brain at any time. When the
mother asked this question, the doctor was in the midst of examining the child, so she could not take a half hour to discuss the danger
and deal with the mother's reaction. Furthermore, the child was
not her regular patient; she was examining her in connection with
an educational placement. So she wanted to make sure that anything she said was coordinated with what the parents had been told
by their own doctors.

The doctor's seeming lack of articulateness stemmed from her
sensitivity to the potential impact of her diagnosis on the mother.
And the mother appreciated this. She told us that of all the doctors
she had taken her daughter to (and there had been many), she
found this one to be the most considerate. In contrast, she said, she
had been given devastating diagnoses and prognoses by doctors
with no regard to how the information might make her feel. For
example, early in the child's life one doctor had told her in a mat-
ter-of-fact way, "Your child will be a vegetable," and then moved
on to other topics.

Considering how the doctor spoke to the mother in comparison with how she spoke in a meeting with other medical staff
makes it clear that her hesitance and other disfluencies did not re-

flect her level of competence but her awareness of the impact of what she was saying on the person she was talking to. But how often do we have a tape recording of the same person talking about the same topic in another setting? And how often, when women talk in tentative, even seemingly confused, ways in order to soften the impact of what they are saying, are they seen as lacking in competence or confidence?

"THEY MUST KNOW SOMETHING I DON'T KNOW"

We judge others not only by how they speak, but also by how they are spoken to. If we hear people asking lots of questions and being lectured to, an impression takes root that they don't know much and that those lecturing to them know a lot. This is why girls used to be told to make boys feel good on dates by asking them about subjects they're expert on and listening attentively to their answers. It is also what Japanese subordinates are supposed to do to make the boss feel important when they spend an evening with him, according to Japanese anthropologist Harumi Befu. Ellen Ryan and her colleagues have found that when a health-care provider behaves in a patronizing way toward elderly patients, observers evaluate the patient as less competent.

If people are being spoken to as if they know nothing, we assume they know nothing. If people are addressed as if they are pretty smart, we assume they're pretty smart. This probably has some basis in most of the conversations we hear around us; it is a reasonable way to approach the world, trusting it to give us clues. But if women routinely take the position of novice or listener to make others feel smart, it is highly likely that those others, as well as observers, will underestimate their abilities.

Even worse, how a woman is addressed by others may have little to do with how she spoke in the first place. A consultant who worked fairly regularly with a small company commented to me that the new manager, a woman, was challenged and questioned by her subordinates more than her predecessor had been. He hadn't noticed any direct evidence that would lead him to question her competence, but he didn't really know the area they were working in. He added, "Maybe they know something about her abilities that I don't know." This seemed to me a double whammy. A woman who assumes a role that has previously been held by men will likely begin work with an aura of suspicion about whether she is up to the job, and this may well lead at least some of her co-workers to press her to justify her decisions. This very questioning then becomes evidence that she lacks competence—regardless of her real abilities.

Women may get more flak not only because their competence is in question but also because they are perceived as more vulnerable. A man who sails competitively commented that in a race, if he's looking for a hole, he picks a boat skippered by a woman or an older man; if you yell at them, he said, they are more likely to get out of the way. In the same spirit, Nancy Woodhull, a media and workplace consultant, points out that when corporate leadership changes and people jockey for position, they are especially likely to try to move in on turf held by women.

TARGET PRACTICE

This insight helped me understand an experience that had puzzled and troubled me. I took part in a joint presentation together with a man whose style was different from mine. When I speak alone, as I generally do, I rarely get hostile comments from audience members because I always make sure to show the positive side of every style I mention and show the logic of *both* speakers when I give an example of a misunderstanding. I am always careful not to make anyone look bad. My co-speaker, however, was more provocative. Many of his anecdotes made either women or men look foolish.

When the question period came, this different tone had sparked a different response from the audience: Some of the questions were hostile—especially from women. But most of the hostile questions were directed at me—including those that took issue with statements he alone had made. At the time, I was hurt and baffled, but in retrospect I could see what probably had happened. These women, riled by his tone and possibly put off by how he talked about women in some of his examples, looked at the stage and saw a large, gray-haired man with a caustic tongue who did not hesitate to ruffle feathers, and a younger woman who was always conciliatory and eager not to offend. I was an easier target. My "open" manner left me open to attack.

A BALANCING ACT

Conversational rituals common among women involve each saving face for the other. One speaker is freed to take the one-down position (ritually, of course) because she can trust the other to, ritually again, bring her back up. Neither has to worry too much about casting herself in the best possible light because everyone is working together to save face for everyone else. I save your face, and you save mine.

Put another way, many of the conversational rituals common among women are designed to make others feel comfortable, and this often involves the speaker taking a one-down role herself, though as we have seen, this is usually a ritual the other person is expected to match. At the same time women who observe these rituals are not investing a lot of energy in making sure they themselves do not appear one-down, which means that's just where they may end up.

A couple of years ago, I arrived at a class I was teaching and found a newspaper journalist waiting outside the door. She told me she had been trying to get me on the phone, but because she had not succeeded in reaching me at my office, she had come ahead to the class because she wanted to sit in and write a short piece about me. Now the number of people who want to sit in on my classes, for various reasons, is considerable, so I have long had a firm policy that I do not permit auditors or visitors for any reason. Since I always conduct classes not as lectures but as discussions among students sitting in a circle, a stranger in our midst is a significant intrusion. There was no question in my mind that had the journalist gotten me on the phone beforehand, I would have told her this. But here I was faced with a poor woman who had made the trek all the way to my class, had waited for a long time, and was now looking at me directly and plaintively. I felt culpable for not having been in my office when she was trying to reach me, and I have a strong impulse to help everyone and inconvenience no one. I had to make a snap decision; I let her in.

At the end of the class, I collected assignments, and a few students had not followed my instructions. To save face for them, I said something like, "I'm sorry if my instructions weren't clear." I suspect some readers will be able to foresee what happened: Lo and behold, in the article she wrote, the journalist took this ritual apology as a literal admission of fault and used it to make me look bad: Imagine, she wrote, here's this expert on communication, and she can't even give comprehensible assignment instructions to her students.

I am sure that some people will think, "It serves her right. She opened herself up to this." And they are correct. The impulses that drove me to make others feel comfortable were driving me in a direction opposite from self-protection, which would have led me to deny the journalist entrance to my class (it was her problem, not mine, if she made the trip without getting permission to sit in), or, once she was there, would have led me to monitor my behavior so as not to say anything that might appear as weakness—the kind of self-monitoring that leads others (including many men) not to apologize, take blame, admit ignorance, and so on.

It is interesting to consider, however, how well my impulse to accommodate the journalist worked for her. She risked rejection by showing up at the door of my class unannounced. In a way, she was counting on me to observe interactional rituals common among women, and in this case, her hunch paid off.

PRESENTING YOUR WORK—AND YOURSELF

All these examples dramatize how ways in which women are likely to talk may mask their true competence in the view of those who are required to judge their performance. When forced to evaluate people they do not work with day-to-day, executive and high-level managers will necessarily be influenced by what little exposure they have had to the people they are judging. In addition to the fleeting impressions of chance encounters, for many top executives this may mean the few times they have observed lower managers directly—when they are making presentations. And this is yet another situation in which knowing a lot doesn't automatically transfer into showing what you know. If most women's conversational rituals have prepared them for private speaking, the importance of formal presentations is yet another aspect of moving through "the pipeline" that puts many women at a disadvantage.

Public speaking is frightening for almost everyone. But standing up in front of a large group of people, commanding attention, and talking authoritatively are extensions of the socialization most boys have been forced to endure, as boys in groups tend to vie for center stage, challenge the boys who get it, and deflect the challenges of others. Many of the ways women have learned to be likable and feminine are liabilities when it comes to public presentations. Most girls' groups penalize a girl who stands out or calls attention to herself in an obvious way.

A woman who works as a trainer for business people coming to the United States realized that a disproportionate amount of the criticism she and her colleagues delivered to the trainees was directed at women, especially in the nebulous category of "professional presence." They found themselves telling women, more often than men, that they did not speak loudly enough, did not project their voices, should stop cocking their heads to one side, should try to lower the pitch of their voices. A few women were told that their way of dressing was too sexy, their manner too flirtatious, if they wanted to be taken seriously in the American business environment. In a sense, they were appearing too "feminine." But there were also women who were told that they were too challenging and abrasive. They launched into questions without a lead-in or hedges; they asked too many insistent questions; they did not tilt their heads at all or seemed to be tilting them in challenging ways. Although the trainers did not think of it in these terms, you could say that these women were not "feminine" enough.

In at least one case, a particular trainee had to be told that she was coming across as both too flirtatious and too confrontational. In wondering why such a large percentage of women in her program (a small one to start with) had the basic skills down cold, yet seemed to be undermining their own effectiveness by their nonverbal behavior, the trainer concluded that they had a very fine line to walk: The range of behaviors considered acceptable for them was extremely narrow. And, perhaps most important, the American professional business culture in which they were learning to fit was not only American but also American male.

All of the factors mentioned by the trainer indicate that making presentations is a prime example of an activity in which behavior expected of women is at odds with what is expected of an effective professional. In fact, the very act of standing up in front of a group talking about ideas is something that was unthinkable for women not so long ago. The nineteenth-century abolitionist Abby Kelley was reviled as a "Jezebel" and "fornicator" because of her public speaking. Because she was physically attractive, men saw her as a dangerous seductress.

Once a woman (or man) does make public presentations, she (or he) is open to challenge or even attack. Many women have been told they cave in too quickly rather than stand their ground. Being able to deal effectively with public challenges is not something that comes easily to many women (or men). And there are regional and cultural differences in styles as well. One man, a sociologist from a small town, was invited to give a lecture at a major East Coast university where he was being considered for a faculty position. The questions from the floor were so authoritative that he became convinced he was talking to people who had obviously done research in his area, research that he had somehow missed in his review of the literature. After the talk, which he was sure he had bombed, he went to the library and scoured the sources for references to these men's work—references that did not exist. To his amazement (he had taken literally the tone of contempt in their questioning), he got the job. So he had occasion to discover that they had done no work in the field at all; they were simply challenging him to see how well he could defend his claims—and were satisfied and pleased with his rebuttals. Although he had successfully defended himself against this ritual assault, he had gotten the impression that they had more basis for their challenges than they actually had.

There are many women who are very successful public speakers. I once noted the different public-speaking styles of two presenters at a meeting—a man and a woman. Both were excellent speakers, but he filled the room with his expansive presence, whereas she brought the room in close. He told stories as if he were in church preaching to a crowd; she told them as if she were sitting in her living room with friends. (An audience member commented on how "natural" she sounded.) She did not tell jokes, as he did, but she was humorous. Whereas he remained straight-faced after saying something funny, she laughed along with her audience. The woman's public speaking was successful in a private-speaking sort of way, whereas his was successful in a more public-speaking, oratorical way.

This is not to say that there is only one way for a woman or a man to give successful presentations. Both women and men must learn to handle this special situation well in order to get recognition for the work they do, but women's socialization is usually more at odds with the requirements of presenting to a group.

Who's to Change?

If one of the reasons women are not promoted is that they are spending more time doing their jobs and less time promoting themselves, can the solution be for women to begin promoting themselves more? Veronica had an observant boss who noticed that many of the ideas coming out of the group were hers, but it was often someone else in the group who trumpeted the ideas around the office and got credit for them. The boss told Veronica she should take more credit for her ideas. But Veronica wasn't comfortable doing that. She tried and found she simply didn't enjoy work if she had to approach it as a grabbing game. She liked the atmosphere of shared goals and was comfortable in the knowledge that she was part of a group effort. Striving to get credit for herself felt like a lonely and not very admirable endeavor. Trying to follow her boss's advice made coming to work a lot less fun.

In a related pattern, I spoke to many women who claimed they simply were not comfortable standing out. And I spoke to men who had noticed women who seemed to feel that way. For example, a man who headed an educational film company called a woman into his office and told her the good news that one of the clients with whom she had dealt in the past had decided to make a large purchase for a new film library. Rather than saying, "Great! I'll give them a call right away," the woman said, "Maybe someone else should follow up this time, since I've already got the highest sales in the group for the month." Even though the sales staff did not work on commission, the manager was incredulous. "They *asked* for you," he said. "They liked working with you before, and you're the one they want. What kind of a company would I be running if I didn't give my clients the person they ask for?" This convinced her, and she accepted the assignment. But she had to think of it in terms of what was good for the company rather than what was good for her—or at least be *assigned* the job rather than appear to be *taking* it.

I saw this same force at work in a talented graduate student who had been working for me as a research assistant in addition to participating in a seminar I taught. One day I told her, in private, that I owed her two apologies. The first was because she had handed me a bill for her services as research assistant as we were leaving class, and I had misplaced it. The second was that I feared I had embarrassed her in class when I unthinkingly corrected a minor grammatical error she had made while speaking. She told me that, since I was bringing it up, there was something that had bothered her, but it wasn't either of the two things I mentioned. It was something else entirely. The students had gathered around me after the last class meeting of the term, discussing who would take the next course. She had expressed frustration that she could not afford to take the course, and everyone knew my policy against allowing auditors. But I had said, "Maybe I can make an exception for you." She had not been bothered by my publicly correcting her grammar or by my neglecting to pay her on time. What bothered her was my singling her out for special treatment.

Favoritism can wreak havoc in any group. But whereas anyone can see that those not in favor would resent those who are, it seems that many women are uncomfortable not only being out, but also being too obviously in. This has resounding implications for promotability. Unobtrusively doing excellent work does not threaten group belonging. But getting special recognition does. It may well spark resentment from co-workers. Resentment, in fact, can result from almost any action that ensures getting credit, especially from those above. In a large organization, everyone is really the servant of many masters. Whereas you are taking direction, or even orders, from an immediate supervisor, that supervisor is answerable to someone above, who is answerable to someone above that. And somewhere in the upper layers are those who determine your fate when it comes to ranking and promotion. Much depends, therefore, on your ability to make contact with the people above your boss. But if you do, you may well incur the rancor of your immediate boss and your peers. And this may be a burden that more women than men are hesitant to risk.

NEVER A BOAST OR A BRAG

Besides the danger of provoking peer resentment (or related to it) is the different ways women and men are inclined to view self-aggrandizing talk. Letting others know about what you have done is almost always labeled boasting by women, and boasting is something most women have learned early on to avoid, as the humble-bee example showed in Chapter One. In contrast, many men assume they have to let others know what they've done in order to get the recognition they deserve. Bragging about his exploits got Othello the hand of Desdemona; Kate had to learn to keep her mouth shut to marry Petruchio—the "shrew" who spoke up had to be "tamed."

The example of a professional couple illustrates the attitudes many women and men have toward displaying or downplaying their own accomplishments. Bridget and Sean were both successful real estate agents, but they had different habits of self-presentation. Sean made sure to let new acquaintances know what he had done; Bridget played down what she had done and assumed people would eventually learn of it from others and like her all the more for her modesty when they did. Bridget thought Sean was boastful; he thought she was foolishly and inappropriately self-deprecating. Neither thought of the other's way of talking as related to gender; they thought they were dealing with issues of personal character.

A widely publicized incident involving political consultant Ed Rollins is evidence that talking about one's accomplishments is a ritual common among men. Rollins managed the campaign of Republican candidate Christine Todd Whitman in her 1993 bid for the governorship of New Jersey. At a breakfast for journalists shortly after Whitman's victory, Rollins boasted that he had won the election for his candidate by his successful efforts to keep blacks from voting—for example, by making donations to African-American churches in exchange for the ministers' agreement not to preach get-out-the-vote sermons. When this boast hit the head-lines, there was talk of knocking the candidate out of office and sending Rollins to jail. So he quickly explained that his boasts had been groundless, designed to embarrass his opponent James Carville, who was campaign manager for the Democratic candidate Jim Florio.

It is not clear whether Rollins was telling the truth when he first made the boast or when he later claimed it had been baseless. Whichever it was—and this may never be known—the case is a revealing example of the ritualized role of boasting. Rollins saw his role of campaign manager as a head-to-head fight with another man, Carville, and wanted to take ostentatious credit for his victory, so he boasted in a group about what he had done—or felt he could get away with claiming to have done. Another famous (or infamous) instance of boasting occurred when police located one of the men who allegedly had arranged an attack on figure-skater Nancy Kerrigan—rival skater Tonya Harding's "bodyguard"—in part because he had boasted openly to fellow students about what he had accomplished.

This incident, and the story of Ed Rollins's boasting, brought to mind an intriguing statement by Rupert Allason, a British member of Parliament who is an authority on the British intelligence services. He was explaining why he thinks women make better spies than men. On the occasion of the appointment of Stella Rimington as the first female director-general of the British Internal Security Service, Allason commented, "Women have always been good security operatives. While men tend to gossip about their job to impress friends, women gossip about trivia and keep their real secrets."

Linguist Penelope Eckert made similar observations of high school girls' and boys' secret-keeping habits. The high school girls Eckert studied told her that boys were better at keeping secrets than girls. Eckert hypothesized that this is not because boys are morally superior to girls but because, given the sex-separate social structure of the high schools, girls have something to gain by revealing other girls' secrets, whereas boys do not. Girls gain status by their social network—whom they are friends with. So showing that you know a girl's secrets is a good way to prove to others that you are friends with her. Boys, on the other hand, gain status by their own accomplishments. They gain nothing by demonstrating that they are close friends with girls, so they have no incentive to repeat their secrets. Instead, the boys are tempted to talk about what they've done or can claim to have done. This explains why, in the situation of a spy or a campaign manager, males' and females' abilities to hold their tongues are not-so-mysteriously reversed.

Whatever the motivation, women are less likely than men to have learned to blow their own horns—which means they may well not get credit for the work they have done, or, as Ed Rollins at least claimed, try to get credit for what they have not done. More women than men seem to have a sense that if they do this, they will not be liked. And the specter of working in an environment where they are not liked may be more than they are willing to risk. The congeniality of the work environment is important to everyone, but the requirement that everyone like each other may be more central to women's notion of congeniality, whereas men may value other types of congeniality, such as easy banter. One man who heads a large division of a corporation commented that in recruiting for diversity, they usually get the minority men they want by offering them the most generous package of remuneration. In recruiting women, however, they are most successful by sending women to recruit other women. If the recruiter can convince a prospective woman that the company provides a positive work environment, it is successful in recruiting her even if she has competing offers that are more lucrative. In addition to providing evidence that a congenial work environment is very important to many women, this may also say something about why women are chronically paid less than men in comparable positions.

THE LESSONS OF A FABLE

The most eloquent and amusing description I know of why someone fails to get credit for her work and how she changes her behavior to rectify the situation is in a short story by the Irish writer Maeve Binchy entitled "King's Cross." As the story opens, an overworked and underappreciated assistant manager in a travel office named Sara Gray is interviewing a prospective secretary named Eve who turns out to be a mixture of the Lone Ranger and Mary Poppins. Eve swoops into Sara Gray's life and transforms it by showing her how to get recognition—and promotion.

The first thing Eve does is insist on addressing her boss as "Miss Gray," even though Sara protests that it sounds "snooty." Eve points out that the male managers and assistant managers all call Sara by her first name, though she addresses many of them as "Mr." When speaking of Miss Gray to others, she adopts a tone of respect bordering on awe that gradually creeps into the attitudes of others in the office. Eve tells Sara that "it is absolutely intolerable the way that people think they can come barging in here, taking advantage of your good nature and picking your brains, interrupting us and disturbing you from whatever you are doing." To put a stop to this, Eve sets herself up at the door to Sara's office and insists that anyone who wants to see Miss Gray must make an appointment.

Eve discovers that Sara has not been taking advantage of available perks such as an account at a taxi firm, a clothing allowance, and a small fund for redecorating her office. With the latter, Eve acquires a conference table and suggests how Sara might use it. She points out that when Sara last developed a wildly successful marketing idea, no one but her boss, Garry Edwards, knew that it had been hers, so he got the credit and the reward, since it came out of his division. Eve counsels:

> Next time, I suggest you invite Mr. Edwards and his boss and the marketing director and one or two others to drop in quite casually—don't dream of saying you are calling a meeting, just suggest that they might all like to come to your office one afternoon. And then, at a nice table where there is plenty of room and plenty of style, put forward your plans. That way they'll remember you.

When Sara prepares work for Garry Edwards, Eve sends copies to others, so everyone knows it's her work. She encourages Sara to get an assistant who can cover her desk, so indispensability will not be an excuse for failing to send her to conferences or, eventually, promote her. She makes sure that Sara's name is on the list of guests to social events attended by executives. When Garry Edwards tries to undo Sara by blaming her for his own mistake, Eve's filing system yields a document proving that Sara had recommended the correct course of action. Garry Edwards is out, and Sara Gray gets his job, which she had, after all, been doing, without remuneration, all along.

This is, sadly for us all, just a fantasy, a work of fiction, though a delightful one to read. How nice it would be if Eve swept into each of our lives and ensured we got the credit we deserve. But the story, oversimplified (and entertaining) as it is, captures some of what individuals can do (and often fail to do) to achieve that felicitous result on their own.

When Connections Equal Advantage

I do not wish to imply that all inequities in recognition and promotion result from the behavior—linguistic or otherwise—of individuals. Some forces are out of our hands, or at least extremely difficult to influence. A phenomenon having little to do with conversational style that may handicap women is mentoring.

An academic position was advertised at a major university. Everyone was welcome to apply. But one candidate was a favorite of someone on the faculty. The faculty member saw to it that his candidate was the last one scheduled for a presentation, and he let him know when the other candidates were giving their presentations. This enabled his candidate to attend the others' presentations and gauge the reaction of the audience—what went over well, what fell flat, what concerns were reflected in the questions asked. He took this information into account in planning his own talk, and he wowed the department enough to get the job. At least one woman who had applied for the job felt that she had been locked out by an "old-boy network."

Similar patterns can obtain in promotion, where one candidate has established a relationship with someone involved in the search. He may be informed of the opening earlier, told what is best to emphasize in his application or interview, and given an advantageous position in the queue. Is this illegal preferential treatment or just "mentoring," a system by which a younger person has a supporter and ally higher up who "brings him along"? If such supporter relationships are likely to spring up between someone established in the organization and someone new to it, it is likely that the older person will be male (since he probably entered the organization when there were few or no women in it) and also likely that the established person will be drawn to someone who reminds him of himself at that stage—who is therefore probably male too. It is not intentional "sexism," yet it is a pattern that favors men over women—not all men, of course, but it is a structure women are less likely to fit into.

At the same time that we seek to understand how ways of talking can work against women, we also must bear in mind that it may be harder for women to get promoted regardless of how they speak. Marjorie and Lawrence Nadler list a number of studies that show that stereotypes work against women. They cite, for example, Lea Stewart, who found that women are often given different task assignments than men with similar positions and qualifications, and the ones they are given are not those that lead to advancement. They also cite Cynthia Fink, who shows that there is a widespread belief that men are simply more suited to management. Finally, Garda Bowman, Beatrice Worthy, and Stephen Grayser show that managers believe women just don't have the decision-making skills or aggressiveness needed to succeed in managerial positions.

Not every woman, or every man, wants to be promoted, though the argument that women don't really want high-pressure jobs has been used to avoid giving them the chance. There are women and men who choose downward mobility, but I do not think there are many people who would choose not to have their work recognized. People whose contributions are appreciated become motivated to continue and increase their efforts, whereas those whose contributions are overlooked are more likely to leave, perhaps citing other reasons for their decision. So failing to recognize the achievements of those with styles that do not call attention to themselves is a loss not only to the individuals but also to the companies.

REMEMBER THE RITUAL

Talking, like walking, is something we do without stopping to question how we are doing it. Just as we cheerfully take a walk without thinking about which foot to move forward (unless a puddle blocks our path), we simply open our mouths and say what seems self-evidently appropriate, given the situation and the person we are talking to. In other words, ordinary conversation has a ritual character, and the conversational rituals typical of women and men, though they obviously have a lot in common—otherwise we couldn't talk to each other—can also be different. And even subtle differences can lead to gross misinterpretation. In a situation in which one person is judging another and holds the key to a gate the other wants to pass through, the consequences of style differences can be dire indeed.

If more and more people understand the workings of conversational style, they will be able to adjust their own ways of talking and stand a better chance of understanding how others mean what they say. But at the same time, the more people gain an understanding of conversational style, the less necessary it will be for others to adjust their style. If supervisors learn to perceive outstanding performance regardless of the performer's style, it will be less necessary for individuals to learn to display their talents. On that happy day, the glass ceiling will become a looking glass through which a fair percentage of Alices will be able to step.

SIX

"She's the Boss": Women and Authority

On a chilly late winter day, two women were walking together from one building to another in order to attend a meeting. They were joined by a man they both knew, who was on his way to the same meeting. Both women said "Hi," but one of them, noticing that he was wearing only his suit jacket, added, "Where's your coat?" The man responded, "Thanks, Mom." The man seemed to be annoyed by the woman's question, and she seemed to be hurt by his rejoinder. "What is it with women?" he may have been thinking. "Why do they always have to take care of you?" "What is it with men?" she may have been thinking. "Why can't you open your mouth to be friendly without their accusing you of being their mother?"

Anne Statham, who interviewed women and men managers, observed that many of the women described themselves as mothers and teachers, whereas many of the men called themselves "coaches." In my own research, women frequently referred to themselves, or were referred to by others, as "mothers" if they watched out for those who reported to them. In commenting on a man who ran a meeting in an authoritarian way, a woman grumbled, "He was like a military sergeant." The military and sports worlds offer us images of male authority. Our primary images of female authority come from motherhood.

A woman who headed a regional sales team had to confront her boss. He had taken to assigning special projects in a neighboring district to one of the men on her team, who would announce to her that he could not do what she had asked of him because he had to complete a project for her boss—a higher authority she could not argue with. She geared herself up and explained to her boss that when he gives assignments directly to someone who reports to her, it makes it difficult for her team to meet its goals. She cannot depend on that employee's work to fit into the plan she has set for her team. Her boss agreed that she had a point. Satisfied, she said, "So you'll tell him to check with me before he takes on something for you?" At this her boss balked: "I can't tell him to ask Mommy for permission."

Perhaps this woman would have done better to say, "So please check with me before giving him projects that will take him away from my team." But what is interesting here is the image that sprang to her boss's mind when she put it the way she did: Checking with a superior—a gesture that should be a matter of course in a work situation—was reframed as a humiliating and inappropriate one, "asking Mommy for permission." The prospect of a man checking with a woman before doing something brought to her boss's mind the scenario of a child supplicant, because a mother is one of the few images we have of female authority—whereas men in authority are as likely to suggest a military commander or a sports coach or captain (in itself modeled on the military metaphor) as a father.

This is not to say that there are no negative stereotypes of men in authority. If a man has a particular characteristic that is noticeable in our culture, he may invoke stereotypes that can be used (often unfairly) to characterize him. If he is short and authoritarian, for example, he may be called "a little Napoleon"—again, a military figure. But simply being male in a position of authority alone does not invoke stereotypes, whereas simply being female in such a position can call to mind stereotypical images of women, including, prominently, that of mother.

A puzzling question remains: Why do many women professionals perceive it as demeaning to be characterized as mothers? One reason may be that mothers are associated with the home, and professional women are trying to escape the old adage that home is their rightful place. But another reason may be that the way many middle-class American mothers talk to their children helps create the image of mothers as relatively powerless.

AMERICAN MOTHERHOOD

Applied linguist Elinor Ochs points out that members of any society learn attitudes toward and assumptions about women from the images they get of their mothers, and these images are shaped by the ways mothers talk to and treat their children. By comparing how mothers talk to their children in "mainstream white middle class" homes and in traditional Samoan households, Ochs shows that because of the Americans' egalitarian ideology, they tend to downplay their own power and authority relative to their children. Many facets of the hierarchical organization of Samoan society give power and authority to women in the role of mother.

First, the middle-class American mother typically tends to her child's needs on her own. In the Samoan household, the mother is the chief caregiver, but she is assisted by other, lower-status family members, such as older children. So the mother may sit and give directions to older children, positioning herself as an authority figure over the lower-status caregivers rather than as servant to the child's needs.

In general, Ochs explains, lower-ranking people accommodate to higher-ranking people. In keeping with this organization, Samoan children are expected to accommodate to adults. But American mothers, Ochs and her colleague Bambi Schieffelin observe, do the accommodating to their children. For example, American mothers typically talk "baby talk" to young children, simplifying their speech to make it more understandable. They also engage young children, and even infants, in protoconversations long before the baby can actually talk back, by providing not only their own side of the conversation but the baby's as well. When babies or children utter sentences or sounds that are difficult or impossible to make out, the American mothers guess at what the children are trying to say and then respond to the guess. Finally, they help their children do things and then reframe the results as the child's single-handed achievement by praising them. A mother may help a child build a castle and then exclaim, "Look at the beautiful castle you made!"—dismissing her own part in the effort and expecting no praise for it.

These ways of talking to children may strike many American readers as self-evidently appropriate, until they are contrasted with what seems self-evidently appropriate to a Samoan. According to Ochs, Samoan mothers do not simplify their register to accommodate to children; they don't talk baby talk to them. (The people they do simplify their speech for are foreigners, such as missionaries—which makes sense, since they feel hosts should accommodate guests). They do not try to carry out conversations with children until the children are capable of doing their part, and if a child utters something unintelligible, rather than guessing at a possible meaning, a Samoan mother typically ignores the utterance or calls attention to its unintelligibility ("I can't understand that."). Finally, in Samoan praising is a reciprocal routine, reflecting the general assumption that activities are "jointly accomplished." If a mother praises a child's achievement with *"Maaloo!"* ("Well done!"), the child is expected to respond in kind: *"Maaloo!"*

According to Ochs, these ways of talking to children contribute to the middle-class American image of women as accommodating to others, as downplaying or dismissing their own contributions, and as helpers lacking in status.

Ochs notes that studies of how African-American mothers talk to their children do not follow the same pattern. Similarly, linguist Carolyn Adger reports that African-American teachers and speech pathologists she has worked with expressed shock at how white mothers they have observed in public talk to their children. One woman overheard a mother in a store trying to get her child out from under a clothes rack by cajoling, "Now we don't want to mess up the clothes." She thought it would have been more appropriate to say, "You get out from under there right now!"

In keeping with this view of mothering, Adger gives the example of an African-American teacher with an authoritarian classroom style who characterized herself as a "mother bear." Unlike "mother hen," which suggests ineffectual clucking and flapping of wings, "mother bear" brings to mind an authority figure who is both nurturing and fierce. And this brings us to the more general question of stereotypical images of female authority.

THE DRAGON LADY

When I heard the same remark twice in one week about two different women, I knew there was something going on. "Before I came to work for Ann," a man who reports to her told me, "everybody warned me to watch out. They called her the dragon lady. But I don't know what they were talking about. I've always found her great to work with." A few days later, a woman at another company commented about the woman she works for, "I've heard people call Marie the dragon lady. But I've never seen anything to justify that. She's the best boss I've ever worked for." I wondered, Why the dragon lady? Not only was there nothing dragonlike about either Ann or Marie, but they were as different from one another as could be, in age, temperament, and personal style. The only thing they had in common was the "lady" part. Being women highly placed in their organizations seems to have caused people to look at them through conventional images of women in positions of authority. Our culture gives us a whole menagerie of stereotypical images of women: schoolmarm, head nurse, headmistress, doting mother, cruel stepmother, dragon lady, catwoman, witch, bitch.

An article about President Clinton's health czar, Kristine M. Gebbie, began by saying she didn't look like a czar, then went on to say she had the air of a head nurse. Although there is nothing inherently negative about being head nurse, the image this term evokes in our culture is decidedly negative: In the tradition of Ken Kesey's Nurse Ratched, the villain in his novel *One Flew Over the Cuckoo's Nest,* it suggests a woman who is arbitrarily authoritarian, life-killingly humorless, and stiffly unfeminine. It is no wonder the reporter did not think Gebbie looks like a czar, since a czar is always male. (Czarina doesn't conjure up a comparable image of authority.) And it is no surprise that the role of someone who is going to take over a problem and solve it should be "czar"—a man who takes control and makes things happen. But why a "head nurse," other than the fact that Gebbie herself was trained as a nurse, which surely was a factor. (If she were an M.D., would she call to mind a "head doctor"?) The writer explains, "There is something at once no-nonsense and fussy about her—her erect posture, her precise and proper answers, her tendency to correct an interviewer's questions." Hmmm. Shouldn't a czar stand erect and have a no-nonsense manner? Shouldn't a czar give precise and proper answers? Correcting an interviewer's questions seems a good way to maintain control when being interviewed. But all these qualities took on a very different effect because they were found in a woman.

"Presto!" a newspaper announced in large type, summarizing an accompanying story. "A stuffy schoolmarm is a contender." I began reading the article and learned that an Illinois gubernatorial candidate named Dawn Clark Netsch had won the Democratic nomination after she managed "to alter her image to a down-to-earth contender from that of a stuffy schoolmarm." But further down, I was surprised to read that the "bookish" candidate, who had previously "talked too much" and sounded "like some kind of egghead," had been a law professor at Northwestern University for eighteen years. This seemed to explain why she might be "bookish," talk a lot, and be denigrated by some as an egghead. But none of these qualities is suggested by "schoolmarm," which has different connotations entirely: stuffy, yes, but a strict disciplinarian rather than bookish, and small-minded rather than an egghead. Forced to choose between a professorial image, appropriate to the qualities the paper attributed to her as well as to her profession, and "schoolmarm," suggested by her gender, the newspaper went for the gender.

Newsweek's review of Margaret Thatcher's memoir about her years as British prime minister began this way:

> For 11½ years, Margaret Thatcher presided over the British government like a strong-minded headmistress. She reshaped the economy, broke the unions and starched up Britain's languid posture in world affairs. Through it all, she thoroughly dominated the "wets" in her own cabinet, clobbering them with a metaphorical handbag whenever they showed too little spine in the defense of conservative ideology—or too much in opposing her will.

Images of authority come drenched in gender. Even when describing situations that have nothing to do with gender—for example, shoring up Britain's "posture in world affairs"—by choosing the verb "starched up," the writer indirectly evoked a housewife doing the laundry, if not a head nurse stiff in a starched uniform. The image of Thatcher "clobbering them with her metaphorical handbag" undercuts the force of her actions, even as it gives her credit for attacking her opponents. A woman clobbering men with her handbag is an object of laughter, not fear or admiration.

THE IMAGE OF AUTHORITY

Part of the reason images of women in positions of authority are marked by their gender is that the very notion of authority is associated with maleness. This can result simply from appearance. Anyone who is taller, more heftily built, with a lower-pitched, more sonorous voice, begins with culturally recognizable markers of authority, whereas anyone who is shorter, slighter, with a higher-pitched voice begins with a disadvantage in this respect. (Here again, cultural convention dovetails with physical attributes. Even before puberty, when boys' and girls' voice boxes are equal in size, young girls seem to raise the pitch of their voices and boys to lower theirs, according to psycholinguist Jacqueline Sachs.) Barbara Mikulski, the United States senator from Maryland who stands 4'11", carries a footstool with her to public speaking engagements, so that the lecterns that add authority to speakers who stand behind them do not hide her from sight. With reference to her senate colleagues who are tall and silver-haired, Senator Mikulski has remarked, "They come with the image." This does not mean that she cannot speak in an authoritative way. Those who have heard her know that she can, and her extraordinary success as a senator testifies to how effective she is. But she doesn't start with this advantage.

The association of authority with maleness goes deeper than associations with physical appearance. It is pervasive in linguistic systems as well, as observed by linguist Kunihiko Harada, who noted this phenomenon with reference to Japanese "particles"— little words that have no meaning in themselves but are often added to Japanese sentences to give them the right emphasis. (There is nothing in English quite comparable, but the effect is something like ending sentences with "y'know," "okay?," "isn't it?," or "right?" The difference is that most Japanese sentences include such particles, and sentences will often seem odd without them.) Many researchers studying the use of particles in Japanese conversation have claimed that certain particles are used by males, others by females. For example, M. Chikamatsu gives the example of a woman saying "I don't want to eat anything":

Nani-mo   itadakitaku   nai   no.
anything   eat (polite)   not   female particle.

As the translations show, "*Nani-mo*" means "anything," "*itadakitaku*" is a polite way of saying "eat," "*nai*" means "not," and the little word, or particle, "*no*" at the end is a polite softener associated with female speech.

In the actual conversations Harada studied between a Japanese man who ran a language school and a young woman teacher who worked for him, the male boss used female particles. When telling the woman that a photography store had to be found to develop a photograph in black-and-white rather than color (as we saw in Chapter Three, an indirect way of getting her to volunteer to find such a store), the boss ended his sentence with the female particle "*no*." Harada believes he did this to avoid seeming too authoritarian when assigning a task. On the other hand, there are other situations in which he used particles expected of men and considered "male"—when he was making decisions or authoritative statements. For example, when the woman subordinate suggested that they wait for a certain piece of information before sending out a mailing, he decided to take her suggestion but stated his decision using the male particle "*ka*":

Jaa,   chotto   matu-ka.
Well,   a little   wait-male particle.

In other words, using the male particle is part of what made his decision sound authoritative.

The Japanese boss using female particles to soften requests and male particles to sound authoritative tells us something about the force of "male" and "female" particles. Femaleness is associated with softeners, mitigation, and politeness, whereas maleness is associated with authority. This means that women who want to sound authoritative must risk sounding male. (It also means that men who want to sound polite must risk sounding female.)

Realizing that the very image of authority is associated with masculinity makes it easier to understand the images of professional women in our society.

This is a quiz. Name all the movies you can think of in which a major character is an ambitious career woman who has risen high in her field. And now: In how many of those movies is this character a likable, sympathetic, warm, and loving person?

In the enormously popular movie *Fatal Attraction*, a dichotomy between a good woman and an evil one was prepared for in the very beginning: The good one is a wife who stays at home, and the evil mistress is a career woman he meets through work. Recall, too, that strange word that was applied to Hillary Clinton—"careerist." What, exactly, is a "careerist"? Is it, on the model of "sexist," someone who discriminates on the basis of careers? Or like "feminist," someone who supports the rights of careers? It is used, of course, to describe a woman who is so focused on her career that she neglects her family or shirks the responsibility of having a family at all. But when you get right down to it, it is just a word that brings to mind the negative image of a woman who has a career rather than a job.

When I asked people for their impressions of the men and women they worked with and for, I noticed a pattern: When they commented on women in managerial positions—but never when they commented on men—people often said, "She's abrasive," or, just as often, "She's not abrasive," "not aggressive," or "has a soft touch." It is one thing to describe how you think someone is— "abrasive," "aggressive," and so on. But why would people mention what someone is not? It makes sense only against the expectation that the person would be that way. So it seems that when a woman is in a high position, there is an expectation that she will be unfeminine, negative, or worse. When she isn't, it is perceived as worth mentioning. And these prevalent images ambush professional women as they seek to maintain their careers as well as their personal lives—and their femininity.

NEGOTIATING AUTHORITY

Even in organizations where the hierarchy is clearly laid out in an organization chart, actual authority has to be negotiated day-to-day, moment-to-moment. Whether those in authority are trusted, respected, or seen as obstacles to be contended with and gotten around depends on how they negotiate authority for themselves, and whether others reinforce or undercut their efforts—which may or may not be a reaction to their own behavior. You will have a hard time finding your footing if others are jiggling the platform on which you are trying to stand.

Individuals in positions of authority are judged by how they enact that authority. This poses a particular challenge for women. The ways women are expected to talk—and many (not all) women do talk—are at odds with images of authority. Women are expected to hedge their beliefs as opinions, to seek opinions and advice from others, to be "polite" in their requests. If a woman talks this way, she is seen as lacking in authority. But if she talks with certainty, makes bold statements of fact rather than hedged statements of opinion, interrupts others, goes on at length, and speaks in a declamatory and aggressive manner, she will be disliked. Our language is rich in words to describe such unwomanly women— words that have been hurled at many prominent women in positions of authority such as Jeane Kirkpatrick, Geraldine Ferraro, and Margaret Thatcher, as well as innumerable women in offices, factories, and studios around the country. Looking closely at how women in positions of authority use language to do their jobs— and how others respond to them—sheds light on our images of women as well as our understanding of authority.

A woman I interviewed owns her own physical-therapy business. There are half a dozen other physical therapists who operate out of her offices, under the name of her company. She pays the rent, buys advertising, and manages the office. She is also the oldest and most experienced practitioner in her group, and she is the one who learns new techniques at conferences and seminars and teaches them to the others. Most important, she invited the other therapists to join her business and can ask them to leave if she feels they are not working out. When I asked her general questions about her experiences dealing with the other therapists, she repeatedly volunteered that she does not take an authoritarian stance. "I treat them like equals," she said, and then, perhaps sensing that the word "like" in "treat them *like* equals" implies pretense, she added, "They *are* my equals. They have the same degree I have. That's why I get along with them, and that's why they like me." She felt that her method worked well with the women who worked with (and for) her.

When I talked to people about their work lives, I asked them, among other things, what they think management is all about, and what makes a good manager or a poor one. When I put this question to women in positions of authority, one of the most frequent statements they offered to explain what makes them good managers is that they do *not* act like an authority figure—insofar as an authority figure is thought to be authoritarian. They told me that they don't lord it over subordinates, don't act as though they are better than those who report to them. I began to wonder why women in authority are so concerned not to appear authoritarian—not to appear as if they think they are superior or are putting themselves in a one-up position, even though that is exactly the position they are in.

DOWNPLAYING AUTHORITY

Women physicians walk this fine line between exercising authority and not appearing too authoritarian, as shown by the research of Nancy Ainsworth-Vaughn, the linguist who tape-recorded physicians talking to patients in private practice. In the study I referred to in Chapter Three, Ainsworth-Vaughn investigated how topics were changed when male and female doctors spoke to their patients. At one end of a continuum were cases in which a doctor got the patient's agreement before moving to a new topic. For example:

> [Doctor and patient are going over the results of some previous tests.]
> Doctor: I think you've got all of this.
> Patient: I've got all of that.
> Doctor: All right.
> Patient: Yeah.
> Doctor: Okay.
> Patient: Um.
> Doctor: All right. And this urine is spilling protein.

At the other end of the continuum were cases in which the doctor switched topics without getting verbal agreement from the patient, or with only a minimal link such as the word "okay":

> Patient: Dr. M had suggested possibly waiting a month. And then, there's times in which I have very (good rest) and then there are times when I can't get any rest because I'm too sore. I have to lay on my back in which I'm not comfortable lying on my back, I like to lay on my sides.
> Doctor: Okay, when are we going to do another CT scan?

Ainsworth-Vaughn found that the men doctors in her study moved on to new topics without getting the patient's verbal agreement almost as often as they got the patient's agreement. The ratio was 1.4 to 1. The women doctors were much more likely to get the patient's agreement before changing topics: Their ratio was 5 to 1. Ainsworth-Vaughn feels that linguistic behavior such as this helps explain why a 1984 study found that both male and female patients were more satisfied with interactions with women doctors than with men doctors. But such behavior also means that the women doctors are constructing a different "demeanor" for themselves as doctors—creating an image of "doctor" as less in control than those who set the agenda for talk without getting the patient's agreement as often.

The term "demeanor" was used by sociologist Erving Goffman to describe the way we show the world the qualities we want others to believe we have. Those in positions of authority must speak in ways that create the proper demeanor for someone in their position. Studies showing that women and men tend to speak differently in the role of doctor (bearing in mind, as always, that the differences are only a matter of degree and may reflect only a small percentage of their behavior as doctors) suggest that they have different senses of the qualities that should go along with being in that position.

CREATING AUTHORITY AS A PREACHER

A particularly interesting study of how women and men tend to use language to create an authoritative stance was conducted by sociolinguist Frances Lee Smith. Smith was interested in how women and men perform in the role of a preacher giving a sermon. She set about comparing the practice sermons performed by students in a preaching lab at a Baptist seminary. In giving a sermon, the preacher has to create authority by using words. Smith was especially interested in how the women would do this, because it was only recently that women began participating in the preaching lab at all. The history of the course reflects society's changing attitudes and expectations. Before 1970, women at this seminary were not allowed to take the preaching lab. During the seventies, taking it was optional for women. In 1980, the course became a requirement for all students seeking the Master of Divinity degree, male and female. Smith realized that women in this course faced a particular challenge, since sermon textbooks themselves identify good preaching with male style, as reflected in the epigram with which she began her essay:

But the minister who is forceful uses language which rings with reality. He is never vague, ethereal, or effeminate. . . . He has the power to stab awake the conscience of men. He speaks like a man!

How then is a woman to give a good sermon? Should she too "speak like a man!"?

In order to compare the sermons of ten men and four women in the course, Smith got most of the students to agree to preach sermons on the same Bible story, "The Ten Lepers." Then she recorded their sermons and transcribed them. Rather than approaching her study by counting up linguistic features in the sermons, Smith began by determining the various "footings" the preachers took in relation to the texts they were interpreting. In other words, how did they position themselves in relation to the material they were preaching about and the task they were performing? She found that the men tended to foreground their authority by putting themselves "on record" as interpreters of the text and by calling attention to the fact that they were in the position of authority, interpreting the text for their listeners (who were, in fact, fellow students in the course).

To emphasize that the gender pattern is a tendency, not an absolute divide, Smith illustrates the "on-record" style with a sermon performed by a woman, Meg, but she notes that Meg was the only woman who adopted this style, along with four men. For example, Meg posed a question and then said, "I've done a lot of thinking about that, and I came up with several possible reasons." At one point, she said, "I'd like to insert something here." In discussing alternate translations for a particular passage, she rendered her own judgment: "And I believe that's a better translation." But Meg also said "we" and "us" often, including the listeners with her as ministers, rather than setting herself apart as the one who interprets Scripture.

The other three women found unique ways to interpret the text without putting themselves "on record," that is, without calling attention to themselves as the one with authority to interpret the text. One woman spoke as if she were telling a story to a group of children. She began, "A little boy grew up in a Samaritan village. He had a happy childhood and sometimes his parents would take him to the neighboring villages, to market, or occasionally they might even go to Galilee to the sea for a vacation." A second woman, rather than stepping outside the text to comment on it in her own voice, retold the story in a literary register. For example: "The clarity of the directions that God gave him were as a stab in his heart." The fourth woman simply downplayed her authority by maintaining a "low-profile" stance.

Although Smith's study is too small to form the basis of wide-ranging conclusions, it is fascinating in showing how speakers create their own demeanor of authority in how they speak, and in revealing a pattern by which the women in her study, with one important exception, managed to exercise their authority—preach a sermon and interpret a sacred text—without explicitly claiming authority to do so.

CREATING AUTHORITY AS A PROFESSOR

Linguist Elisabeth Kuhn examined the way male and female university professors established their authority, and she came to conclusions comparable to Smith's for student preachers. Kuhn noticed that the American women professors she taped avoided giving their students direct orders at the beginning of the term. Instead, they spoke of "the requirements" of the course, as if these were handed down directly from the institution, and then told the students how they could fulfill the requirements. This is how three different women professors introduced their syllabi—written outlines of the courses:

"We are going to talk about the requirements."

"I also tell you what the course requirements are, since I'm sure you're interested in that. Um, there is going to be a midterm and a final. Okay?"

"Now, let me say a little bit about the requirements for the course. I think if you look on the bottom of the second page, the cues are all there. . . . There are two papers, the first paper, ah, let's see, is due it's back here [while looking at her sheet] at the beginning."

Kuhn contrasts this with the male professors in her study who also handed out lists of requirements in the form of syllabi but made it explicit that the syllabi set forth decisions they personally had made:

"I have two midterms and a final. And I added this first midterm rather early to get you going on reading, uh, discussions, so that you will not fall behind."

"I want you to read NN's XX. But I have not assigned a textbook for you to go out and buy because I assumed either you have a copy of XX which will include the NN, or you will be delighted to go out and provide yourself with it. . . . I'm gonna ask you to do one midterm, which will primarily be a reading check to make sure that you're with it."

Just as the women as preachers found ways to interpret the Scriptures without stating explicitly that they were doing so, the women professors used impersonal statements like, "There is going to be a midterm and a final," and "There are two papers," to avoid stating directly that they had devised and imposed the requirements. By using personal statements such as "I'm gonna ask you to do one midterm," the men professors called attention to their authority by going "on record" as the ones setting the requirements for the course.

"WE'RE ALL EQUALS"

In all these studies, women were found to downplay their authority while exercising it. It seems that creating their demeanor in a position of authority is yet another conversational ritual growing out of the goal of keeping everyone on an equal footing, at least insofar as appearances are concerned. This doesn't mean that women or men who speak this way really think everyone is equal; it means they have to do a certain amount of conversational work to make sure they maintain the proper demeanor—to fit their sense of what makes a good person, which entails not seeming to parade their higher status. If they have to tell others what to do, give information, and correct errors—all of which they will have to do on the job, especially if they are in a position of authority—they will expend effort to assure others that they are not pulling rank, not trying to capitalize on or rub in their one-up position. In contrast, since men's characteristic rituals have grown out of the assumption that all relationships are inherently hierarchical, it is not surprising that many of them either see less reason to downplay their authority or see more reason to call attention to it—to ward off inevitable challenges.

Choices of ways of speaking that highlight or downplay authority are not deliberate decisions that are thought through with each utterance but are rather habitual phrasings learned over time that become automatic, seemingly self-evidently appropriate ways to say what you mean.

I cannot emphasize enough that the appearance of equality I am referring to is ritual, not literal. I am not implying that individual women doubt their superior position in the hierarchy. The woman who owns her own physical-therapy business knows that she is the most experienced therapist in the group, and that she is the owner of the business. When she says, "I want them to feel independent, to maintain their self-esteem," she is acknowledging that it is in her power to determine how independent they feel, since they are in fact dependent on her for their jobs. She simply feels it is appropriate not to rub their noses in their dependence.

Those whose characteristic conversational rituals place less value on denying hierarchy (including many men) may find women's protests that they treat others as equals to be hypocritical. Accusations of hypocrisy are often a sign that cultural differences are at work; it is the universal impression one gets from observing those whose rituals are unfamiliar. "Hypocrisy" is acting in a way that is not a sincere reflection of how you feel. In other words, the way it seems "natural" to talk and the way you see someone talking don't match up. Though this could certainly be the result of true hypocrisy—putting on an act for some ulterior motive—it is also the unavoidable impression made when people have different ideas of how it is "natural" to talk, given a particular context and set of emotions.

Another liability for women in authority is that if they do not talk in ways that highlight the power of their position, they are more vulnerable to challenges to it. Like many conversational rituals common among women, talking as if "we're all equals" but still expecting to receive the respect appropriate to the higher-status position depends on the participation of the other person to respect that position. The president of a women's college had a long and difficult meeting with a student who protested her choice of commencement speaker. Finally, the president said, "What it comes down to is that you don't accept my right to make this decision, after considering your point of view and everyone else's." The student thought about it and agreed. "When I see you on campus after hours dressed informally, I forget about your position," she said. "If you were an older white man, it would be easier." In addition to dressing informally when she went to her office evenings and weekends, the president probably also spoke in ways that did not continually create a stance of authority, and this no doubt contributed to the student's forgetting the power of her position.

SAVING FACE IS A TWO-PERSON JOB

Part of the reason that many women in positions of authority speak in ways that downplay rather than emphasize the power of their position is simply an expression of the ethics characteristic of many women's conversational rituals that I discussed in Chapter Two: the desire to restore balance to a conversation and take into account the effect of one's words on the other person. Whereas one might expect the person in the subordinate position to take more care about not offending a boss, research has found that women in superior positions often take more care to avoid offending when talking to subordinates than to superiors.

Speech communication researchers Karen Tracy and Eric Eisenberg devised a business letter that contained a number of errors. They invited thirteen male and eleven female college students to role-play informing co-workers of the mistakes in the letter—in other words, to deliver criticism. They then examined their results to see how much effort the speakers spent trying to avoid hurting the feelings of the person they were criticizing. A way of delivering criticism that evidenced minimal concern with the other's feelings began like this:

Hi. Oh I just looked over this letter and I just found a couple of mistakes on it. And, ah, here I'll show 'em to you.

Ways of showing more concern for the other's feelings included addressing the person by name, asking about themselves or their family ("How are you doing today?" "How's the family?"), thanking them ("I really appreciate you writing this letter for me"), complimenting this piece of work ("It was done very nicely") or their work in general ("I know you can do a really good job because you've done it before"), and belittling the significance of the errors ("Other than that, it's a fine letter").

You might expect people to be more careful about how they deliver criticism when they are in a subordinate position. This is exactly what Tracy and Eisenberg found—for the men in their study, but not the women. Whereas the men showed more concern for the feelings of the person they were criticizing when they were role-playing a person in the subordinate role, the women showed a great deal more concern about the other person's feelings when they were playing the role of superior. It seems that the women were keenly aware of the power inherent in their authority and expended effort to avoid wielding it carelessly. Of course, men can do this too, and no doubt many do, but if Tracy and Eisenberg's study is reflective of the real world, women are more likely to do it.

An example of just this way of talking comes from my own tape recordings of office talk. A woman I will call Marge, who heads a division, noticed that her secretary had made a mistake in a list of office assignments:

> Marge: Oh, but you've still got Mitch and Evan in the same office, you know!
> Secretary: Are you *kidding*? Oh, darn.
> Marge: [Laughing] You know, it's *hard* to do things around here, isn't it, with all these people coming in!

Although she told the secretary directly that she had made a mistake, Marge hastened to soften the criticism by providing a reason for why she might have made the mistake—and by laughing, to show that it was not a serious error and there were no hard feelings.

Marge spoke in a way that saved face for her secretary. Though it might seem that saving face is primarily something one does for oneself, saving face works especially well if two people do it for each other, as often occurs in ritual exchanges characteristic of women's conversation. And this highlights the importance not only of how you speak, but how others speak to you.

Continuing to use Goffman's terms, "demeanor"—behaving in a way that shows you have desired qualities—must be balanced by "deference": other people's behavior acknowledging that you

180

have those qualities too. In terms of "face" (another concept Goffman wrote extensively about), you speak in ways that present a certain face to the world, but the world must do its part in supporting that face. If others refuse to treat you as deserving of authority, you can't "hold up" your face on your own.

I once had a nightmare that I walked into class to teach, and the students would not look at me or listen to me. They all sat with their chairs turned to the back of the room, so I could not teach. (Perhaps I was haunted by the memory of a junior high school teacher whose grimacing expression of despair is still graven in my memory, as she stood at the front of the class sighing and pleading in vain with the gleeful boys to stop running around the room and throwing things, and sit down and listen to her.) When entering a room in which students are noisily talking to each other, many teachers feel a momentary panic that the students will not stop talking to listen to the teacher. And if they did not, the teacher could not teach, no matter how commanding the performance.

A woman who worked in sales (I will call her Jane) explained that she got off to a rough start in her job because her co-workers did not "position" her with the customers as the person responsible for a new product line. In her words:

> We had a customer that was interested in that product line, and when that customer was there, they never properly introduced me as the person who was going to be handling that line. . . . I sat in on the meeting and the customer said, "So who is my key contact on this?" and they said, "uh, uh," and I said "Ahem!"

When pressed, someone replied, "Well, Jane and myself." But the "myself" was not supposed to be the contact for the new line; only Jane was. Apparently, the members of the sales staff were uncomfortable about sharing their established customers with a new person. The effect of their reluctance illustrates the necessity of everyone in a group cooperating to establish the authority of an individual in the group.

The study by Shari Kendall of conversations involving a woman named Carol who was technical director at a national radio network caught in action how one woman's ways of handling authority contrasted with the style of a male co-worker, Ron, in a parallel position. Kendall's analysis also captures how both speakers' ways of talking work together to support (or undercut) a stance of authority for either or both of them.

As I mentioned briefly in the preceding chapter, Carol, the technical director of a show, was discussing with Ron, her counterpart who had responsibility for the master control room, a potential problem in the telephone hookup for an upcoming call-in talk show. (Carol foresaw potential problems that Ron did not—problems that did, in fact, materialize.) Kendall shows that whereas Carol talked in a way that established both her own competence and Ron's, Ron talked in a way that established his own competence but called Carol's into question.

Both Ron and Carol lowered their voices periodically in the conversation, but they did it in different contexts. Ron tended to speak loudly when he was giving information, an activity that established his authority—even though in several cases, Carol already had the information he was giving her. But he lowered his voice when he was speaking in ways that did not position him as an authority: conceding a point, assenting, asking for information, and acknowledging information that he should have known.

The times that Carol lowered her voice were completely different. During the conversation, she repeatedly suggested solutions to the problems they were facing. By lowering her voice, Carol downplayed her suggestions, so as not to threaten Ron's competence, since he did not think the extra precautions were necessary. For example:

Carol: All right. I've got a call in to Andy and, uh, I'm going to pursue, mildly pursue, the double—double /?/ the backup, in case.

Kendall points out that lowering her voice went along with other ways that Carol mitigated her suggestions for a backup, such as hesitation ("uh") and false starts ("double—double"). She also downplayed what she was planning to do by changing "pursue" to "mildly pursue."

In contrast, Ron spoke in a way that enhanced his own authority and undercut Carol's. As he gave her information, he not only spoke loudly but also frequently said "Okay," "you follow?" and "you see this?"—expressions that Carol never used. Asking "you follow?" and "you see?" implies the listener might not be able to follow or understand. Kendall points out that not only did Carol definitely follow and understand what Ron was saying, but at this point in the conversation he was arguing for a position that she had argued for earlier. He also undercut her authority by repeatedly questioning her about information she had already given him:

> Ron: But that's all you know that it was ordered— And you *did* tell the phone company that we had an Adtran— um
> Carol: Yes.
> Ron: I S C M.
> Carol: Well, they know that now 'cause they went in and reconfigured our Adtran.
> Ron: *They've seen it?*
> Carol: They've seen it.

Kendall points out that Ron's repeated questioning sounded as though he were challenging Carol's knowledge—and consequently her authority. His way of speaking stands out in these conversations precisely because it contrasts so sharply with Carol's. Because she is talking in a way that saves face for him but his way of talking threatens her "face," an observer might conclude that she is less competent than she is, and he more so.

THE EFFECT OF DOWNPLAYING AUTHORITY '

It is possible that Ron spoke to Carol exactly as he would speak to anyone in her position, or to any woman in her position. But it is also possible that the way he talked to her was influenced in part by the way she spoke to him. In other words, it could have been her very downplaying of her own authority that encouraged him to downplay it too (and perhaps even to question it).

In response to my interest in one of the conversations she had analyzed between a woman doctor and a male patient, Nancy Ainsworth-Vaughn offered to send me the tapes and transcripts of the conversation. But she was concerned that I might get the wrong impression of the physician, that I would see her as less competent than she really was. Ainsworth-Vaughn cautioned, "She makes a very different impression in talking with other patients—very poised, knowledgeable, but warm and empathetic. So don't assume that the self she constructed in these encounters is anything like the whole story. She has tremendous respect from her co-workers; the nurses recommend her to their friends. . . . A nurse's recommendation is a pretty good indicator of competence. . . . Just wanted to say all this because I would hate to see this doc go undervalued."

I asked Ainsworth-Vaughn what it was about the way the doctor spoke in this encounter that led her to fear I might undervalue her. She responded, "She laughs good-naturedly and supports topics rather than initiating them. . . . She plays down being board certified. All this is jointly constructed. [The male patient] is initiating so many topics she hardly can fit one in. *He* plays down her board certification. . . . When the topic of her success comes up, he changes the topic to whether she went shopping while she was in Minneapolis taking the boards."

Using the sociolinguistic term "jointly constructed," Ainsworth-Vaughn pointed out that the impression the doctor made in this encounter resulted not only from her own verbal behavior but from the patient's as well. The doctor seemed less accomplished because the patient underplayed her accomplishments; she seemed not to control the conversation because he kept raising topics. But Ainsworth-Vaughn found, in examining this physician's interactions with other patients, that she did typically follow patients' leads in determining an agenda for the conversation, and that this was an effective means of discovering patients' concerns and conditions. In Ainsworth-Vaughn's words, "I've also been thinking about the doctor's habit of following her patient's conversational lead. This works out beautifully in most situations, e.g., when she has to discuss very bad news with the patient, she allows the patient to initiate a topic that relates to the news (which the patient knew about but obviously didn't want to start right out with)."

Once again, the ritual nature of conversation is key. The doctor's willingness to follow the patient's lead allows patients to express their concerns and reveal crucial information that might not come out under questioning, since the doctor, not being in the patient's skin, might not know what questions to ask to bring it out. But allowing patients to establish the lead depends on their goodwill to hold up the doctor's face. She does not wield her authority, but she depends on the patients to respect it nonetheless. Patients inclined to bring the doctor down a notch have far more opportunity to do so with physicians who allow them to take the lead. Wearing the mantle of authority lightly allows it to be more easily pushed off your shoulders.

WHY DOWNPLAY AUTHORITY?

Considering the responses women in authority get from others provides possible explanations for why they often create authoritative stances as they do. Part of the reason surely lies in the way others react to them.

Because of their experience playing in groups of boys when they were children, many men develop a sensitivity to being told what to do. When boys play, the high-status boys get and keep their status in part by giving orders to the other boys and making them stick. Working for and with other people necessarily entails getting others to do what you want and dealing with others' efforts to get you to do what they want. This introduces a constant potential source of tension and battles of wills. Since many men associate being given orders with attempts to establish a one-up position—in other words, to dominate—the situation becomes especially sensitive when the person giving orders is female. A woman who owns and runs her own interior-architecture and design firm discovered this: "If I tell a painter, 'You know, that color looks a bit off,' a hundred percent, without fail, he'll turn around and say, 'Hey, lady, you can't tell me what to do.' "

In the preceding chapter, I mentioned a woman surgeon who discovered that she got better cooperation from nurses if she treated them "with respect" than if she barked orders the way many of her male counterparts did (with satisfactory results, for them). I heard similar strategies from many other women I talked to. A woman who worked successfully as the manager of a factory explained:

> What I found was that if you demonstrate a little bit of respect for them, they're fine, but when you come in and tell them, "You do this and you do that," they resent it. And if I said, "Listen, Deborah, I need to figure out whether we can get this lot worked in and we can get this machine up to speed. What do you think we ought to do?" And they'll tell me. I'll say, "Well, why don't we try this? Do you think this would work? I'll tell you what. Let's try this, and if this doesn't work, let's try your way." And then they would really work towards making whatever effort—they went into an effective effort rather than resenting, and starting from this negative thing, "You tell me what to do and you act like I don't know. I been running this machine for fifteen years. How dare you?"

This woman did not think of her style as differing from men's. She was simply explaining her philosophy of management, in her words, her "natural instincts." But others' research, as well as my own observation, indicates that there are often patterns to women's and men's philosophies of management, just as there are systematic differences in how others react to the same ways of talking when heard from women or men.

Judging from the excerpts she presents from her interviews with twenty-two women and eighteen men managers, Anne Statham also found women claiming that their management style was not authoritarian. She quotes one woman as saying, "I don't care to have that type of attitude . . . you know, crack the whip. I feel more family-oriented to the whole lot of them." Statham points out that previous studies have divided managers into "task-oriented" and "person-oriented" categories. This dichotomy almost ensures that women will be found wanting, as any evidence that they are "person-oriented" is then taken to imply they are not "task-oriented," not a very good advertisement when times are hard and companies are concerned with the bottom line—getting the task done. Statham concludes that the women she interviewed were both: They regarded focusing on people as the best way to get the task done. As one female manager put it, "If my people are happy, they are going to do a better job for me—and they do." Statham notes that half the women she interviewed did not describe themselves as people-oriented; it was their secretaries who did.

Statham contrasts this with the styles of the men she interviewed, which she calls "autonomy-invested" and "image-engrossed." She concluded that the men were "autonomy-invested" because, whereas the women talked about their jobs in terms of making sure their employees were happy and maintaining close relations with them, the men emphasized the importance of independence for their employees as well as themselves. She quotes some of the men:

"hire people with personalities that fit your needs and let them go . . ."

"hire people who take pride in their work . . . and get out of their way . . ."

"search for good people and stay out of their way . . ."

"if you don't give people that freedom, they are not growing
. . . If you are going to move forward, you have got to let
people take risks."

"The more you interfere, the less gets done."

"I want them to become less dependent on me, so I can
become more independent."

It does not surprise me that so many of the women in Statham's study talked in terms of staying involved with their employees whereas so many of the men talked about autonomy. This supports the pattern that has been described by many researchers, indicating that American men are likely to place relatively greater value on independence, whereas American women are likely to place more relative value on involvement. But I wonder if it is right to see "autonomy-invested" as opposed to "people-oriented." It seems from the men's statements quoted above that they feel giving their subordinates freedom is best for them, personally, as well as for the company, so they are being person-oriented in a different way. The women assume it is best for people to maintain involvement with them, whereas the men assume people are happier and more productive when granted independence.

The similarity in phrasing used by so many of the men (saying, one way or another, "Hire good people and get out of their way") is evidence that ways of talking are relatively routinized: What we say seems self-evidently the right thing to say because we have heard others express similar sentiments. Further evidence for this view lies in Statham's report that the secretaries she interviewed said they liked working for their women bosses because they gave them more autonomy! As one secretary put it, "She doesn't question what I do. She has confidence . . . that makes you feel good."

The other contrast Statham observed was in what she refers to as the tendency of the men to talk about the importance of their jobs or their division to the company, something only one of the women

did. She calls this "image-engrossed," but concern with the importance of one's job is not necessarily only a matter of image. The
pattern by which men were more likely to mention the importance
of their job or division, something I noticed in my own observations
as well, probably says more about women's and men's senses of the
right demeanor to display than it does about their relative valuing of
demeanor at all—that is, image. The greater likelihood that men
may mention the importance of their division goes along with the
prohibition already discussed that many women feel against saying
anything that could be construed as boasting.

"Don't Hate Me, I'm Not Perfect"

Barbara Matusow (her real name), a writer at *Washingtonian
Magazine,* showed me pages from a journal she had kept in the
early 1970s. At that time, she was a producer at WRC-TV in
Washington, D.C., the only female producer of a local television
news show at the station. This is what she wrote one day in her
journal:

> Today was a really good day. Several people who had merely
> tolerated me before passed over the magic line into hatred
> today, but in not a single instance did it crush me. Or even
> faze me.

One of the incidents Matusow recorded in which she weathered
hatred took place in the control room. Having made a number of
complicated last-minute changes in the show, she saw that the director had not completely grasped what he had to do to adjust, so
she began explaining the situation directly to the audio engineer.
The director "exploded in rage, yelling, 'There's only one director
in a control room, baby!' " Matusow, however, kept her cool:

> I, a monument of calm, returned to my chair. Not seething
> with the injustice of the attack. No thought of later explaining

my actions to any of the parties involved. Just serenely, almost happily cresting on the wave of his palpable, evident hatred.

Don't get me wrong. I will never learn to *enjoy* hatred. I don't want to. But it is fairly exhilarating to be able to stare hostility straight in the face and manage to remain unmoved.

It's taken me thirty-five years to learn this trick.

Being hurt by anger and criticism is not gender-specific. Secretary of defense nominee Bobby Ray Inman withdrew his nomination because he did not want to deal with what he regarded as extreme and unfair attacks. This sparked a new round of criticism of him for being too "thin-skinned." In this connection, columnist Meg Greenfield wrote that "thin skin is the only kind of skin human beings come with." But she went on to say that "people in authority need to have learned how to 'take it' and just keep on doing what it is they were meant to be doing in the first place." Surely, this applies equally to everyone. But there is evidence that women are less accustomed to dealing with conflict and attack. Athletic coaches, for example, frequently inspire athletes by verbally abusing and insulting them (a practice that outraged the mother of a girl who played in Little League, according to the mother's "My Turn" column in *Newsweek*). And there is also reason to believe that women in positions of authority receive more hostility.

In recalling the poet he said had been his greatest teacher, Philip Levine notes that John Berryman did not care if he was disliked. "In private," Levine recalls, "he once remarked to me that teaching something as difficult as poetry writing was not a popularity contest. 'Even a class as remarkable as this one,' he said, 'will produce terrible poems, and I am the one who is obliged to say so.'"

Wanting to be liked may be one reason many women find it appropriate to be extra nice when they're in a position of authority, assuring others that they are not throwing their weight around. As we have seen, this is a legitimate concern. Another way of ensuring that your high status does not threaten your being liked is making sure that you do not appear to "have it all." This is a concern that frequently surfaced when I spoke with women in power. One woman who was head of a nonprofit charity told me that she senses that many of the other women in the organization are hostile to her. She said, "I'm well respected by my superiors and peers at other nonprofits, I'm well paid, I have power and influence, and I have an intact marriage to boot. If I were thin too, I wouldn't last a minute." This belief that she had to have at least one major flaw in order to be accepted echoed precisely the statement by Oprah Winfrey—with reference to the same flaw: "My weight was always my apology to the world. It was my way of saying, 'Okay, I'm rich. I've got a good-looking boyfriend, and I've got a great life but, see, I've got this big weight problem, so you can still love me.' "

In dealing with this dilemma, some women fall back on verbal variations on the conversational ritual "What, this old rag?" They try to be appropriately modest by denigrating their own accomplishments and possessions. But while it may work well for them by making them more likable, this ritual can work against them by interfering with a demeanor that exudes authority.

THE DIFFERENCE BETWEEN HOLDING AUTHORITY AND SEEKING IT

A particularly enlightening study was conducted by sociologists Arlene Eskilson and Mary Glenn Wiley. They figured out a way to compare situations in which women felt they had earned their status to those in which they felt they had not. The researchers examined who talked more in groups of three that had to perform a task together. In one situation, the three members drew lots to determine who would be the leader. In the other situation, the experimenters gave them a test and announced that one of the three had performed best on the test. (In fact, the person had been chosen at random.) That person was also given information relevant to the task that others did not have. The results showed that when women (and the others in their group) felt they had earned the role of leader by their own performance and possessed crucial information, they talked as much as men did in the role of leaders, but when women (and the others in the groups) felt they had been given the role at random, they did not.

I was intrigued by this because it reflected my own attitude toward talking on the radio. When invited to be a guest on a talk show because of my expertise, I am completely comfortable in that role. But I never call in to talk shows, even though I often listen to them and think of ideas to contribute based on my expertise. When I am on a show as an invited expert, everyone else in the context is supporting my authority for me. But if I were to call in, I would have two choices. I could establish my authority myself ("Hello, I'm Deborah Tannen, I'm a professor and the author of books. . . ."), but this would seem boastful to me, and I would be embarrassed if I was not recognized. The alternative would be to risk being dismissed if I didn't identify myself as an authority ("Hello, I'm Deborah and I'm calling from Washington, D.C."). Faced with two equally unpalatable options, I don't call in.

This may reflect another barrier to women being seen as appropriate for positions of authority. There are many women who would do exceptionally well if they were given a role of authority but who never get the chance because they do not act as if they want or deserve it before others grant them the position. I observed this in a company in which a woman division head discussed with a male regional manager the question of who on his staff should be promoted to office manager at a particular site. The division head suggested a woman in the office, but the regional manager said that this woman didn't want to be promoted. He had heard her say as much repeatedly. The division head suggested that he ask her, and the regional manager was surprised to report back that she had eagerly accepted. He had taken her disclaimers literally, whereas she had probably been disclaiming interest in promotion in order to avoid seeming too ambitious, and to save face if she were not offered one. In many organizations, those making decisions about promotions into leadership positions look for leaderlike behavior as well as evidence of a desire to be promoted, but many people (including many women) do not exhibit leaderlike behavior unless they have been granted the leadership position, and refrain from expressing interest in jobs they have not been offered. This may be related, as well, to the comment that I heard from many of the people I interviewed that women they knew who were extremely capable on the job did not "interview" well.

JUDGING A BOOK BY ITS COVER

Although all these forces are at work when individuals speak one way or another, it would be misleading to imply that everything that happens to us is a reaction to something we said or did. Much as this goes against our beliefs in how the world should be, sometimes others treat us in ways that have far less to do with who we are as individuals than with their assumptions about who we are based on the group we seem to belong to.

We would all like to believe that we judge others and are judged by competence, performance, and hard-and-fast results, not stereotypes. But there is overwhelming evidence from studies in many different fields that people's judgments of others are influenced by appearance and other characteristics that cause us to see them as members of groups about which we have preexisting assumptions.

All other things being equal, when confronted with a woman and a man they do not know in managerial positions, many people assume the man is more competent than the woman. Veronica Nieva and Barbara Gutek reviewed a large number of studies in which this conclusion was reached. Subjects were asked to evaluate hypothetical people who are described identically, except for their sex. Study after study had similar results: Well-qualified people in managerial roles were evaluated more highly if they were identified as male. But when managers were identified as unsuccessful or not well qualified, then evaluators were harder on men than women—

as if they expected less of women to start with.

In these studies, it is simply the image of women as women that affords them low status, not anything they have done as individuals. Offensive as the realization may seem, expectations about us, based on preconceptions, can affect and even determine how we are heard—and if we are heard at all. A German man who lived in Japan for many years and spoke Japanese fluently reported that the Japanese assumption that foreigners cannot learn Japanese made it impossible for some Japanese people to understand him when he spoke their language—if they were looking at him. When he spoke Japanese on the telephone, no one ever had trouble understanding him. But frequently, when he spoke to people face-to-face, they simply stared at him in incomprehension. Convinced he could not be speaking Japanese, they simply failed to process what he said.

The effect of expectations on comprehension is also supported by research. Speech-communication professor Donald Rubin was concerned with complaints by students at his university that they had trouble understanding foreign-born teaching assistants. Rubin suspected that their preconceptions about foreign-looking speakers being difficult to understand might be playing a powerful role. To test this idea, he tape-recorded a four-minute lecture given by an American-born woman from Ohio, then played the tape to two groups of students at two different times. As the students listened to the lecture on tape, they saw projected on a screen a photograph of the person they were told was the lecturer. In one case, they saw a photograph of a Caucasian woman, in the other, a Chinese woman. Then he gave the students a comprehension test to see how much they had been able to learn from the identical lectures, given their differing assumptions about the person giving it. He found that the students who thought they were listening to a Chinese lecturer scored lower on the comprehension test than those who thought they were listening to a white American—and their lower scores were about the same as those for a third group who had heard a lecture given by a real Chinese teaching assistant with a heavy accent. In other words, the students' assumptions about the person they were listening to had a stronger effect than the way the speaker actually talked.

In addition to how much was understood, the students' evaluations of the abilities of the speaker reflected those assumptions. Rubin found that students who thought they were listening to a foreign-born teacher also rated her teaching skills lower than those who thought the woman delivering exactly the same lecture was American-born.

SAME WORDS, DIFFERENT REACTIONS

These studies showing that we tend to react differently to the same way of speaking if we think the speech is coming from different speakers helps explain why women and men can get very different reactions even if they speak the same way. When people told me about men who had "strictly business" or "no-nonsense" styles, they simply said, "He's a strictly business type," or they referred to his profession: "He's a typical accountant." But when they were commenting on the same style in a woman, I frequently heard, "She's got a pseudomasculine style." Because this style was expected of and associated with men, women who adopted it were seen not as trying to be efficient, competent, and businesslike, but as trying to be like men.

One man I interviewed mentioned the same characteristic—directness—in talking about three people in his company. But it was a complaint in the case of the two women and a compliment when applied to the man. About one woman he said:

> Well, her style was very direct. I think very direct and abrupt. Because that was one of the criticisms I had of her . . . was a, somewhat of a lack of tact. Because she could make statements which were right, but not tactfully made. And she tended to upset—or ruffle some feathers.

At another point in the interview, he said he didn't like working with a particular woman because her failure to engage in small talk made her seem too direct: "It was more, 'Okay, here's the question, here's the answer. That's the story.' No small talk." I asked, "Do you think she also had a very direct style?" He answered,

> Yes. Yes, she was very direct too. Very much. Here's the task at hand, here's what needs to be done. Okay, we're done. There wasn't a lot of side stuff.

And yet, in telling me why he particularly admired a man he worked with, he mentioned the same quality—directness:

> And I had a great deal of admiration for him. I think he's direct, he's aggressive, he's very intelligent. . . . On the other hand, he does carry a big hammer! And if he needs to, he'll use it and you'll get squashed!

I have no way of knowing whether the people this man was referring to really did talk in the same way. No doubt there were many aspects of their styles and personalities that were different. But it is clear that the quality of directness made a different impression on him when it was used by the man and by the two women.

Another facet of this dynamic is that individuals within a culture may be punished by others if they do not conform to expectations for their sex. Anne Statham notes in her study of male and female managers that individuals of both sexes who departed from the norms for their own sex were viewed negatively by subordinates of the same sex. A male manager whose style approximated those of the women was seen as "fairly meek" and "weak" by men who worked for him, though he was highly praised by women subordinates. A woman manager whose style was more like those of the men in the study was criticized for neglect by a woman who reported to her (she "never shows any personal interest in me . . . has only asked me to lunch once") and by her secretary for having "superior airs." The woman herself felt that women subordinates resisted accepting decisions she made independently.

Similar findings were uncovered by Susan Schick Case in a study of men and women managers talking together in groups of ten at a management school. Case concluded that two of the most influential members of the groups were a woman and a man whose styles combined ways of speaking expected of the two sexes. (She gauged influence by who talked more, how much, to whom, about what, and in what way.) The ways the particularly influential man spoke included hesitating, using rising intonation at the end of statements, mitigating statements with qualifiers, expressing feelings, and talking about himself. He also used "masculine traits" like swearing and joking. The particularly influential woman's style included using complex sentences, slang, resisting interruptions, and talking to the group as a whole. Her style also had many feminine aspects: She did not swear, did not talk "about competition, aggression, taking charge or one-upmanship," and her talk was often personal; Case found her to be the most supportive group member linguistically, but the only woman in the group who never said "Mm-hmm." Case further describes her style in this way:

> She contributed 83% of all female usage of interruptions and all the incidents of disallowing interruption. That is not to say that she always disallowed interruptions. But the times she allowed interruptions accounted for only 18% of the female total. Although very assertive, her style was not confrontative, thus placing her in the bottom quartile in arguing, confronting, and attacking. She stated her own ideas, but also built on others' utterances and asked questions to elicit ideas, both female traits.

All in all, Case's description sounds quite appealing. So it comes as a surprise to learn that this woman was widely disliked and provoked openly hostile comments from others in the group whom Case describes as "male group members with prototypical male-style speech." Here are some of the things they said about her:

"What you putting on airs being like one of those men?"

"You're a woman who takes a man's role."

"You're playing the role of a man in the group. There's an issue of competition."

"Castrating bitch."

The men whose speech combined male and female traits, including the one Case singled out as being one of the most influential group members, did not, apparently, elicit the anger that this woman did, but neither were they pleased with the receptions they got. One man whose speech Case calls "balanced" measured in the middle in terms of influence, but he was the least influential of the men. Another man whose speech exhibited what Case considered both extreme male and extreme female qualities was responsible for 75% of the swearing and one third of the interruptions but also had the highest pattern of building on others' talk. His use of approximations and qualifiers was the highest for males in the study, as was his tendency to speak personally (using the pronoun "I") and, accordingly, his "willingness to accept personal experience as proof, something the women did readily." Yet he was not happy with the reaction he got from the group either: "I feel trapped," he told Case. "I can't be myself in this group. Makes me feel stopped up. I can't be what I am . . . I'm damn uncomfortable."

This study suggests that men and women who do not conform to expectations for their gender may not be liked.

WHEN EQUAL IS DOMINANT

Although many women avoid being as aggressive as some men may be, and those who do speak assertively may get more negative responses than men who speak in similar ways, nonetheless many

women in positions of authority, and women in the business world
in general, do gradually adapt their ways of speaking to the norms
of the world they inhabit—norms that may be different from those
they previously followed. And this has consequences for the reception they get when they use their new speech styles at home. A
woman in the army who had been promoted to drill sergeant had a
hard time getting recruits to follow her orders at first, but over time
she changed her style and became successful at her job. And the
change carried over to her way of talking at home, where it began
creating problems in her marriage.

I have heard from many women in positions of authority who
say the assertiveness required on the job causes problems at home.
An attorney told me that she finds herself questioning her mother
in a way that her mother protests, "You're not a lawyer now." Her
husband too at times reminds her, "You're home now." One
woman said that her husband told her, "Go out, come back in, and
try saying that a different way. I'm not your secretary." Another
woman told me that her husband became angry because instead of
waiting on the sidewalk while he hailed a cab, she stepped into the
street and raised her own arm, as she had come to do automatically
when she needed to hail a cab in the course of her work. A third
woman told of a similar experience: She and her husband arrived
at an expensive restaurant for dinner. As usual, she had made the
reservations. (This was no problem.) But as they approached the
maître d', it was she who gave their name and helped the maître d'
locate it on his list by pointing to it. By the time they were seated,
her husband was livid. "Don't you ever do that again," he seethed.
"You are the only woman in this whole restaurant who did that!"

In the case of the last example, I had to ask for clarification, to
be sure I understood what exactly had angered the woman's husband. (It was that she took charge, dealing with the maître d' herself rather than hanging back and letting him do it.) But if women
and men are to relate to each other as equals, shouldn't they be
following the same norms in talking to each other? If the husband
in the first anecdote thought his wife had adopted too imperious a
tone in speaking to him, why was it acceptable for him to use such

an imperious tone in telling her to try it differently?

In considering these examples, I wondered why these women's husbands felt their wives were trying to dominate them, when the women did the very things that the men themselves wanted to do? I got a glimpse of a possible explanation while I was a guest on a radio talk show discussing how women's and men's differing conversational styles could lead to misunderstandings. A man called in to say that he and his wife got along very well because they agreed there could be only one boss in the house, and he was it. The talk-show host, a woman, fielded the question herself. She responded at length that she didn't see why anyone had to be boss: Relationships are, after all, a partnership. When he needs something, she should listen; when she needs something, he should listen. Both should share equally in resources and rights. When she was done, pleased with the self-evident rightness and clarity of her statement, she took another call. It was a man who said, "That's what's wrong with you women. You want to dominate us." The host said, "Excuse me for a moment. I'm going to scream." Which she then did: long, high-pitched, and wordless, right into the microphone.

It was a scream of frustration and bewilderment. The host had just talked about wanting to be equal, and here she was accused of wanting to be dominant. This made no sense, unless you assume that all relationships are necessarily hierarchical—in other words, as the first caller had put it, there has to be a boss in every relationship, and there can be only one. If you begin with these assumptions, then a woman's refusal to take the subordinate role means, ipso facto, that she wants to be the dominant one. The result is damaging for women who do not fit stereotypical images of self-deprecating femininity, and also for women who do: A woman who is simply trying to be appropriately feminine in her manner is seen as submissive, and a woman who is not is seen as dominating and reviled for it.

There is one final liability that makes it harder for a woman in authority than for a man, all else being equal (which it may not be). Unless there is something special about a particular man who holds a managerial position (for example, he may be a member of a minority group, may have been promoted from within or have come from a rival company, or may have a background different from that of the people who previously held the post), then a man in a position of authority will be judged as a boss. When a woman is in a position of authority in a field mostly populated by men, then she is judged as a woman—and, in the minds of some, as Woman: All women are implicated by what she does. This too results from women being marked.

In Caryl Churchill's play *Top Girls,* Marlene is visited at the office by Mrs. Kidd, the wife of her colleague Howard, who wanted and expected the promotion Marlene just got. Mrs. Kidd informs Marlene that Howard is "in a state of shock" over being bested by a woman, and that he is taking it out on his wife:

> It's me that bears the brunt. I'm not the one that's been promoted. He's not being dominated by me, I've been right behind him, I put him first every inch of the way. And now what do I get? You women this, you women that. It's not my fault.

In the world of the play, it is unusual for a woman to get promoted over a man, so Howard sees Marlene not just as an individual who happened to be promoted over him, but as a *woman* who surpassed him, and his anger is directed at her not only as an individual, but as the representative of all women. And he vents his anger at the representative of all women in his home—his wife.

Another way that women in positions of authority come to be seen as Woman rather than as individuals emerges when two or more women are seen together. Some years ago I was standing in the hall talking to the two other women who taught in my department. One of our male colleagues encountered us on his walk down the hall and said, "What are you three cooking up?" He was joking, of course, yet the sight of the three women in the department talking to each other suggested to him some kind of plotting, maybe an insurrection. Apparently, this impression is common when women constitute a minority in a particular situation and are found talking to each other, including women in the United States House of Representatives. In his article about women in the House, journalist David Finkel wrote, "And when they are on the floor, they are keenly aware that if four, three, even two of them stand together, it is only a matter of time before a male colleague will wander over and ask what they're doing . . ."

WHAT'S A WOMAN TO DO?

All this means that women in positions of authority face a special challenge. Our expectations for how a person in authority should behave are at odds with our expectations for how a woman should behave. If a woman talks in ways expected of women, she is more likely to be liked than respected. If she talks in ways expected of men, she is more likely to be respected than liked. It is particularly ironic that the risk of losing likability is greater for women in authority, since evidence indicates that so many women care so much about whether or not they are liked.

Many of the constraints I have discussed apply equally to women and men. A man who quietly does a good job but is not good at letting others know about the job he is doing may go unrecognized. And there are many men who for reasons of cultural background, upbringing, or personality are not comfortable "blowing their own horn," not good at speaking up at meetings, too succinct and understated to command attention. But their situations are really not the same, because if such men were to take assertiveness training and alter their styles, they would enhance not only their chances for success. Everything they did to enhance their assertiveness at work would also enhance their masculinity, in others' eyes. But a woman is in a double bind. Everything she does to enhance her assertiveness risks undercutting her femininity, in the eyes of others. And everything she does to fit expectations of how a woman should talk risks undercutting the impression of competence that she makes.

Before the 1992 national election, there were two women in the United States Senate: Democrat Barbara Mikulski of Maryland and Republican Nancy Kassebaum of Kansas. Senator Mikulski is frequently called "tough" because of her hard-hitting style (a style that would be unremarkable, and probably unremarked, in a male senator). Senator Kassebaum has a style closer to that expected of women, one that would be characterized as "a soft touch." Each became an object lesson for the other. "You should be more like Barbara," their colleagues told Senator Kassebaum, encouraging her to be firmer and more assertive. "You should be more like Nancy," they told Senator Mikulski, encouraging her to soften her approach. This complementary and conflicting advice dramatizes the damned-if-you-do-damned-if-you-don't double bind that women in authority confront. As more and more women, each with her own unique style, take their seats in the Senate and in other positions of authority, we can hope that each woman will be free to be more like herself.

SEVEN

Talking Up Close: Status and Connection

A woman and a man were talking about the manager of a large division of their company. The woman was saying that this manager had connections in many of the company's departments, so she was successful at fulfilling her agenda. "What you mean," the man offered, "is that she has clout." "Not really," the woman clarified. "I mean she's built relationships with people that she can call on when she needs to get around rules or hurry things up." "That's what I said," the man retorted. "She's been there long enough to develop clout." "No," the woman objected, becoming irritated. "I'm not talking about clout. I'm talking about relationships." "But what it comes down to," the man retorted, equally irritated, "is clout. She can make things happen."

In a sense, this is the kind of conversation I wrote about in *You Just Don't Understand,* where I showed that women and men often walk away from the same conversation having seen different aspects of it. In this conversation, the man was focused on status— who's in the one-up position, and who's one-down? (Having "clout" means being one-up, so you can get others to do what you want.) The woman is focusing on connection: The person they are talking about can get things done because she has "built relationships," established connections to others. But there is a danger in this formulation. It can be taken to imply that status and connection are parallel and mutually exclusive. They aren't. They are two different dynamics of interaction—dynamics that dovetail and often entail each other. The manager being discussed in this example did have clout, which resulted in part from the relationships she had built up.

Competing for status can be a means of establishing connection, which is more or less what happens in sports and in boys' social groups. People can also compete for connection, which is more or less what happens in popularity contests, and in girls' social groups, according to sociologists and anthropologists who have studied them. Rather than thinking of status and connection as mutually exclusive opposites, to understand the dynamics of talking at work we have to explore the ways they are intertwined.

A woman was at home when her husband arrived and announced that his arch rival had invited him to contribute a chapter to a book. The woman remarked on how nice it was that the rival was initiating a rapprochement by including her husband in his book. He responded that she had got it wrong: By taking the position of editor, the one in control, and casting him as merely a contributor, the rival was actually trying to solidify his dominance, "get me under his thumb." He thought she was naïve. She thought he was paranoid.

Whose interpretation was right? The answer is, both. But they were focusing on different aspects of the relationship. She was asking herself how close or distant the two people would be as a result of the transaction and concluded it would bring them closer. He was asking who would be in control and concluded that he would be in a one-down position. I don't know what the editor of the collection had in mind; to determine that, I'd have to know how he would react if their roles were reversed. But regardless of what the editor thought, inviting someone to contribute to a book you are editing could be seen as either an exercise of power or an invitation to rapprochement. In that sense, it is ambiguous. Even more, it has elements of both; it "means" both at the same time. The linguistic term for meaning more than one thing at the same time is "polysemy" (pronounced pul-LIH-sih-mee), from *poly,* Greek for "many," and *semy,* Greek for "meaning"). Using this term, the invitation was "polysemous" (pul-LIH-sih-mus).

The same double meaning explains my surprise when a man born and raised in Europe expressed his annoyance at what he called Americans' obsession with knowing everyone's roots, expressed in their continually asking others where they are from and where their parents were born. He said it is an attempt to get power over you by pinning you down. I was surprised because to me asking someone's background is a means of establishing connection, finding a point of reference from which to select topics of conversation and discover areas of shared experience. In fact, it can be either or both. (I suspect this practice is more common in the Northeast, where this man lives, than in the Midwest, South, and West, where such questions are less common and can even be considered rude.)

If you have a friend who repeatedly picks up the check when you dine together, is she being generous and sharing her wealth, or is she trying to flaunt her money and remind you that she has more of it than you do? Although the intention may be kindness, her repeated generosity may make you feel bad by reminding you that she has more money. It also can establish a sense of obligation and therefore feel like control. Many people feel that if a man pays for a woman's meal or theater ticket, then the evening becomes a date, and she owes him something in exchange. (This quid pro quo was made explicit in a 1963 guide to behavior for young women which cautioned, "Remember . . . that the evening is costing him a sizable amount, and that it's up to you to see that he's enjoying every minute.") Both of you are caught in the web of the ambiguity of status and connection. Even if you believe your friend's motive was purely generous, you may still feel denigrated by her generosity because the fact that she can act on this impulse is evidence that she has more money than you. Both interpretations exist at once: connection—she is paying to be nice—and status—her generosity reminds you that she is richer and makes you feel obligated. That is why offering to pick up the check is not just ambiguous but polysemous: It means both at once.

The double meaning of generosity explains an observation that initially surprised me: Greta Paules, an anthropologist who wrote a book about the culture of waitressing called *Dishing It Out,* found that waitresses in a restaurant chain were offended not only by tips that were too small, but also by tips that were too large. They felt that a customer leaving an unusually large tip was implying that the amount of money left was insignificant to the tipper but significant to the waitress. And this they found insulting.

WHAT'S IN A FIRST NAME?

Status reigns when one speaker addresses the other by first name but is addressed by title–last name. For example, a patient addresses his doctor as "Dr. Henderson," but the doctor calls him "Sidney." Perhaps the doctor's receptionist assigns these forms of address by saying, "Dr. Henderson will see you now, Sidney." In many offices, the secretary addresses her boss as "Mr. Birch," but he calls her "Mindy," not "Ms. Burns." The same goes for teacher and student, or the executive in an office building and the night watchman who lets him in after hours. What suggests power is not the formality of the address, "Mr. Birch," but the asymmetry: The two people do not address each other the same way. A kind of connection is established by symmetry: Two nurses call each other by first names; a doctor telephones another doctor he doesn't know well, and they address one another as "Doctor." Regardless of formality, the mutuality of addressing each other in the same way implies shared experience or equal status.

Nowhere is the double meaning of status and connection clearer than in the use of first names. I recall a colleague reporting at a faculty meeting his committee's shortlist of four candidates for a faculty position: Turner, Smith, Jones, and Annie. He referred to the three men by their last names, the one woman by not only her first name but a diminutive, even though she was older and more experienced than the other three candidates. Two of the men were graduate students who had not yet received their Ph.D.'s, and one was a recent Ph.D. who had been teaching for a year; the woman was an experienced faculty member at another institution who had held her Ph.D. for half a dozen years.

Women frequently notice that they are referred to by first name more readily than their male counterparts are. They tend to see this as evidence that they are not respected as much—placed lower on the status dimension. But I suspect that as often as not, those who refer to women by first names believe they are doing so not because they don't respect the women but because they feel friendlier toward them. It is not an either-or matter; both dynamics are operating.

Columnist Judith Martin, who writes as Miss Manners, expressed the opinion that doctors should address patients by title–last name, not first name:

> A doctor who remembers that his patient has his own mantle of dignity—which is admittedly not easy to think about a naked person clutching a sheet and wearing an alarmed expression—will not be patronizing in his form of address. He will not call patients by their first names while expecting to have his own title used. . . . You will notice that Miss Manners has used the pronoun *he* about offending doctors. This is because she has noticed women doctors who have behaved better. They may be a statistical error.

I heard Judith Martin express the same opinion on a radio talk show, after which she was deluged with calls from women saying how deeply they resented being addressed by first name by their doctors and the doctors' staff. (This shows that women are not oblivious to being put in a one-down position.) The talk-show host said she was surprised at the overwhelming response this topic sparked, but Ms. Martin said she was not at all surprised; she knew how strongly feelings ran on this topic.

I was not surprised either, because this practice was a frequent topic of complaint among professional women I knew. But I was surprised when I interviewed women doctors. I entered the conversations curious to learn whether Martin was correct in her impression that women doctors were more likely to address patients by their titles and last names. (Although my personal experience with women doctors has been mixed, the ones I interviewed all told me they did.) But the topic that most exercised the women physicians I interviewed was their resentment at being addressed by first name by their patients—either first name alone or title–first name, as when a mother said to her child, "Sit down for Dr. Joan." Several resisted my suggestion that those who use first name might do so because they find women more approachable. They were sure it was a lack of respect.

One physician had a telling anecdote. She had been angered when a crucial piece of surgical equipment was removed due to budget-cutting, without her being consulted. She confronted the chief and his assistant, a young man. The chief remained calm and said he'd look into it. The assistant, however, became angry in return and said, seething, "Harriet, good-bye." There was no question in her mind that the assistant used her first name as a deliberate put-down, to remind her that she was a woman and therefore in a lower position, because the chief and his assistant never addressed her by first name.

These examples illustrate the status-based power of first-naming, but also the rhetorical power of *changing* how you address someone. With a usual pattern as background, you can dramatize your displeasure by switching to first name, as the doctor's assistant did, or to title–last name, creating distance by becoming more formal. (This is the effect when a mother switches to full name and says to her son, "John Henry Allington, you get in here this minute.")

The double meaning of first names—friendliness versus lack of respect—is at play when people choose a means of reference to the first lady. Almost without fail, ordinary people in conversation refer to the president as Clinton and his wife as Hillary, not Mrs. Clinton or Hillary Clinton. For example, referring to Hillary Clinton's commission on health care, the chair of the American Medical Association, Dr. Raymond Scalettar, was quoted as saying, "We have not had any direct contacts with Hillary's commission." Even as he states that he has never met or spoken to the chair of a major federal commission, Dr. Scalettar nonetheless refers to her by first name. (Notice I did not just refer to him as "Raymond.")

Most people, I believe, if they thought about it, would say that they do this not because they don't respect Mrs. Clinton but because they find her more approachable, or assume that she should be. In this first-name-is-friendly spirit, an article in *The New York Times* reported, soon after President Clinton took office, that some senators were delighted that they got to address the first lady that way: "You can't imagine how great it is to talk with her, to call her 'Hillary,'" one senator was quoted as saying. On the other hand, another article reported some senators' resentment that the first lady was addressing them the same way: "Did you hear, they muttered among themselves," an article in the same newspaper reported the day before, "that she had actually been calling some senators by their *first* names?" This response suggests the flip-side sense that using first names shows a lack of proper respect.

People who see one interpretation or the other—the status view (first-name-shows-lack-of-respect) or the connection view (first-name-is-friendly)—tend to see their interpretation as the right one, the other as "reading things in." It's like the drawing that can be seen as a chalice or two faces. Though we can see both pictures when they are pointed out to us, we can't see them both at once. Yet they are both there, all the time.

DOMINANCE HIERARCHIES AND NETWORKS OF ALLIANCES

In order to grasp how inextricably intertwined are the dynamics of status on one hand and connection on the other, it is illuminating to consider primate behavior. The point is not to equate human and animal behavior, but rather that the behavior of primates provides insight into the dovetailing of dominance hierarchies and networks of alliances.

In a book entitled *How Monkeys See the World,* Dorothy Cheney and Robert Seyfarth show that both male and female monkeys have dominance hierarchies, and that negotiating their position in the hierarchy is a matter of forging and monitoring alliances. Females, for example, inherit their rank from their mothers, but in many monkey populations, high-ranking females have larger families, so one reason for treating a high-ranking female with respect is the fear that her family members will come to her aid if she is angered. High-ranking females also have more friends: They are better at forming alliances with monkeys outside their own families, which is easy for them to do since other females prefer to form alliances with those of high rank. The role of alliances in maintaining rank is dramatic: Although a female's rank rarely shifted, in the cases where it did, a high-ranking female had lost her allies to predators or disease.

Just as dominance is based in part on alliances, so alliances cannot be forged without competition. Grooming each other is the monkeys' primary means of establishing bonds, but competition arises for grooming partners, since monkeys prefer to share the pleasure of grooming with others of high rank.

Competition for alliances is a dynamic pervasive in girls' friendships, as the research of sociologist Donna Eder and of anthropologist Penelope Eckert has shown. Eder, for example, presents a conversation in which sixth-grade girls are fighting about whether or not one of the friends was combing another girl's hair:

Tami: Why were you combing Peggy's hair yesterday?
Heidi: I didn't.

Tami: Yes, you were!
Heidi: I was not.
Tami: You were feathering it back.
Heidi: I was not.
Tami: You were *too*.
Heidi: I was *not*. You can go ask Peggy. [Peggy walks by.]
Peggy, was I combing your hair yesterday? [Peggy
shakes her head no.]
Tami: Whose hair were you combing?
Heidi: I wasn't combing anybody's hair.
Tami: Who was combing Peggy's hair?
Heidi: I don't know.

The argument about hair combing was clearly a dispute about alliances: who is closer friends with whom.

The ability to maintain alliances helped Jay Leno gain the position he wanted as successor to Johnny Carson on NBC's *Tonight*
show, according to the book *The Late Shift* by Bill Carter. This is
how a reviewer summarized Carter's analysis:

Mr. Leno played an inside game, building friendly relationships with NBC executives, local affiliates (whose support
was crucial) and advertisers. He was the guy everyone liked,
and he was always willing to help out with a free promotional
spot, a few minutes of stand-up at an affiliates meeting, an
interview with the local press. So when Mr. Carson announced his retirement, Mr. Leno stood, if you will, as the
machine candidate. Along with his title as Mr. Carson's permanent guest host and his considerable skills as a stand-up
comic, he had an influential booster club of television insiders.

Even if you are not looking for a promotion, having social
contacts with many people means that when you need them, the
channels of communication to them are open. If you see them at
lunch, you can ask for information or present your view of a situation in an informal way. If you have had lunch with them in the

past, and your relationship is friendly, you can call them directly (knowing they will take your call) and ask for what you need or what you want to know.

I saw one woman, highly placed in her organization, who brimmed with this form of friendliness. She regularly organized lunches at work and dinners at her home with many of the executives at and above her level, including the company president. When a problem arose involving their departments, it was easy for her to call them up and resolve it quickly, one-on-one. It seemed to me that this was simply an extension of her naturally sociable temperament, but it served her well on the job. A similar kind of camaraderie can be established through playing golf, a phenomenon well enough recognized in corporations that, according to an anecdote reported to me, a rising young star, identified for advancement, was sent for a weeklong stint at golf school in California at the company's expense.

In other words, hierarchies and alliances, status and connection, are intertwined and inextricable. In trying to understand the dynamics of interaction, we must see these two forces as inseparable, each one implying the other.

HIERARCHY HAS TAKEN A BAD RAP

For Americans, "hierarchy" usually has negative connotations. But all human relations are more or less hierarchical and also involve connection. The American sense that hierarchy is bad may result from our democratic ideology by which "all men are created equal." Yet most people would agree that a mother-child relationship is, at least potentially, a lovely thing. Would one therefore want to insist that it is not hierarchical? Does the mother's superior status and power over her child undercut their closeness? Realizing the hierarchical nature of the mother-child bond is particularly ironic, since much of what is written about women—especially if it is attempting to romanticize them—focuses on women's ability to bear children and attendant "nurturing" qualities. Yet nothing is more hierarchical than motherhood, and "nurturing" frames the nurturer as more capable, more competent—in a word, one-up. Imposing discipline is an inevitable part of nurturing, though American culture has tended to separate them, associating discipline with the father and nurturing with the mother, regardless of who actually does either or both in particular families.

In a classic work on Japanese psychology, Takeo Doi points out that the Japanese regard the mother-child relationship as the prototype for all others, including the one between superiors and subordinates in the workplace, so the notion of hierarchy has a positive connotation for them. According to linguists Ron and Suzanne Wong Scollon, the same is true for Chinese. The Japanese, like the Chinese and members of many other cultures of the world, are most comfortable in hierarchically ordered groups or relationships. What is uncomfortable is not knowing your place in the hierarchy, and hence not knowing how to speak or how to behave. A person who is oblivious to hierarchy would be regarded not as morally superior but as a social misfit. In this schema, knowing one's place in a hierarchical network is a prerequisite for being human—with equal emphasis on "network" and "hierarchy."

Americans tend to assume that hierarchy precludes closeness, so employers and employees cannot "really" be friends, and if they do become friends, complications arise that must be worked out. I myself was inclined to assume that hierarchy is distancing, so that taking a one-up position is synonymous with pushing someone away. But the Japanese perspective made me rethink that assumption.

Sociolinguist Suwako Watanabe compared how American and Japanese students spoke in group discussions with others of the same background. She concluded that the Americans in her study saw themselves as individuals participating in a joint activity, whereas the Japanese students saw themselves as members of a group united by hierarchy. When I first read Watanabe's words, I was caught up short: How could hierarchy unite? But her study, and a little thought, made clear that feeling you are in your rightful place in a hierarchy can feel as safe and close as being in your family—a quintessentially hierarchical institution.

Part of the reason Americans feel hierarchy is negative is that we tend to think of its benefits as flowing one way only: The person in the superior position has the right to tell a subordinate what to do, and the person in the subordinate position has to obey. In this spirit, if someone says he is being treated like a child, he is sure to be heard as registering a complaint, synonymous with saying he is being humiliated. In fact, Murray Bookchin argues, in a book entitled *Remaking Society,* that hierarchy is the source of society's ills.

But in the minds of Japanese, Chinese, Javanese, and members of many other world cultures, there are obligations as well as privileges that go along with both the superior and the subordinate roles. After all, parents have to do a great deal for their children, just as surely as they have power over them. And it is awareness of the privileges associated with the child's role that gives the term "dependence" a positive rather than negative connotation in these cultures. The English title of Takeo Doi's book, *The Anatomy of Dependence,* about what he regards as the key theme in Japanese character, *amae,* sounds to American ears slightly embarrassing if not downright insulting. The positive connotations of the word "dependence" in Asian culture, however, come through in the following statement that Ron Scollon tells me one of his Chinese students in Hong Kong wrote in a paper: "Parents generally give more freedom to their daughters than to sons to have dependent behaviors, for example, touching, crying, and seeking help."

In our assumption that equality is good and hierarchy is bad, Americans tend to regard the sibling relationship as the ultimate in reciprocity. Such statements as "We're like sisters" or "He's like a brother to me" are usually understood as references to closeness, not hierarchy. It is as if to say, "We're so close, there are no power games between us." And yet anyone who has had a flesh-and-blood sibling knows that age differences resulting from birth order are the ultimate in hierarchy: Older siblings can both protect and torment younger ones, who, in return, idolize or resent them or both. And none of this means that they cannot be close.

215

Anthropology provides many examples of cultural contexts in which hierarchical relationships are seen as close and mutually, not unilaterally, empowering. For example, anthropologist William Beeman shows that Iranians often struggle to "get the lower hand." Taking the lower-status position evokes a cultural schema by which the higher-status person is obligated to offer protection, so "getting the lower hand" is a way of getting someone to do things for you—exactly our notion of power. It's a game of one-downmanship. Anthropologist Judith Irvine describes a similar process among the Wolof of Africa as "self-lowering." A Wolof noble may try to grab the lower position to forestall requests for gifts.

Yet another such culture is described by anthropologist Clare Wolfowitz: the Javanese community in Suriname. Wolfowitz explains that a style of speech called "respect/deference" is experienced not as subservience but as an assertion of claims. It is typified by the grandchild-grandparent relationship, one that is both very unequal and very close. (Equality, in contrast, is associated with relatively distant relationships that are formed in the public sphere rather than in the family.)

IT'S ALL IN THE FAMILY

The relationships that form a backdrop to office relations are illuminated by this sampling of cultural perspectives. Although Americans do not tend to think of office relations in terms of the mother-child relationship as explicitly as do the Japanese, nonetheless family relations are probably the model through which we understand all others. If you remind co-workers of members of their family, it can have either a positive or a negative impact. Indeed, the implications of reminding people of members of their family can be complex, as complex as family relationships themselves.

I could see the positive effects of associations with family members when I asked a man who was very highly placed in his organization why he was particularly interested in making sure that women got a fair shake in his organization. He said it was because he had two daughters. "When I saw them coming up at their jobs," he said, "I realized they weren't playing on a level playing field."

Individuals may benefit from reminding others of family members, and such reminders need not follow gender lines. A physician experienced first negative and then positive effects of reminding a supervisor of his son. She recalled her experience as the only woman in her internship program:

> I remember walking down the hall with a very, very, very powerful patriarchal domineering physician who told his patients what and where to do. And I had been on his service, as they call it, for about three weeks, and he was a bombastic kind of an individual, and we were walking down the hall, and suddenly he turned to me, and his—he was infuriated. He was angry. And he looked at me and he said, "What I wanna know is why my son can't be like you."

Eventually, this professor became her ardent supporter. As she put it, "He thought I was the world."

This woman also described how at first she was physically tested, put through more physical trials than her male counterparts. She was, she recalled,

> challenged—could I stand up longer than anybody else in the surgical assist? Could I be on o.b. call just a little bit longer than anybody else? . . . I would go down to look at my scrub, in surgery, and I would start at 8:00, and I would get the long cases. So that very frequently I wouldn't get the lunch break. And it was—it was subtle. I mean, nobody really—but sometimes guys would look at it and say, "Gosh, you know you're really getting the longest cases."

I asked her if this had been a sort of hazing ritual, and she answered:

I think that it started out as a hazing, but then what happened
was you know you can turn a weakness into a strength. What
happened was, I did so well that then some of the men—
older men became very paternalistic. And then they wanted to
give me the good cases. . . . Nobody had—I mean it wasn't
written on paper, but there was a point at which you passed
and from then on, it was no question that I became a favorite
child.

According to this physician's account, her being female drew attention to herself in first a negative but then a positive way. The word
"paternalistic" suggests the fatherlike aspect of a superior watching out for a subordinate. Indeed, the superior who compared her
with his son came to think she was "the world" just as a favorite
child is "the world" to a doting parent. The phrase "bringing up"
a younger colleague, commonly used in business, also suggests par-
enting.

If younger colleagues can remind older ones of their children,
older colleagues, especially bosses, can remind younger ones of
their parents. I heard references to this in a positive spirit—the senior being seen as protective and helpful—as well as a negative one,
by which the senior may be seen as, in the words of one manager,
"arbitrary and unreinforcing, like my father." Gender, again, is
not necessarily a determining factor here. A graduate student who
got into a conflict with a woman supervising professor said that the
professor "reminded her of her father, a high-school football coach
who wanted [her] to excel at sports but couldn't show any pleasure
when she did."

A parentlike stance can be projected in many ways, including choice of metaphors. An executive was recruiting a high-level
manager for a directorship. After explaining that the new position would entail far more responsibility for the candidate than
his current one, he assured him, "Don't worry; I'll put limits
around you so you can't hurt yourself." The metaphor he chose
suggested a parent baby-proofing a house or setting the baby up
in a playpen.

EVER-SHIFTING STATUS

On the model of parent and child, the question of who's in power is not always clear. A parent can order a child to do things—the ultimate test of status—but parents also do many things for children: feed them, dress them, reach things for them. One who does such things for an adult is, in effect, a servant. For that matter, servants also have power over the people they serve, like the secretary who controls whose calls get through to the boss. (My mother recalls that when she was dating my father, there was another woman who also liked him, but my mother worked as his secretary, so when the other woman called, she simply said he was not in.) In the British movie *The Servant,* Dirk Bogarde, in the apparently low-status role of servant, was able to completely take over the life of the person he "served."

It is not surprising that the screenplay for this movie was written by Harold Pinter, since many of Pinter's plays concern power struggles, and many of them explore the complexity of power relations between servants and masters. Another example is his play *No Man's Land,* in which a wealthy alcoholic is attended by his butler and (male) secretary who at times appear and act more like his jailers than his servants.

Relative rank or status modulates how the most social of conversational signals are managed. This can be seen in Thurgood Marshall's recorded reminiscence about how he learned of his appointment to the Supreme Court. Marshall recalled the morning when Ramsey Clark, the attorney general, called Marshall's office and told his secretary not to let anyone else in because he wanted to talk to him. Clark then came to Marshall's office, "and we had pleasantries and all, and I said, 'Well, what're you up to, Ramsey?'" Clark then asked what was on Marshall's calendar for the morning and told him to forget it and go directly to the White House to talk to President Johnson. This is how Marshall described that meeting:

> I went in, and he [President Johnson] was over there at the ticker-tape machine, and I waited a little while, and I coughed, and he said, "Oh, hi, Thurgood. Sit down. Sit down." So we chatted just a few minutes, and I didn't ask him what was on his mind. I let him speak. And all of a sudden he said, "You know something, Thurgood?"
>
> I said, "No, sir, what's that?"
>
> He said, "I'm going to put you on the Supreme Court."

Johnson seemed to be savoring his power to appoint Marshall by springing the announcement on him and also by stating it in an offhand way. What I want to emphasize here is that with both Ramsey Clark, who was then attorney general, and with Lyndon Johnson, who was president, the conversations began with pleasantries. But whereas Marshall cut off the pleasantries and asked the attorney general directly what he wanted ("What're you up to, Ramsey?"), he did not ask the president why he wanted to see him so suddenly, but just "let him speak." Also evident in Marshall's account is the assumption that in order to maintain his independence as a justice, Marshall could no longer socialize with the president. He quotes Johnson as saying, "I guess this is the end of our friendship," to which Marshall replied, "Yep. Just about. Be no more of that."

As a sign of the difference in power, Clark came to Marshall's office, but Marshall went to the president's. And when he got there, he didn't announce his presence but simply stood there waiting to be recognized. When Johnson showed no sign of noticing him, Marshall still avoided speaking first, but rather made his presence apparent by coughing, an intentional use of a vocalization that in principle could be involuntary. The question of who waits and who makes others wait is a bone of contention in many work settings, because it is one of many ways that relative power and status are revealed and negotiated.

"Just a Dime Waiting on a Dollar"

Darrell, who was new in his job at a loading dock, was working with Vic loading pallets and lining them up in the right place in preparation for transferring them to a truck. When they were done, Vic announced, "I'm going to go get the truck." He expected Darrell to wait there, so when he returned with the truck, they would immediately start to load it. But instead of waiting, Darrell went to make a phone call. When Vic returned with the truck, he had to stand around waiting for Darrell. Later their boss asked Vic to unload a shipment that had arrived unexpectedly, and to get Darrell to help. Vic refused: "I'm not working with that asshole!" The supervisor had to mediate the dispute before work could proceed.

It was easy to see why Darrell might have resented being put in the one-down position of having to wait for Vic, and why he would have preferred to go do something and return to find Vic waiting for him. The one who waits is one-down, as a patient waits for a doctor, and as Thurgood Marshall waited for President Johnson to turn to him. An important executive does not want to wait while the telephone rings in the office of someone he is calling, so he gets his secretary to place the call and make the person he's calling wait while she puts her boss on. (One executive quoted a retired colleague who used to say, when they were waiting to see a superior, "Just a dime waiting on a dollar.") Those who manage to make others wait are jiggling the lines of power to get them aligned to their own advantage. But that also makes it clear why Vic would have been so angered. Perhaps he thought that Darrell was the one who should wait, not only because the phone call delayed loading the truck, but also because of Vic's seniority.

The supervisor who told me this story related it to another pattern she had noticed. She said that when she asked women to do something, they usually stopped what they were doing and helped right away. But it was common, in her experience, for men to put off doing what she asked. She had learned that when she gave orders to men, she had to state exactly when she needed the task done—now, or if not now, when. She went on to say that the men on her crew frequently tussled with each other when one asked another to do something; typically, the person who was asked wanted to put off fulfilling the request and make the person who was asking wait.

It is not surprising that this supervisor found men more likely than women to resent waiting, since, as we have seen, men are more likely to be sensitive to being positioned as one-down. Since waiting is associated with being one-down, making others wait not only reflects higher status, but can be a way to create higher status for oneself. So the simple matter of getting someone to do something at work becomes an arena for negotiating status.

"THANKS FOR THE COMPLIMENT"

Another such arena, though very different on the surface, is the act of complimenting—a brief, pleasant way of showing goodwill toward another person. Linguists Robert Herbert and Stephen Straight found that compliments tend to flow from those of higher rank to those of lower rank. Herbert quotes an 1882 etiquette book that makes this explicit:

> [B]etween equals, or from those of superior position to those of inferior station, compliments should not only be acceptable, but gratifying. It is pleasant to know that we are well thought of by those who hold higher positions, such as men of superior talent, or women of superior culture.

Although we would not today speak of anyone being "of inferior station" (nor would we assume that men can have talent whereas women can only have culture), nonetheless the tendency for more compliments to be given by those of higher rank remains.

Inextricably, a compliment can also be interpreted in the spirit of status. For one thing, those who offer compliments can seem to be setting themselves up as in a position to judge, so someone of lower rank who compliments someone of higher rank can appear to be cheeky. For another thing, sociolinguist Janet Holmes points out that compliments can be interpreted as evidence that the complimenter is envious or wants the admired item. For this reason, in some cultures it is considered rude to offer compliments, since custom requires that an admired item be given as a gift. An American woman who married a man from India was badly misunderstood when she met her mother-in-law for the first time. Trying to be nice, she helped her mother-in-law unpack and told her how beautiful her saris were. The mother-in-law complained bitterly to her daughter, "What kind of woman did he marry? She wants everything!"

WHO CALLS THE CHATS?

In the course of a workday, talk shifts continually between work and social topics, and these shifts too can reflect and negotiate status relations. Charlotte Linde noticed in her study of police helicopter crews that when the immediate demands of work subside, the crew may engage in social chat, which will stop if work requirements intrude. And she found that the switch from work talk to social talk was more often initiated by the pilot, who functioned as a superior in command. For example, if it was quiet, the pilot might begin free conversation by noticing the view ("This reservoir or lake or whatever looks pretty"), returning to a previous topic ("So you gonna, uh, look for another car or try to get that one fixed?") or commenting on the mission just completed ("That guy was kinda calm and cool for havin' just ripped down somebody").

This is exactly the pattern that sociolinguist Janice Hornyak noticed in a study of talk in an all-female office at an accounting firm. As the women in the office shifted between work and personal talk, the shift was always initiated by the highest-ranking person in the room, the office manager. If she was busy, nobody else began telling personal stories or chatting. But if the office manager was ready to take a break and chat, the others followed suit. No one worried about whether the office temp had work to do or not, or whether her work required concentration that would be interrupted by social banter.

In this way, hierarchies are reflected, reinforced, and created throughout a workday, in even the most automatic and casual conversation.

"WHAT ARE YOU GOING TO DO ABOUT IT?"

Talk intended to create connection always runs the risk of offending co-workers who have different styles, but the risks are even greater in hierarchical relationships. Complaining about situations at work may be perceived as creating connections—"We're in this together"—among people at the same rank, but it can be taken as a literal complaint—and therefore either a request for action or an implicit criticism—when addressed to a boss.

A fire chief who listened to a lecture I gave was interested in my point that some people engage in complaining to create rapport. He recalled a woman who worked for him who was aghast when he acted on a complaint she had made. "I was just sounding off," she said. "I didn't want you to *do* anything." But the more he thought about it, the more convinced he was that he had no choice but to act when a subordinate told him about a problem. After all, he said, that is his job; he could be faulted for negligence if he didn't take action to solve a problem reported to him.

Applied linguist Lena Gavruseva analyzed a conversation in which this double meaning of complaining was key. The conversation took place between John, the editor of a small local newspaper, and Dan, a young writer who had recently been hired. In the middle of a friendly chat, John mentioned that another writer at the paper had just gotten a new computer and added, "You just have that little shitburner of an XT." He then asked, "How is your computer?" Taking his cue from John, Dan matched his boss's tone and replied, "It sucks." But John took this as a literal complaint and began a line of insistent questioning about what was wrong with the computer. The conversation went like this:

John: How is your computer?
Dan: It sucks. I mean—
John: Why?
Dan: I— 'Cause it doesn't—
John: Why, it's slow?
Dan: No, it's not that. It's just like there are all sorts of keys that don't work and stuff.
John: What do you mean keys that don't work?
Dan: Like the caps lock doesn't work.
John: It can— You want it to?
Dan: No, it doesn't.
John: You want it to?
Dan: Okay.
John: All right. What else would you like?
Dan: um, I don't know. It was just sort of—
John: No no no, come on.
Dan: Like I can't turn it off because—
John: You would like—you'd like to be able to turn it off? Why? 'Cause it bothers you?
Dan: And it's—it's frozen up on me like three times.
John: Yeah?
Dan: Yeah.
John: Like is there a pattern?
Dan: No, I mean maybe there is, I haven't noticed it. I—I don't know. It hasn't done it for about a week or so, so don't worry. I'm just griping. I'm just griping. I've never—I've got no particular complaints because it—all I need to—I'm not—I'm not one of these, I'm not a computer junkie, so I don't really care.
John: So if you want your caps-lock key to work, there's no problem. I can come in and do that.

Dan: No, I don't really need a caps lock.
John: It'll take me twenty-five seconds.

Dan had interpreted John's profanity (his reference to Dan's "shit-burner of an XT") as an invitation to engage in friendly complaining, a ritual of camaraderie. But John took it literally as a complaint, and perhaps even a criticism of him as boss for providing inadequate equipment. It is also possible that John's response was an automatic impulse to put Dan back in his place, because his use of profanity ("It sucks") in describing his computer's failings might have struck John as impudent. In the companies where I observed, the general pattern was that the higher a man's rank, the more likely he would curse.

HUMOR TO THE RESCUE

Gavruseva, who interviewed both speakers, shows that Dan was getting increasingly uncomfortable with the line of questioning, but something snapped when John said he could fix the caps lock on Dan's computer in twenty-five seconds. At that point in the conversation, which had been proceeding very quickly, with many of the turns coming fast on the heels (or stepping on the toes) of the one before, there was a two-and-a-half second pause—a very long silence in a fast-paced conversation. Then Dan said:

Dan: I'd like to s— Okay, I challenge you to do it. I think it's broken.

Dan then repeated the challenge, making it more formal and therefore less serious:

Dan: I challenge you, John Ryan.

Dan was using the cover of humor to talk back to his boss, redressing the power imbalance that had been taking shape.

John joined in on the joke, responding in the exaggerated, mock-tough voice of a radio-play gangster:

John: Yes, the John Ryan challenge? [2-second pause] You are a fool if you think you can challenge *me*, Mr. Computer!

John agreed to make fun of his own self-assurance with regard to fixing the computer. Humor was used to smooth over the mounting tension and restore the balance of power that had been threatened when Dan had begun to feel that he was being "shown up" and put "on the spot" (as he expressed it to Gavruseva).

Joining in Small Talk

What happened next is interesting. After another two-and-a-half-second pause, Dan turned the conversation to another topic. Knowing that John had recently been sick, Dan inquired about his health:

Dan: How are you feeling today, John?
John: What's that?
Dan: How are you feeling? Are you still—
John: um, Actually my guts started grinding, and I thought, "Hey, it's back," but I had like a heavy night last night. I mean I went to bed at six and only came out to like piss and drink water, and eat a can of tuna fish. I mean it was bad. I get a gastrointestinal thing at both ends. It was—it was spewing. It was violent.
Dan: [laughing] Not simultaneously. Please tell me no.
John: No no no, but it was intense. And it made me so glad that there was no girlfriend around, nobody could take care of me. There's only one fucking thing I hate, it's being sick and somebody wants to take care of me.

Asking John how he felt served not only to change the topic but to focus on an area in which John was not heroic and full of mastery but rather vulnerable. By giving so many details about his intestinal ailments, John agreed to the realignment. When he added how glad he was that there was no girlfriend around trying to take care of him, and did so using language few men would use in front of women, he realigned himself with Dan, setting them apart from hypothetical women. Although editor and newly hired young writer were not the same rank, they were both men and could bond on that basis.

This example shows how small talk can be used to restore a balance of power, but it also strikes me as a conversation that would be unlikely to take place between two women. That does not mean, however, that women's small talk might not also serve the purpose of restoring balance. The following example shows how a very different kind of small talk was used by women to mask (and reinforce) power differences and to include an intruder in a conversation.

The conversation took place in the office where Janice Hornyak was working as a temp while recording talk as part of her research. The three women in the office were taking a break from work, listening to one of them telling a personal story, when a fourth woman, June, arrived with the day's mail. A clerical worker in her early twenties, June did not have high status in this organization. Tina, who had been telling the story, stopped midstream, but found another way to make June feel welcome. Calling out in high-pitched voices, drawn-out vowels, and singsong intonation, she and Heather complimented June on her clothes:

June:	Hii.
Tina:	Hey! Ah, we gotta see this getup. Come on in.
Heather:	C'mere, June!
Tina:	She—she—she's—uh, that's cute.
Heather:	Love that beautiful blouse!
Janice:	Hey, high fashion today.
Tina:	Cool.

June: Hi. I had the blouse /?/ and didn't know what
             to wear it with. And I just took the tag off
             and /?/ said /?/ I'm gonna wear it with a vest.
Tina: And that hair too.
Janice: Oh, that's neat.
Heather: Is that your Mom's?
[Tina laughs.]
June: No I got this from uh /?/
Tina: What is it?
June: /It's from/ Stylo.
Tina: I've heard of it.
June: The one in Trader Plaza that has all that wild
             stuff.
Heather: What'd you do to your hair?
June: Added /?/. Judith said, "You just are bored,
             you have to do something."
[All laugh.]

Just as John extended a friendly hand to Dan by including him in
"boy talk" replete with graphic details about being sick and grumbling about how irritating women's ministrations can be to a man
in that state, Heather, Tina, and Janice extended a friendly hand to
June by including her in "girl talk" about clothing and hairstyle.
These two different types of small talk are fairly similar in overall
function—establishing rapport—yet are quite different in tone.
They are also fairly typical of other instances of small talk among
men as compared to women in the range of companies where I
observed.

These small-talk episodes are an essential element in keeping
the interactional wheels turning at work. But speakers' relative
rank never stops influencing how they all talk, even when it is not
in focus. Tina was the head of the office and, in fact, the owner's
daughter. So it is not coincidental that she was the one who initiated the talk about June's clothes, and she and Heather, the next in
rank, who used the most exaggerated, singsong intonation in ad-
miring them. It seems unlikely that June herself, when walking into
the office to deliver mail, would have called out to Tina or Heather

229

and initiated an extended interchange about their clothes and hair, and it does not seem surprising that throughout the interchange, both June (the mail clerk) and Janice (the office temp) spoke in relatively low-key tones.

IT LOOKS DIFFERENT FROM UP (OR DOWN) HERE

Let's return to the conversation about the computer with a broken caps-lock key. Lena Gavruseva's analysis allows us to see how Dan and John's different positions in the hierarchy altered their perceptions of the conversation. Gavruseva asked Dan why he continued to complain about his computer if he didn't really care whether or not it was fixed. He said he had to play along so as not to "rebuff" his boss. This miscommunication led to another. John interpreted Dan's way of talking as evidence of his personality rather than his reaction to John. He felt that Dan really wanted the computer fixed but was too wishy-washy to make a demand in a more assertive way.

Like many people in the superior position, John was unaware of the impact of his own status and power on a subordinate. This can be equally true for those with relatively authoritarian styles and those who foster an atmosphere of equality. There is little that people in power can do to assure subordinates to ignore their power, since their gatekeeping role cannot be revoked. A person in a superior position who extends the olive branch of equality is in a position to yank it back.

I saw this happen some years ago, following a lecture I had delivered. I was taken to dinner by several managers at the nonprofit organization that had invited me to speak, together with the organization's president, who was hosting the dinner. When we were seated at the restaurant, the president made a grand gesture and invited everyone to order drinks before dinner, saying, "Let's live it up; I'll take care of it." But when one of the managers began perusing the wine list to order wine with dinner, the president rebuked him: "Hey, c'mon, don't try to take advantage—the budget isn't that big!" The manager was left feeling foolish and out of line, reminded that he did not hold the purse strings, even though he would not have thought to suggest wine had it not been for the president's suggestion that they order drinks.

Anything that is done in an organization in which some people have power over others can be affected by that hierarchy. It might make sense to express concerns to a superior who can offer help and encouragement, but any expression of insecurity can become the basis for holding you back, not giving you a particular assignment at a later date. In fact, the repercussions of a chance remark can get magnified into an ineradicable stain, as someone I will call Anthony discovered.

Anthony had been assigned to a task together with Justin, whose working style was so different from his own that it was driving him crazy. Anthony was the kind of person who liked to be prepared well in advance, but Justin was a last-minute type who never had his part ready until the night before the deadline. Not wanting to bad-mouth Justin, Anthony asked not to be assigned to work with Justin again by saying he preferred to work alone. Though he was accommodated in this, he got a reputation for being a loner, not a team player, and found himself passed over not only for team assignments but also for promotion. The gesture of connection—trying to put a positive face on his request not to work with a particular co-worker—was passed through a status filter by which he was negatively evaluated when promotion decisions were made.

Much of the power associated with higher rank resides in the gatekeeping aspect of the superior's role. In addition to helping or teaching, a boss has the right—and often the obligation—to determine the future of subordinates' careers. This intertwining of status and connection is nowhere more apparent than in teaching, which requires both helping and gatekeeping. Teachers help students learn, but at the end of the term they assign grades, and in some situations decide or help decide who can advance to the next level or remain in the school. Students may later be dependent on teachers for letters of recommendation even after they've left the program. So whenever students ask teachers questions, in addition to getting information, they are giving impressions of their ability. If a student asks for help, the teacher may comply but also conclude that the student doesn't know as much as other students who do not seem to need help.

The same double vision can blur the role of "coach" in a business environment, where a higher-ranked employee is assigned to guide a newer one. Insofar as the coach has the ear of those who make decisions about promotion, or has a voice in those decisions, the helping aspect of the coaching role is complicated by gatekeeping overtones. Having the power to pass judgment on someone's work and convey that judgment upward can become a filter through which all "helping" utterances are passed, so that suggestions for improvement can be heard as criticism. Moreover, taking the role of teacher in itself positions the coach as one-up.

"DON'T TALK WHILE I'M INTERRUPTING"

Status and connection are inextricably intertwined in some linguistic strategies that most people feel they instinctively understand, including interruption.

It's almost a truism that interrupting others is a way of dominating them. It is rare to find an article on gender and language that does not make this claim. Tellingly, however, linguists Deborah James and Sandra Clarke reviewed all the research they could find on gender and interruption and did not find a clear pattern of males interrupting females. Especially surprising was their conclusion that the studies that investigated how much interruption took place in all-female as compared to all-male conversations actually found more interruption, not less, in all-female groups. James and Clarke note that in order to understand this pattern, it is necessary to ask what the speakers are *doing* when they talk over other speakers. Does the interruption show support for the other speaker, or does it contradict or change the topic? Overlapping talk can be a way of exerting status or establishing connection. (I prefer to use the term "overlap" to avoid the interpretation—and accusation—implicit in the term "interruption.")

Some speakers consider talking along with another to be a show of enthusiastic participation in the conversation, creating connections; others assume that only one voice should be heard at a time, so for them any overlap is an interruption, an attempt to wrest the floor, a power play. The result of this difference is that enthusiastic listeners who talk along to establish rapport can be perceived by others as interrupting—and are furthermore blamed for bad intentions: trying to "dominate" the conversation.

The key to whether an overlap (something neutral) becomes an interruption (something negative) depends on whether or not there is symmetry, or balance. If one speaker repeatedly overlaps and another repeatedly gives way, the resulting communication is unbalanced, and the effect (though not necessarily the intent) is domination. But if both speakers avoid overlap, or if both speakers overlap each other and win out equally, there is symmetry and no domination, regardless of speakers' intentions. The very engagement in a symmetrical struggle for the floor can be experienced as creating rapport, in the spirit of ritual opposition analogous to sports. Further, an imbalance can result from differences in the purpose for which overlap is used. If one speaker chimes in to show support, and the other cuts in to take the floor, the floor-taking overlapper will tend to dominate by determining the topics and expressing more ideas and opinions.

To know whether an overlap is an interruption, you must consider the context (for example, cooperative overlapping is more likely to occur in casual conversation among friends than in a job interview), speakers' habitual styles (overlaps are more likely not to be interruptions among those with a style I call "high-involvement"), and the interaction of their styles (an interruption is more likely to result between speakers whose styles differ with regard to pausing and overlap). This is not to say that one cannot use interruption to dominate a conversation or a person, but only that overlap is not always intended as an interruption and an attempt to dominate.

"CAT GOT YOUR TONGUE?"

Silence has been seen as evidence of powerlessness, and doing most of the talking can seem synonymous with dominating. Researchers have counted numbers of words spoken, or timed how long people have talked, to demonstrate that men talk more than women and thereby dominate interactions. Undoubtedly, there is truth to this observation in some settings. But the association of volubility with dominance does not hold for all people, all settings, and all cultures. Silence can also be the privilege of a higher-ranking person, and even an instrument of power. Imagine, for example, an interrogation in which the interrogator does little of the talking but holds much of the power.

The potential double meaning of talking a lot or a little or even remaining silent is highlighted in Margaret Mead's analysis of "end linkage," a concept developed jointly by Mead, Gregory Bateson, and Geoffrey Gorer. Universal and biologically constructed relationships, such as parent-child, are linked to different behaviors in different cultures. One of the paradigm examples is the apportionment of spectatorship and exhibitionism—that is, the question of who performs and who watches silently. In middle-class American culture, children, who are obviously the weaker party in the constellation, are expected to exhibit while their more powerful parents are spectators. Consider, for example, American children who are encouraged (or forced) to demonstrate for guests how well they can recite the alphabet or play the piano. In contrast, in middle- and upper-class British culture, exhibition is associated with the parental role and spectatorship with children, who are expected to be seen and not heard.

Amusingly, according to Cheney and Seyfarth, the assumption that higher-ranking individuals vocalize more holds for at least some monkeys in some settings:

In Amboseli, high-ranking female vervets are usually (but by no means always) more active and aggressive participants in intergroup encounters than low-ranking females, and they also give more *wrr* calls.

For people in a work setting, it is often the case that the higher-ranking people talk more, but not always. At a meeting, the high-ranking person may dominate discussion, or may sit silently, taking it all in and keeping the others guessing about the impression they are making. In one company, I observed a man who influenced the direction a meeting took even though he spoke little. The fact that he was British may well have played a role in how little he spoke. It was sometimes hard for him to find a way into American conversations, which were faster-paced than those he was used to. Indeed, one day when I was shadowing him, he conducted a telephone conversation with a compatriot back in England on the speaker phone, so I could listen in. The slow pace and long pauses that characterized their conversation surprised me. I frequently thought that pauses I heard were pre-closings, indicating that the conversation was winding down, but it kept on going. When the call ended, I asked his impression of the interchange, and he said it had been very comfortable, just the right pace for a pleasant conversation. Hearing those nice long pauses, I could easily see why he would have a hard time getting the floor in American conversations that leave no gap for him to step into.

This example shows that the amount people talk can result from style differences rather than their individual intentions. Pacing and pausing is an element of conversation that differs greatly depending on regional, cultural, and subcultural background. When you talk to others who leave longer pauses than you expect, you become uncomfortable and start speaking to fill in the pauses, with the result that you do all the talking—and blame them for not doing their part. When you talk to others who leave shorter pauses than you expect, then they start speaking to fill what they perceive as comfortable silence, and you end up not getting a word in edgewise—and blame them for hogging the floor.

Yet another apparent sign of power is the question of who

raises the topics that get discussed. This too can result from style differences, since whoever speaks first tends to set the topic. A speaker who thinks the other has no more to say on a given topic may try to keep the conversation afloat by raising another topic. But a speaker who was intending to say more and had simply paused for breath will feel that the floor was taken away and the topic aggressively switched. This could also occur if one speaker is overlapping cooperatively, as explained in the previous section, but is perceived to be interrupting. In other words, any style difference that results in an interruption can also result in two speakers polarizing into a voluble one and a taciturn one, and in the apparent interrupter controlling choice of topics. Yet again, the impression of dominance might result from style differences.

FIGHTING TO BE FRIENDS

It is frequently observed that male speakers are more likely to be confrontational by arguing, issuing commands, and taking opposing stands for the sake of argument, whereas females are more likely to avoid confrontation by agreeing, supporting, and making suggestions rather than commands. As I discussed in Chapter Two, cultural linguist Walter Ong argues that "adversativeness"—a tendency to fight—is universal, but "conspicuous or expressed adversativeness is a larger element in the lives of males than of females." In other words, females may well fight, but males are more likely to fight often, openly, and for the fun of it.

But what does it mean to say that males fight more than females? One thing it does not mean is that females therefore are more connected to each other. Because status and connection are mutually evocative, both fighting with each other and banding together to fight others can create strong connections among males, for example by affiliation within a team. In this regard, a man recalled that when he was young, he and his friends amused themselves after school by organizing fights among themselves. When school let out, the word would go out about who was going to fight whom in whose backyard. Yet these fights were part of the boys' friendship and did not evidence mutual animosity. (Contrast this with a group of girls banding together to pick on a low-status girl, without anyone landing a physical blow.)

I think, as well, of my eighty-five-year-old uncle who still meets yearly with his buddies from World War II, even though the members of his battalion are from vastly different cultural and geographic backgrounds. It is difficult to imagine anything other than war that could have bonded men from such different backgrounds into a group whose members feel such lasting devotion. Indeed, a man who was sent to Vietnam because of an error gave this as the reason he did not try to set the record straight and go home: "I found out I belonged in Vietnam," he said. "The bonding of men at war was the strongest thing I'd felt in my life."

Folklore provides numerous stories in which fighting precipitates friendship among men. Robert Bly recounts one such story which he identifies as Joseph Campbell's account of the Sumerian epic *Gilgamesh*. In Bly's rendition, Gilgamesh, a young king, wants to befriend a wild man named Enkidu. When Enkidu is told of Gilgamesh,

> . . . his heart grew light. He yearned for a friend. "Very well!" he said. "And I shall challenge him."

Bly paraphrases the continuation: "Enkidu then travels to the city and meets Gilgamesh; the two wrestle, Enkidu wins, and the two become inseparable friends."

A modern-day equivalent of the bonding that results from ritual opposition can be found in business, where individuals may compete, argue, or even fight for their view without feeling personal enmity. Opposition as a ritualized format for inquiry is institutionalized most formally in the legal profession, and it is expected that each side will do its best to attack the other and yet retain friendly relations when the case is closed.

These examples show that aggression can be a way of establishing connection to others. Many cultures see arguing as a plea-surable sign of intimacy. Linguist Deborah Schiffrin examined con-versations among lower-middle-class men *and women* of East European Jewish background in Philadelphia and found that friendly banter was one of the fundamental ways they enjoyed and reinforced their friendship. A similar ethic obtains among Ger-mans, who like to engage in combative intellectual debate about such controversial topics as politics and religion, according to lin-guist Heidi Byrnes, who was born and raised in Germany. Byrnes points out that this has rather negative consequences in cross-cultural contact. German students try to show their friendliness to American students by provoking heated arguments about Ameri-can foreign policy. But the Americans, who consider it inappropri-ate to argue with someone they have just met, refuse to take part. The German students conclude that Americans are uninformed and uncommitted, while the Americans go away convinced that Germans are belligerent and rude.

Linguist Christina Kakava shows that modern Greek conver-sation is also characterized by friendly argument. She found, by taping dinner-table conversation, that members of a Greek family enjoyed opposing each other. In a study we conducted together, Kakava and I showed that modern Greek speakers routinely dis-agree when they actually agree, a practice that explains my own experience—and discomfort—when I lived in Greece.

I was in a suburb of Athens, talking to an older woman whom I call Ms. Stella, who had just told me about complaining to the police because a construction crew working on the house beside hers illegally continued drilling and pounding through the siesta hours, disturbing her midafternoon nap. I tried to be nice by telling her she was right, but she would not accept my agreement. She managed to maintain her independence by restating her position in different terms. Our conversation (which I taped), translated into English, went like this:

Deborah: You're right.
Stella: I *am* right. My dear girl, I don't know if I'm right

or I'm not right. But I am watching out for my
interests and my rights.

Clearly, Ms. Stella thought she was right, but she did not want the
lively conversation to dissipate in so dull a way as her accepting my
statment, "You're right," so she managed to disagree: "I don't
know if I'm right or I'm not right." Disagreeing allowed her to
amplify her position as well.

This was typical of conversations I found myself in when I
lived in Greece. I vividly recall my frustration when I uttered what
to me were fairly automatic expressions of agreement and support
and found myself on the receiving end of what seemed like hostile
refusal to accept my agreement. I frequently felt distanced and put
down when my attempts to agree were met with contentious responses. In an effort to make things right, I would try harder to be
agreeable, so that my conversations became veritable litanies of
agreement: Exactly!, Absolutely!, Without a doubt! But my Greek
interlocutors probably were puzzled, irritated, and bored by my
relentless agreement, and stepped up their contentiousness in their
efforts to liven up the interactions.

As evidence that contentious argument helps create connection among Greek friends, I offer an example taken from the study
by Kakava, who was also a participant. The other two speakers
were her friends, two brothers she calls George and Alkis. George
was showing off a belt he had received as a gift, and the three
friends argued animatedly about its color:

George: I've got burgundy shoes, but the belt's got black in
it too.
Kakava: Does it have black in it? Let me see.
George: It has a stripe in it that's kind of black.
Alkis: Dark brown.
George: It's kind of dark.
Alkis: It's tobacco-colored, dummy! It goes with
everything.

George: Tobacco-colored? What are you talking about?!
         Are you color-blind?!

Conversations in this spirit often give Americans the impression that Greeks are fighting when they are just having an animated conversation.

The discussion of fighting, silence, and interrupting is intended to show that it is impossible to determine what a way of speaking "really means" because the same way of speaking can create either status differences or connection, or both at the same time.

"Is It You or Me?"

Again and again, when I have explained two different ways of saying or doing the same thing, I am asked, "Which way is best?" or "Which way is right?" We are all in pursuit of the right way of speaking, like the holy grail. But there is no one right way, any more than there is a holy grail—at least not one we can hope to find. Most important, and most frustrating, the "true" intention or motive of any utterance cannot be determined merely by considering the linguistic strategy used.

Intentions and effects are not identical. When people have differing conversational styles, the effect of what they say may be very different from their intention. And anything that happens between two people is the result of both their actions. Sociolinguists talk about this by saying that all interaction is "a joint production." The double meaning of status and connection makes every utterance potentially ambiguous and even polysemous (meaning many things at once).

When we think we have made ourselves clear, or think we understand what someone else has said, we feel safe in the conviction that we know what words mean. When someone insists those words meant something else, we can feel like Alice trying to talk to

Humpty-Dumpty, who isn't fazed by her protest that "glory doesn't mean a nice knock-down argument" but claims with aplomb, "When I use a word it means what I want it to mean, neither more nor less." If others get to make up their own rules for what words mean, the earth starts slipping beneath our feet. One of the sources of that slippage is the ambiguity and polysemy of status and connection—the fact that the same linguistic means can reflect and create one or the other or both. Understanding this makes it easier to understand the logic behind others' apparently willful misinterpretations and makes the earth feel a little more firm beneath our feet.

EIGHT

What's Sex Got to Do with It?

Every time we open our mouths to speak, we are taking a leap of faith—faith that what we say will be understood by our listeners more or less as we mean it. Often we are lucky, and the leap lands us safely—at least, as far as we can tell. But linguist A. L. Becker, borrowing terms from the Spanish philosopher José Ortega y Gasset, points out that everything we say, every utterance contributed to a conversation, is both exuberant and deficient. Our utterances are exuberant in the sense that others always take away meanings we did not intend or suspect, because they have associations with words and expressions that we do not have. And everything we say is deficient in the sense that others necessarily miss some of the meaning that we feel we have expressed, because we have associations with words and expressions that they do not, so we assume meanings they do not understand or suspect.

Nowhere are these ambiguities as palpable as in matters of sex, including what has come to be called sexual harassment. Just mentioning the term sets off predictable and intractable emotional reactions of anger or indignation, although these emotions may be aimed at different aspects of the phenomenon—anger at what is perceived as sexual exploitation, or at what is perceived as exploitation of the new preoccupation with it. The indeterminacy of language, the inscrutability of people's "real" intentions, the liability of conversations we thought were about one thing coming back at us, refracted through someone else's mind, as if they were about something else entirely—all these, and the deepest and strongest currents of sexual relations and myths—muddy the waters in which women and men swim together at work.

SAYING ONE THING AND BEING HEARD AS SAYING ANOTHER

After the second round of Clarence Thomas's confirmation hearings, when talk of sexual harassment had become ubiquitous, my dean quipped, "That's the last time I'll kiss you hello." He was (playfully) reflecting the concern many men have felt at that time and since: that attention to sexual harassment is putting a chill on office relations, which won't be fun anymore. Why, they wonder, do so many women want to spoil the fun? But those who are concerned with the dangers of sexual harassment are not suggesting that no friendly kisses be allowed in the office (though I have heard good arguments against kisses and hugs between faculty and students). They are simply asking that people try to be sensitive to how others respond to their behavior. The same moves that are harmless in most situations, when done in a certain way, become sources of discomfort if done in a different situation or in a different way—and of course the preferences and styles of individual others are crucial.

A young American woman had a summer job as a student intern at the Latin American branch office of an American company. Although the man she worked for was nice to her and gave her a job she liked to do, she was uncomfortable working there because when he came to work in the morning, he went around the office and kissed the secretaries (all women) in greeting, including the new intern, whom he had just met. Now kissing cheeks in greeting is common in this Latin American country, but her boss was from the United States. Furthermore, those who were native to that country practiced this greeting ritual in social situations with friends and acquaintances, not at work. It seemed to the young woman that the American either sincerely believed he was acting appropriately according to local custom (misapplying a practice he had observed in other settings) or was taking advantage of his position as boss to avail himself of the pleasure of kissing a bevy of women each morning—women who could not easily tell him to desist, since he was their boss, and if they offended him by objecting, there were innumerable other women in need of jobs who would be willing to put up with a daily kiss on the cheek in order to keep their jobs.

The American college student was not dependent on the boss in this way, since her job was just a summer internship, not necessary for her livelihood. Nonetheless, she could not think of a tactful way to tell him she didn't like his kissing her, so she avoided him in the morning. But one day he approached her, and when she put her hand out to shake hands with him, he tried to pull her toward him for a kiss. She blurted out, "I don't like it when you do that." This solved the problem, more or less. He never tried to kiss her again. But relations between them remained strained for the rest of the summer, and he stopped greeting her in the morning at all. This is a relatively happy ending, as these things go. There were no reprisals, no continued advances, and no indication the boss had intended anything more than a good-morning kiss on the cheek in the first place. But to people who feel the need for friendly relations in order to enjoy work, the incident would mean a loss of comfortable happiness on the job.

Once again, we come up against the indeterminacy (or, to use the term I introduced in the previous chapter, polysemy) of language and other symbolic systems. Part of what makes sexual harassment so complex is that the same symbols can have one meaning in one context or to one person and a very different meaning in another context or to another person. The same phrase or gesture can be interpreted as a show of kindness, gratitude, or love; a move in a seduction; a demand for sexual compliance; or a sign of disrespect. The young woman who didn't like her boss kissing her contrasted this bad experience with a good one involving another boss. She liked the other boss very much; he treated her with more distance and formality, which she interpreted as respect. And when that summer ended, he sent her roses to wish her luck back at school. Sending roses to a young woman could have been a gesture of romantic interest or (because any symbol that can be sent sincerely can also be faked) a move in a seduction. But in the context of their professional relationship, this woman regarded it as a welcome gesture of friendship.

Sending flowers, like any other symbolic gesture, is a cultural ritual developed over time. As sociologist Erving Goffman has pointed out, our systems of courtship and courtesy are intertwined, both based on the same "arrangement between the sexes" that our culture has developed. So it is easy for something intended as a courtesy to be confused with courtship, and equally easy for the license provided by courtesy to be manipulated to phase into courtship. Furthermore, the rituals associated with men and women have developed differently, many of them growing out of the situations in which members of the genders most often met in the past: in romantic contexts. Because meeting as peers at work is relatively new, fitting the old rituals into the new context can be problematic. When regional, ethnic, and age differences are added to the ambiguity inherent in communication, the brew becomes truly daunting.

MEN CAN BE HARASSED TOO—BUT IT'S DIFFERENT

When the Clarence Thomas hearings took place, I was asked to appear on radio and television to talk about the role of language in sexual harassment. I had previously spent the major part of a year appearing on such shows and writing articles on the topic of women's and men's conversational styles and had rarely gotten a negative response. Nearly everyone seemed to appreciate my even-handed approach: Women's and men's styles are equally valid; each has its own logic; problems occur because of the differences in style. But when I made public statements about sexual harassment, I had to say that things were different for women and men. I received several letters of complaint from men who felt I was slighting them. "Men can be sexually harassed too," they accurately protested. Michael Crichton's novel *Disclosure* dramatizes this. But it also shows that, although the situation can occur, its fundamental elements are different from those that underlie harassment of women by men.

Maureen Dowd summarizes the premise of *Disclosure* in a book review:

> Meredith Johnson, the cool, beautiful blonde who is the new boss at Digital Communications in Seattle, summons one of her division managers, Tom Sanders, to her office for their first business meeting.
>
> She has a chilled bottle of chardonnay waiting. Her skirt is riding up her thigh. She kicks off her heels and wiggles her toes. She crosses and uncrosses her legs several times, explaining that she doesn't wear stockings because she likes "the bare feeling." She half parts her full lips and looks dreamily at him through preternaturally long lashes. She tells him that he has "a nice hard tush." She asks for a neck massage.

Dowd comments about the Crichton book, "Here is the novel Hollywood has been waiting for: Sharon Stone as Bob Packwood." But compare her description of the novel's action with a description of Bob Packwood's behavior, according to an account in *The New York Times Magazine*:

> While running for reelection in 1980, Bob Packwood was eager to meet his campaign chairwoman for Lane County, Ore. The Senator invited Gena Hutton to dinner at the motel where he was staying in Eugene for a get-acquainted meeting. Hutton, a 35-year-old divorced mother of two, had brought along pictures of her children and even her cats.
>
> Then it was time to go and Packwood offered to walk her to her car. "As I started to put the key in the car door," Hutton recalls, "he just reeled me around and grabbed me and pulled me close to him." For an instant, she thought he was offering a good-night hug. But then the Senator planted a full kiss on her lips, wriggling his tongue into her mouth.

Packwood's behavior toward Hutton was aggressive. He grabbed her, pulled her toward him, and pushed his tongue into her mouth. In contrast, the woman in the Crichton novel, although clearly abusing her power, is seductive: She doesn't begin by lunging at Tom, but by luring him to her. Rather than forcibly pulling him toward her and doing things to him, she invites him to move toward her and do things to her. ("She asks for a neck message.")

Later in Dowd's summary, Meredith is described as physically attacking Tom: "She pushes him onto the couch and pinions him there." But this physical assault comes after the seductive behavior previously described, not out of the blue as in the alleged Packwood example. And if Tom Sanders does not push Meredith Johnson off him, it is not because he is not big and strong enough to fight her off, but because he is unwilling to ruin his career by hitting his boss. Gena Hutton, in contrast, was smaller in stature and weaker in strength than Bob Packwood, as is usually the case when a woman and a man have an encounter. Hutton did not accept Packwood's invitation to enter his motel room, but if she had, and if he had wanted to, he would probably have been physically capable of throwing her down and "pinioning" her, and she would probably have been physically incapable of fighting him off.

Behaviors associated with the sexes in our culture are differently apportioned. Men's sexual behavior is expected to be aggressive, women's seductive. Imagine the scene of the Crichton novel with the genders reversed:

> Tom Sanders, the cool, beautiful blonde who is the new boss at Digital Communications in Seattle, summons one of his division managers, Meredith Johnson, to his office for their first business meeting.
>
> He has a chilled bottle of chardonnay waiting. His trousers are riding up his calves. He kicks off his shoes and wiggles his toes. He crosses and uncrosses his legs several times, explaining that he doesn't wear socks because he likes "the bare feeling." He half parts his full lips and looks dreamily at her through preternaturally long lashes. He tells her that she has "a nice hard tush." He asks for a neck massage.

It would not be surprising if Meredith Johnson, observing Tom Sanders behaving this way, would burst out laughing or determine he had come unhinged. Even the initial description, "cool, beautiful blonde," is incongruous when applied to a man, because it is only with women that physical attractiveness is the key feature, which is why the word "beautiful" has come to be associated with women—except, perhaps, to describe a young man from the perspective of someone who might be drawn to him. A description of a male boss would more likely be in terms of his size and appearance of power.

WOMAN AS WITCH

It might seem puzzling, at first, that Michael Crichton's character Meredith, a woman boss who sexually harasses a man who works for her, is portrayed as young and beautiful. Dowd suggests it is Crichton's way of finessing the irony that "while women think power is sexy in men, men often find power threatening in women." In other words, had the "carnivorous supervisor" been a large, physically overpowering older woman, the image of her making sexual advances toward Tom would have been less titillating for readers, a problem that would not have arisen if the genders were reversed.

But there is another reason, I think, for the way Meredith is portrayed. And it too comes down to cultural stereotypes and collective memory. A cultural icon deeply associated with female characters in folk tales and popular culture is the witch. In her book *Reflections on Gender and Science,* Evelyn Fox Keller quotes a character in a play published in 1659, Walter Charleton's *Ephesian Matron,* who is railing against witches in the form of woman: "You are the true *Hiena's,* that allure us with the fairness of your skins; and when folly hath brought us within your reach, you leap upon us and devour us."

It is the fear of being devoured by a woman he is attracted to, fear inspired by the very attraction he feels, that can stir such atavistic anxiety in a man. The fear results from the loss of control entailed by attraction. In other words, it is precisely the beautiful, alluring woman who is terrifying to men (especially when she is "cool," impervious to losing control as a result of sexual attraction herself), in a way that a large, physically threatening woman would not be. Although such a woman might frighten an individual man in a real-life encounter, the thought of a large, unattractive woman trying to seduce a man would not strike terror in most men's hearts but would be more likely to make them laugh; rather than tapping into deep fears, it would simply seem incongruous and therefore funny.

The woman as witch is also, I think, at the heart of another popular literary work about sexual harassment written by a man: David Mamet's play *Oleanna.* In it, a college student named Carol destroys a professor named John by falsely accusing him of sexual harassment and then rape. The action takes place in the professor's office. In the first act, Carol is insecure and self-effacing, confessing that she is unable to follow the course material and terrified of failing. "I can't understand," she wails. "I sit in class, in the back, and I smile, but I don't know what anyone's talking about. I'm just stupid." The professor is touched. He fears it is his fault, not hers, that she doesn't understand, so he tries to make amends. He reassures her: He'll tutor her privately; she will get an "A." At the end of the act, in his attempt to comfort her, he puts his arm around her shoulders. In Act II, we learn that Carol has filed a sexual-harassment suit against John, just when his tenure (the key to a professor's career) is hanging in the balance.

It is easy to imagine a real-life situation in which a professor might put his arm around a student to comfort her, and she might take offense, though hard to imagine her going so far as to file a complaint. Later in the play, however, Carol ups the ante and threatens to accuse him of rape. The action that follows leaves the realm of reality and enters the world of nightmare. In Act II, Carol is transformed. She is articulate, self-assured, and on the attack. Now it is she who is standing, lecturing, interrupting, and he who is sitting, helpless, speechless.

When I first saw this play, I found Carol's transformation from Act I to Act II baffling. I could only regard it as incompetent playwriting. But the description of witches makes it comprehensible. The play captures what it is about the issue of sexual harassment that so frightens men. Like a witch, a woman can lure a man with the fairness of her skin and a pretense of weakness, then leap upon him and destroy him. (This is the same deep fear that is embodied in the story of Samson and Delilah.) The professor in Mamet's play explains that he has always felt that authorities were out to get him: parents who told him he didn't understand and made him feel stupid, bosses, and now the tenure committee. The play shows that the ability to yell "sexual harassment" gives women students that kind of power over him, since any one of them could, in theory, fabricate a charge and destroy him.

This is why women and men seem so often to be holding on to different legs of this elephant. The aspect of sexual harassment that taps into women's fears is the specter of assault, verbal or physical, by a man from whose clutches they cannot easily escape. This aspect is likely to be dismissed by many men. Indeed, some men find it insulting because they hear the statement "the *possibility* of violence against women is ubiquitous" as an (obviously unfounded) accusation that all men are rapists. The aspect that holds power for most men is the possibility of a false charge, a possibility that many women dismiss as unlikely to happen, since bringing charges is so damaging to the accuser. For their part, many women are insulted by men's concern, which they hear as an accusation that women are manipulative liars. In fact, it is far more common for women to be physically assaulted or sexually harassed than for them to bring false charges, but these realities do not change the power each fear holds for the individuals who identify with one party or the other.

I believe that most men do not wish to use their status and position to hurt and exploit women. But many good men worry, What would I do if someone brought a false charge against me? Not realizing that those who are guilty of serious sexual harassment are doing things they would not think of doing, they ask themselves, "What kind of remark have I made, in innocence, that could be misconstrued?" Again, the relative infrequency with which women make false charges is not relevant here; it suffices that the possibility is theoretically real, and there have been enough such cases to dramatize the possibility. In other words, each group tends to dismiss the other's deep fears as unlikely to occur. Their own fears, however, thrive on the awareness of possibility.

HIS AND HER VIEWS

The production of *Oleanna* that I saw ended with the professor physically beating the student, as the audience cheered him on. Physical assault, or the possibility of it, is often an undercurrent, if not an explicit element, in sexual harassment, and assumptions about violence often distinguish women's and men's characteristic responses to the same scenario.

Washington Post columnist Bob Levey wrote about an incident in which a woman entered a taxicab around midnight one night in Washington, D.C. Once seated in the cab, with the door shut and the trip under way, she noticed that the driver's license was not displayed, as the law requires it to be. When she asked to see his license, the driver not only refused to produce it but became angry and began yelling at her, continuing to verbally berate her for the rest of the trip. When she arrived safely at her destination, the woman jumped out of the cab and later filed a complaint. At the hearing, she explained that she always feels in danger when she is out alone at night, and being closed in a taxi with a strange man yelling at her was terrifying. She did not feel free to flee the cab before she reached her destination, because that would have left her in even greater danger. Levey felt that so long as the driver had not hit her, but only yelled, his offense was minor. Curious about whether others would agree with his interpretation, he conducted an informal survey. He asked all the women and men he ran into for their opinion and found complete unanimity—by gender. All the women agreed that having a strange man hurl verbal abuse at a woman passenger late at night was frightening and constituted a serious offense for a taxi driver. All the men agreed that yelling alone was not serious.

Although this incident did not involve sexual harassment per se, Levey's findings are similar to those of studies showing that most men do not believe sexual harassment has occurred unless there has been a physical move, whereas women often include verbal moves in the category. Why this difference in perspective? I believe it has to do with a sense of threat that most women are aware of, dimly or sharply (depending on the context and their own experiences with men), hovering about them—a threat that most men do not constantly live with and therefore do not understand. The fear of rape is the extreme form of it; the fear of male violence is the nub.

The connection between sex and violence in the movies and on television has been much discussed lately. But this connection also leaks out in countless casual remarks made by men. A man who ran the purchasing division of a large supply firm took a liking to one of the women on the sales force. When she came to place her requisitions—which she had to do to get her orders filled—he often teased her by joking references to throwing her down on the floor and making mad, passionate love to her. The fact that he was raising the specter of sexual relations with her was disturbing in itself, but the references to throwing her down were what really "threw" her, even though she did not fear he would literally attack her. It is likely that the purchasing agent thought he was joking about sex, not violence, and that he did not think of himself as threatening attack. But whether he thought about it or not, the act of throwing someone down mixes passion with physical assault.

A man told me he was riding in a car with a friend when an attractive young woman crossed the street in front of them. "I want to nail her properly," his friend said. When I heard this, I was taken aback. Nail her? I thought. Is that the impulse that an attractive woman engenders? Nailing? Another man told me that a co-worker said, in describing a woman they both work with, "She's wearing her knock-me-down-and-fuck-me shoes." I was pretty sure the woman thought she was wearing her "look-at-me-and-notice-me" shoes. Maybe even her "admire-me-and-love-me" shoes. But knock me down?

The reason that women's dressing in a sexy way may provoke fantasies of violence in some men was clarified for me by an articulate college student named William King. King had been sitting in a car with a friend when a woman crossed the street in front of them. Here's the conversation as he recalled it:

Friend: Look at her strut, man. She really thinks she's something.
King: Yeah.
Friend: I'd like to take her out and show her a thing or two.
King: Right.

King's analysis is that his friend resented the sexual power that he perceived this woman had over him; in King's words, it made his friend "feel one-down. So he responds by envisioning her as his sex slave, where *he* calls all the shots."

This helps explain the association of physical assault with sex (and the reason more men than women regard wearing provocative clothes as "asking for it"), but it makes it no less troubling.

THE THREAT OF VIOLENCE

Whether or not it is associated with sex, women often perceive the specter of violence lurking when they are in the company of men, however vague and in the background it may be. In fact, Erving Goffman points out that the threat of violence is the flip side of chivalry: Both are posited on women's presumed physical weakness, relative to men's presumed strength. Many men don't understand this and are insulted by it. Simply hearing this statement makes some men feel hurt or angry. Many men would never intentionally hurt anyone and are upset and repelled by physical violence. (Anyone who thinks women have a corner on nonviolent philosophy need only think of the great pacifists Mahatma Gandhi, Bertrand Russell, and Martin Luther King, Jr.) Some men respond with indignation, "How dare you stereotype all men as violent?" But the point is not that all men are violent. It is the awareness of the *possibility* of violence, the knowledge that *some* men (no matter how few—though statistics on domestic violence indicate that the numbers are not small) are violent, that creates this aura—even for women who have never been hit. Because men are typically bigger and stronger, and because as girls we experienced the greater likelihood of physical assault from boys than from girls, the awareness of the possibility is there.

I remember, as one of the most terrifying moments of my childhood, when an older boy I did not know pinned me against the brick wall of the corner grocery store in my Brooklyn neighborhood. I no longer recall what he wanted, but I vividly recall the overpowering force of his hands pressing my wrists to the wall, his face in my face, and the ruse I used to talk my way out of it. (I told him that the sign on my house identifying my mother as an "electrologist" meant that she was a lady judge.) Of the many boys I encountered in my years of growing up in a densely populated neighborhood, this was the only one, as far as I can recall, who physically assaulted me. (Throwing snowballs and chasing were another matter.) Yet I never again walked alone to that corner; when my mother asked me to go to the store, I'd agree only if she let me go to the one around a different corner. And forever after I found the presence of boys I didn't know intimidating.

The young woman who had the summer internship in the Latin American country used the word "intimidating" to describe the impression made by the boss who kissed her on the cheek. This word recurs so often when women speak of relations with men, I began to wonder what it really meant. I came to believe it refers, even if only indirectly, to the vague sense of physical threat that many women feel around men, even if there is little or no danger of actual physical violence.

"Intimidating" is the word used by Captain Carol Barkalow, who was among the first group of women to graduate from West Point, to describe the style of a section chief under her command at an air-force post in Germany:

> One day, Sergeant Wood stomped into my office and said, "You know, Lieutenant Barkalow, if a firefight ever breaks out here, I'm going to shoot all the women."
>
> As though this were not an attempt to frighten me, I calmly asked, "Sergeant Wood, why would you do that?"
>
> "So they won't be in my way," he said.
>
> "Sergeant," I told him, "you're a bag of hot air. If you're ever caught in a firefight, the only thing on your mind will be saving your own ass."

It seems safe to assume that then–Lieutenant Barkalow knew that this sergeant would not shoot her or the other women on the base. Yet in his attempt to "test" her and "show her his power," he simply referred to the possibility of violence against women.

A woman who was the highest-placed female executive in her investment firm told of a heated disagreement with a male colleague over whether to open a new office in Chicago. As the man's anger mounted, his face turned red and came ever closer to hers as he leaned across her desk. She found herself so shaken that she had to repeat to herself reassuringly, "Stay calm—he can't hit you." (Of course he *could* have, but it was unlikely he would.) Later, she was amazed less by the fact that he had become so angry or that she had been so frightened than by the fact that the threat of physical attack had leaped so readily to her mind, since she had never experienced physical violence.

The hovering awareness of violence against women has particular relevance when a woman has risen beyond the level expected of women, reinforcing the point that physical attack, or the threat of it, is a show of anger (or fear) against a woman who is perceived as trying to get power over men. This was shockingly evident in a cartoon that appeared during the 1992 presidential campaign in *New York Newsday*. The cartoon, in its concept, was sympathetic to Hillary Clinton. Spoofing Republicans' attempts to cast her in a negative light, the cartoon portrayed her as having been mugged: A woman's body was flat out on the ground, her attaché case lying beside her, with the name "Hillary" written on it. The attaché case was particularly unsettling. Perhaps the cartoonist's intention was simply to use it to identify Mrs. Clinton, but as a familiar symbol of professional employment, the case's presence beside the prone body seemed to imply Mrs. Clinton had been attacked in retribution for having failed to know her place.

When my book *That's Not What I Meant!* was published, it received only two reviews: one in *MS.* magazine, the other in the ultraconservative newspaper owned by the Reverend Sun Yun Moon, *The Washington Times*. The headline under which *The Washington Times* review appeared was "Debbie Does Dialogue," deliberately echoing a well-known pornographic movie; I was referred to throughout as "Debbie"; and the review ended with the sentiment that my husband should have beat me:

> If she had come at him with the formidable vocabulary . . . she displays in this book his resentment might well have gone

beyond the merely verbal. Nor would the patient reader . . . have been without sympathy for such a reaction.

Significantly, the offense for which the reviewer felt physical assault was warranted was a "formidable vocabulary"—in a word, being uppity, too big for a woman's britches. Holding a Ph.D., being a university professor, and having attained status and recognition in my scientific field all counted for nothing—or, more likely, were the very characteristics that provoked the impulse to bring me down by reminding me of my sex and therefore my vulnerability. In the eyes of the reviewer and the paper's editors, being female was reason enough to be compared to a pornographic film star and envisioned as the object of wife-beating.

IT'S ABOUT POWER—AT ALL LEVELS

It is commonly said that sexual harassment is not about sex, but about power. I believe this is true, but the fact that it involves sex is not irrelevant. Rather, sex entails power in our culture. Most important, the corresponding statement is not always true—that sexual harassment necessarily involves the threat of reprisal from one in power toward one in a subordinate position. Although this is undoubtedly a frequent constellation, and perhaps the most frightening, it is not the whole story. Sexual harassment can be experienced at any level of power: It can be encountered among peers, and it is a frequent form of insubordination perpetrated by those of lower rank against those above them in a hierarchy.

Having a high position is not protection from sexual moves that make someone uncomfortable. There is the now well-known case of the state senator from New York who described publicly the many times her male colleagues made her job harder by reminding her she was female. One experience occurred when she needed to get past a man already sitting in his seat, in order to reach her own in the State Senate chamber. He refused to move, so she had to climb over him to get to her seat. Assuming she was wearing a knee-length skirt, one can imagine the compromising position this put her in. As happens with many women, I think, it apparently did not occur to her that she could challenge him by simply refusing to climb over him—sitting in someone else's seat, perhaps, and explaining, if that person arrived, that this colleague would not let her get to her seat. (It probably would not have come to that: He would likely have moved if he saw she would not climb over him.)

Even members of the United States House of Representatives are not immune: In an article about women in the House, Congresswoman Jill Long is quoted as saying that a male colleague "complimented me on my appearance and then said that he was going to chase me around the House floor. Because he was not my boss, I was not intimidated. But I was offended, and I was embarrassed."

These public officials were made uncomfortable by sexual references or behavior on the part of colleagues. Similarly, although a study done in 1993 found that 73% of female residents said they had been sexually harassed primarily by male physicians, many women physicians I interviewed said they experienced as much or more behavior they considered harassment from fellow students, interns, and residents as from their professors. One physician who was the only woman in her medical-school class recalls that the worst offenders were two psychiatric residents. She recalled one in particular:

> I went on rounds with him one day, and he actually said "/There's a/ smell of a woman." And he turned to me and he said, "It's you." He said that women are estrous, and he said, "I thought I could smell a woman." It was—and he was a—it was really foul. It was a very—it was a dirty foul play. It was a curveball. I didn't know what to say. And so I did what all women do when they don't know what to say. I didn't say anything. But I felt humiliated. I was so embarrassed, and I remember feeling immensely anxious. I could feel my heart starting to beat. It was almost as though I'd been found out.

As this physician pointed out when she told me about this and other experiences, men at her own level were able to humiliate her simply by calling attention to her female sexuality.

This seems also to explain why simply leaving pornographic materials in sight can be disturbing—and, yes, intimidating—to women. A woman working on a Ph.D. in linguistics had been asked to share a textbook with another student. Since she had a car and he did not, she offered to deliver the book to him when she was finished with it. When she arrived at his house to hand over the book, she was appalled to find herself surrounded by pornographic magazines. He blithely asked her to sit down, but there was no surface on which she could sit without first handling a magazine that had been left spread open to reveal a woman in a pornographic pose.

Another woman was hired as manager of a department composed entirely of men—some of whom left pornographic pictures of women in places where they knew she would come across them. What is the logic by which leaving pornographic pictures is a form of harassment? These materials were meant to shock and embarrass, to make the woman feel uncomfortable. But how is it different from any other form of hazing that men in subordinate positions might use to test a new boss or "give him a hard time"? It is that pornography, or any reference to sex, reminds the new manager that she is a woman, that they are thinking of her as the object of sexual desire, and, most intimidating, that sex can be used as a format for physical attack. The graduate student who found herself surrounded by pornography in a fellow student's apartment reported that, besides humiliation, what she felt was fear.

More difficult for some to understand is why materials need not be pornographic, but simply explicit, to make women uncomfortable, especially if there is a component of violence. Congresswoman Marjorie Margolies-Mezvinsky describes an experience that took place during her freshman term:

Last summer, the freshman class was invited to the Motion Picture Association of America for a screening. Because the class is so large, we were invited to come in two groups. The

259

first group saw *In the Line of Fire.* Those of us who went the next night saw Michael Crichton's *Rising Sun,* in which a videotape of a woman being raped is replayed repeatedly.

"It was an appalling choice and all of us felt the same way. We sat there with our colleagues and we were embarrassed," says [Utah Congresswoman] Karen Shepherd, who was particularly disgusted with the movie. . . . "The very next day, we all had to come on the floor and work alongside the men and pretend we don't live in a culture that portrays women in that way. It's very, very difficult," says Karen.

What made the experience so distressing is that it brought to the fore the ways that the women, newly elected to Congress, were different from their male counterparts, and more vulnerable.

FEMALE IS FAULTABLE

Because of this constellation of phenomena—that by reminding a woman she is a woman and therefore seen as sexual, one-down, and (most important) physically vulnerable—being female is in itself "faultable"—a term coined by Erving Goffman to capture the sense in which someone can be embarrassed or made to feel in the wrong because they have a particular characteristic. Although there are situations in which a man may become "faultable" because he is male—say, when the topic turns to sexual harassment or rape and he feels that everyone of his gender is being impugned—a woman can become faultable for being female in any situation at any time. (Comparably, being Jewish or African-American is faultable at any time in our society in a way that being Christian or white is not, although there are situations in which it could be.)

One way that women's sexuality is often called to attention is a subtle matter of fleeting glances. A woman told of interviewing a young man for a job as assistant; the poor fellow was rather nervous, and, among other types of evidence of this, his eyes kept flicking down to her chest. It seems unlikely that this young man did this intentionally, to make her uncomfortable. After all, he was applying for a job, and if he offended her, she would not hire him. The most probable explanation was that it was an involuntary tic, a sign of his own discomfort. Most women recognize the experience of having a man's eyes continually drift to her chest. Although it might be a sign of interest, admiration, or invitation, most women take it as a fleeting but irritating reminder, "You're a woman, and I'm thinking about your sex rather than your brains, your authority, the words you are saying to me."

Although men as well as women can be upset by unwanted sexual advances and uncertain how to deal with them, there is a way that bringing sex to the fore is especially compromising to women. Why are women the ones who are the objects of obscene phone calls? While on a national television call-in show, I received an obscene phone call in which the caller simply made reference to a sexual body part. Why would this be so much less likely to happen to a man in a public position? Why did a visitor to Congresswoman Rosa DeLauro's office sign her guest book as "Dick Hurtz, 131 Penis Drive"? (Is there a veiled threat of sexual assault in the last name, which was spelled to suggest "hurts"?) Did he do the same in the guest books of congressmen? Reminding him that he is a sexual being does not seem to be regarded as compromising to a man. Quite the contrary, many men regard their sexuality as a form of prowess, not vulnerability. So simply being reminded that he is a sexual being (as distinguished, of course, from sexual behavior that might be considered inappropriate) would be, if anything, enhancing to his image rather than compromising—and that is probably why nobody bothers to bring it up.

Evidence that women's sexuality is regarded as "tainting" is widespread. In a related, though quite different example, a newspaper reported that Graham Leonard, the bishop of London, was distressed when his church decided to ordain women. "Because any bishop's hand would be 'tainted' after placing them on the head of a woman undergoing ordination, he reasoned, the Archbishop of Canterbury could appoint 'flying bishops' to enter the dioceses of dissenting bishops [i.e., those who did not want to ordain women] and do their dirty work for them."

A sense that females can be contaminating made life difficult for the physician I quoted who had been humiliated by a psychiatric resident. Earlier in her training, as the only woman intern at a Catholic teaching hospital, she was not allowed to live in the interns' residence, where the difficult life of a doctor in training was made easier by the ministrations of a live-in housekeeper. As the physician recalled years later:

> And there was a housekeeper there that—that tidied up the rooms . . . and literally took on the mother role. She would make sure that there were snacks there for fellows who were on call, and she was very protective, and absolutely wonderful. She did their laundry, or if they needed to do things—she was marvelous, she was a house mother. Guess what? Not for me, they wouldn't let me stay there. They would not let me stay in that residency.

Even worse, she was not allowed to set foot in the interns' residence:

> The housekeeper said that she would not tolerate me there, and the sense of it was, there was a very clear sense that I would contaminate these men.

It is interesting that the housekeeper did not feel her own presence was tainting, probably because she saw herself as moving in a different realm within the same building, just as women and men in some cultures inhabit the same house but keep to different parts of it. The female resident would have entered "the men's house" in the same realm as the men.

The possibility that a female can be perceived as contaminating is a resource that can be drawn upon to make life more difficult for any woman by anyone, regardless of where they are placed in hierarchical relation to her.

"WHO'S IN CHARGE HERE?"

In the examples I have just given, the relative rank and consequently of power among the participants varies but is fairly clear-cut. Many cases, however, are ambiguous, and the introduction of sexual references or propositions can become moves in the negotiation of power.

What is the distribution of power between a writer and editor? In some ways, editors have power over authors. They decide whether or not to accept a book for publication; they assign tasks to authors and give them deadlines; they tell authors what they must do to their manuscripts to make them acceptable.

In this spirit, the most egregious experience I myself have had occurred with an editor. I was writing my very first book, and the editor insisted I meet him in his hotel room to discuss the draft of my manuscript that I had sent him. I demurred, arranging to meet him in the hotel cafeteria instead. But as we sat in the cafeteria booth discussing the manuscript, he proclaimed that it was impossible to work in the noisy environment, and we should move to his room. Intimidated by his position and unused to raising objections to what sounded like nonnegotiable demands, I followed him to his room. At first we continued discussing my draft, but when we were done, he announced that he had to change, stood up, and began removing his clothes. I sprang for the door but did not walk through it, fearful of offending him. Instead, I stood there with my back to the room and my head buried in my manuscript, keeping him in my peripheral vision so I could bolt if he made a move toward me. He did not. But I did no more work on that book so long as this editor was in place, since it would have required contact with him. I returned to the book when he vacated his position for reasons unrelated to me.

In this scenario from my own life, the editor held the power. I was young and not yet published, and I was eager not to offend the man who kept the gate I wanted to pass through. My book would not be published until he approved it. But the power relations between author and editor seem to be reversed in the following incident. An editor told of an experience in which an author insisted on dropping off his manuscript at her home. When he arrived, he began telling her about the sexual fantasies he had been having since the first time he laid eyes on her. Surprised, I asked if this had happened before, and if her female colleagues ever had similar experiences. She said that sexual advances from authors were not unusual, and that they were troubling. In her words, "It is certainly sexual harassment when an important author makes an uninvited pass at an editor. It's not that they're in a position of authority over you exactly, but they know that they're important to the press and that you will be blamed if they take their business elsewhere."

The relative "importance" of the author is crucial: Unknown authors need to be published more than the presses need to publish them. But presses need established authors with recognizable names, so if these authors leave one house, they can easily get another to publish their work. The "importance" of the authors varied in the two examples.

The doctor-patient relationship is often studied as a classic example of a situation of asymmetrical power: The doctor is in the powerful position, the patient subordinate (although the power balance is complicated in private practice where the patient is paying and can switch doctors). This is reflected in a range of patterns: Doctors typically keep patients waiting, and they wear white coats as symbols of their position while patients wear ordinary clothes or no clothes at all. Commonly, doctors are addressed by title–last name while they address patients by first name. Furthermore, those who have studied conversations between doctors and patients have found that doctors are more likely to interrupt, ask direct-information questions, do more of the talking, change the topic precipitously, and generally control the interaction. But on all these dynamics, women doctors fall somewhat further along the continuum toward what we think of as "powerless" behavior rather than "powerful." According to my own interviews, they are more likely to be addressed by first name by patients. They are also more likely to be interrupted (as sociologist Candace West has shown) and to enlist the patient's agreement before changing topics (according to a study I discussed earlier by linguist Nancy Ainsworth-Vaughn).

In keeping with the image of doctors as the ones in power, and of sexual harassment as flowing from the powerful to the powerless, many surveys have found that a small percentage (but comparatively large numbers) of male doctors, like ministers, judges, therapists, professors, and coaches, press sexual advances on women in their charge. Two particularly egregious examples were recounted in full-length books: *Doc* tells the real story of a highly respected physician in Wyoming who systematically raped many of the women who came to him for gynecological appointments. Choosing naïve and sexually innocent Mormon women, he hid behind a cloth and simply inserted his own body part in place of the gynecological instrument. (When the author of this book appeared on a radio talk show, many women listeners called in to tell about their own experiences in which doctors sexually abused them.)

Barbara Noël tells in *You Must Be Dreaming*, a book written with Kathryn Watterson, of her personal experience with Dr. Jules Masserman, a former president of the American Psychiatric Association and co-chair of Psychiatry and Neurology at Northwestern University. Dr. Masserman drugged his patients with sodium amytal, saying the drug would help them overcome resistance to the truth of their problems. One day Noël awakened while undergoing a treatment—and discovered the doctor on top of her, having sex with her. Eventually, twenty-eight other ex-patients (three were men) came forward with similar stories of having been drugged and subjected to sexual abuse from Dr. Masserman.

The constellation in these examples seems clear: Male physicians are in a position of power, so a small percentage abuse that power by taking sexual advantage of women patients. Yet a recent study published in *The New England Journal of Medicine* found that 77% of women doctors surveyed felt they had been sexually harassed by male patients. In other words, women experience sexual harassment from men over whom they theoretically have power as well as from men who have power over them.

Although the nature of the harassment is far less egregious than in the examples above, the study shows that women physicians are frequently the object of unwanted sexual attention from their patients. The survey of women family physicians in Ontario, Canada, conducted by Susan Phillips (a physician) and Margaret Schneider (a psychologist) found that 321 of the 417 doctors who responded to their questionnaire said they had been sexually harassed by patients. (Some groped them, requested unneeded genital exams, sent sex-related objects and letters, and physically assaulted them.) The doctors reported having minor incidents occur monthly, with the most extreme occurring a few times a year. The study by Phillips and Schneider did not give examples of actual conversations, but sociolinguist Nancy Ainsworth-Vaughn seems to have captured a mild such example on tape.

As part of an ongoing study of doctor-patient conversations, Ainsworth-Vaughn recorded the interactions between twenty-three patients and eight physicians in a private-practice setting, with the agreement of all concerned. One of the twenty-three patients was a man who regularly brought up sexual topics and jokes with a female physician. His ritual greeting had sexual overtones: "So whatta you been doing and who have you been doing it to?" On one occasion, something that occurred in the examination reminded him of the movie *Young Frankenstein,* and he took the opportunity to speak lines from the film: " 'Would you like to roll in the hay?' [laughs] 'Oh, great knockers.' Remember that?" This physician told Ainsworth-Vaughn that she was not troubled by this patient's jokes; she regarded them as simply an expression of his personal style. But the nurses in her office found his suggestive remarks offensive. One jokingly told the researcher, "We draw lots to see who will have to put him in [the examining room]." Indeed, most women to whom I showed the examples felt that references to "rolling in the hay" and "knockers" would make them uncomfortable in a professional situation. They felt that the patient was trying to put the doctor down, to counter the power imbalance in the doctor-patient relationship, an interpretation that is supported by the emphasis this patient placed on the need to avoid being intimidated by doctors, when Ainsworth-Vaughn interviewed him. A psychiatry resident at the University of Southern California stated explicitly that she perceives propositions from patients during physical exams to be in this spirit: "They have to put you down to make you lower than them."

Which is it? Is a proposition a sign of affection, of a desire to get closer, or is it a put-down? Is it a put-down when a woman patient propositions a male physician during a physical exam, or lets him know she is romantically interested in him? (It could be considered sexual harassment, whether or not it is deemed a put-down.) Since the same linguistic means are used to create both messages, both interpretations are possible. In fact, the two might go together: Because he likes the doctor, he wants to bring her down to his level so he can get closer to her. It is less likely for the proposition by a female patient toward a male doctor to be taken as a put-down because of the stereotypical constellation of sexual relations in our culture: A man "conquers" a woman, subdues her. This is part of our cultural heritage that lives on in people's consciousness even if it is no longer explicitly subscribed to by everyone. In any case, there is always an actual or potential element of fear present for women in the face of male sexual aggression, which is less likely to be part of men's reaction to women's sexual aggression. In the survey of Canadian women physicians, 26% reported feeling frightened by the sexual behavior of male patients.

The fact that physicians are typically alone in examining rooms with unclothed patients presents an ambiguity that must be resolved by an unspoken agreement on the part of both parties to ignore the potential for sexual relations, just as the audience at a theater must agree not to speak for the period of the performance, since any one of them could disrupt the play by speaking out. This explains why simply bringing up sexual topics can be offensive (like the "knockers" joke): It breaks this unspoken agreement.

CULTURAL SCRIPTS

Stereotypical cultural scenarios are powerful and hold us in their grip. This was discovered by a woman executive who took a client to lunch at an expensive New York restaurant. By the time they finished their main course, the client became agitated about his tight schedule. The weather was bad, and he feared he would have trouble finding a cab and therefore might be late for his next appointment. The executive hosting the lunch encouraged him to leave right away and called for the check after he left. When she handed over her credit card, the waiter said, "I should meet a woman like you." She was shocked that although nearly all the diners in the restaurant were there on expense accounts, this waiter had responded to the stereotypical script that when a woman and man dine out, they are romantically involved. Yet awareness of such scripts is only practical. One woman explained that she decided early on in her business career to arrange only lunches, not dinners, with male clients unless she knew them (and preferably their wives) extremely well. She had learned that it is easier to mistake the situation for a romantic one in the evening.

The cultural script that casts women and men as romantic partners in particular settings is there, in the background, even though most people are able to put it aside when the sexes mix in work settings. But it cannot be denied that these scripts complicate cross-sex relations at work in a way that they do not among same-sex colleagues, unless participants are lesbians or gay men. Perhaps one of the reasons so many people have such irrationally negative responses to homosexuality is precisely that—it introduces this complication in settings in which they otherwise would feel free of them. A man and a woman who close the door behind them to have a private meeting find themselves in a situation in which sex is possible—as do two women or two men if they are gay. In most work settings, parties agree not to act on or make reference to this possibility, unless they are romantically involved. When one and not the other gets the idea and acts on it, either physically or verbally, the result is sexual harassment.

If status and connection are bought with the same currency (as shown in the previous chapter), it is hard to think of a situation in which they are more inextricably intertwined than in an office affair—especially when it is between two people who are in a reporting-to relationship. Perhaps any love relationship, like any relationship at all, is in part a struggle for power, as people become more and more dependent on each other, and they must negotiate whose preferences will guide their joint actions.

Since people spend so much time working, it is not surprising that many collegial relationships turn into love relationships. Individuals who in the past might have expected to meet prospective partners through extended family and religious organizations are now far more likely to find them where they work. A 1993 study by the Japanese Ministry of Public Welfare concluded that 42.3% of Japanese marriages are between couples who meet at work. I am not aware of any statistics or studies in this regard for Americans, but everyone knows of many long-standing relationships and marriages that have emerged from workplace acquaintance, my own included. (I met my husband, who is an English professor, at an academic institute.) The shared interests and schedules that often accompany a shared profession may be excellent for happy relationships. But there are some situations in which workplace romances can cause ripples in the dynamics of status and connection.

An affair between a boss and a direct subordinate can wreak havoc in an organization. (This awareness must underlie the military ban on fraternization of any sort within a chain of command.) One liability is favoritism (a phenomenon that creates dissension in organizations no matter what its source): Employees get preferential treatment, either because the bosses wish to please their loved ones or because love has made the bosses see their beloveds as more capable than they are, or out of fear of the loved ones' anger if they do not get what they want (especially if the affair has ended and the boss is married). Just as likely, real excellence can be dismissed as favoritism, actually preventing the partner in the subordinate role from deserved advancement. The most common stereotype is the boss with his secretary, someone he has power over. But if the boss is married, having an affair can give a subordinate power over him. (An office affair also gives the subordinate this kind of power—the power to expose—if the affair is homosexual and the boss is "in the closet," trying to keep that hidden.)

Though actual affairs are common enough when people work together, the presence of women and men, for heterosexual co-workers, or of same-sex co-workers for lesbians and gay men, introduces an element of attraction that can either confuse or enhance office interactions. In her story "The Crossword Puzzle," Alice Mattison describes such a feeling by a (happily married) woman who works as a typist in a law office, toward one of the young attorneys in the office:

> Once when Jasper was finishing a brief in a hurry he asked me if I could stay late and type. I was delighted. I couldn't be quite casual about him—I always could say exactly when we'd last talked, and I remembered what we'd said. It wasn't sexual. I often felt like touching him, but only to straighten him up. I'm not looking for someone. But there's that good middle category: men you don't stay up nights thinking about but who seem more definitely placed before your eyes than most men, as if they're in bold type.

The presence of this attraction was not hurtful in this story: "We work well together," the protagonist remarks.

A very different, and more troublesome, kind of tension was described to me by a woman who observed that some men like to have what she called "decorative women" around them. Such men tend to hire women they find attractive, regardless of their abilities. According to her, the presence of women whose abilities are not up to those of the others, and who are extremely attractive, can throw an office into disarray. This phenomenon obtained in the group-practice office that a surgeon joined upon receiving her degree in hand surgery. She was the only woman in the practice, and her presence introduced a new level of disorientation for all involved. The office had consisted of a two-tiered structure: The surgeons were older men (their appearance was not at issue); the secretaries and receptionists were extremely attractive young women. The surgeons told the newest member of their practice that they believed it was not possible to find women to work for them who were both attractive and competent, so they had decided that between the two, it was more important to have women who were attractive. In other words, decorative. The problem was that the newest surgeon was a young, attractive woman—and a very capable surgeon. Neither the secretaries nor the other surgeons seemed to know how to treat her.

Another physician told me that when she placed an advertisement that said "physician seeking office assistant," one after another young woman appeared wearing low-cut blouses and minute skirts. When they discovered that the physician interviewing them was female, they became uncomfortable, and during the interviews tugged at the necks of their blouses and hems of their skirts, trying to cover themselves up. She learned to avoid this embarrassing situation by advertising "Woman physician seeks office assistant."

Among the complaints I heard from women about jobs they had held was the sense of injustice suffered when a boss paid more attention to a prettier co-worker. I myself have seen some of my fellow professors act very strangely when a woman who took part in a small working conference dressed and acted in an overtly sexual way. Of the eight men in the group, three seemed to be vying for her attention in more and more bizarre ways—to the exclusion of noticing any of the other women present. It was difficult both for the other women and for the men not involved in the resulting competition to get their ideas heard.

The value of "decorative women" in a work environment is institutionalized in some countries. For example, Japanese businessmen often hire pretty young women simply to stand around while they do business. Sociolinguist Itoko Kawakami notes that most Japanese women in the world of work are young, partly because most women leave when they marry but also because their main purpose is decorative. Women office workers are commonly called "flowers of the workplace." It is not just that women are encouraged to quit when they marry, but that they are encouraged to marry before they are too old to continue at work.

THE INDETERMINACY OF LANGUAGE

These multilayered meanings of gestures and actions are always a potential source of confusion and misunderstanding when people try to work together. The situation can be especially frustrating when it comes to language, because we expect language to be clear-cut. After all, we have dictionaries to tell us what words mean. We want language to be firm so we can feel in control of our messages: This means that, period. For conversational-style differences to confuse everything seems, at times, more than we can bear.

Those who look for hard-and-fast lists of what is acceptable and what is not will never be satisfied. Ways of talking that are upsetting, even traumatizing, for some are not offensive to others, and neither of these views is "right." A woman who was a shift manager in the shipping department of a factory, and the only woman on her shift, mentioned that there was always lots of talk about sex among the men on the shift, and she didn't mind it. She did, however, feel she had to tell the men who reported to her not to hug or put their arms around the women office and clerical staff who occasionally came through the shipping department, as she sensed that this was making some of them uncomfortable.

One woman told me that she had never had a problem with sexual harassment. But it soon became clear that this did not mean she had not been harassed. She went on to relate several experiences and how she had dealt with them. Because she had been able to handle them to her satisfaction, she didn't feel they had been a problem.

That some women do not find references to sex, or other ways of talking, offensive, does not mean that no woman has a right to respond to them that way. Nor does it mean that there is necessarily no problem. Some women report that they simply join in when men "talk dirty," but that may cause problems they did not foresee. An airline pilot told me that if a woman pilot joins a crew, the talk changes; pilots who normally exchange plenty of talk he would call "dirty" clean up their act. But if a woman pilot chooses to talk that way herself, he said, she gets "a bad reputation."

"YOU JUST DON'T UNDERSTAND"

Knowing how sharply conversational styles differ, I am always reluctant to issue advice. I cannot know all the elements in any situation, and a way of talking that will work well with one person may prove disastrous with someone else. But if pressed to suggest something to be done to solve the intractable problems I have discussed here, I would urge women and men to appreciate the deep but differing fears the phenomenon referred to as "sexual harassment" engenders in the other. Men should try to understand women's abiding fear of male violence and their reluctance to offend by stating that something makes them uncomfortable. This, I think, is what lies behind the familiar refrain that some men "just don't get it." But women, for their part, should try to understand men's fear of being falsely accused, of having a woman they felt protective toward turn on them and destroy them. This is a sense in which some women just don't get it. The hardest thing about these parallel efforts is the implied insult of both images: Men are as offended by the image of man-as-predatory-beast as women are by the image of woman-as-witch: a temptress and deceiver who entices only to destroy. We all feel that we personally are not reflected in these stereotypical images. But they have been graven in our collective cultural experience. Even though statistics indicate that men beat women far more often than women bring false charges, both fears are not without basis and are aggravated by the cultural myths and images that surround us, from fairy tales on.

When harassment occurs at work (or when office affairs break up), it is typically the woman who either puts up with the uncomfortable situation or leaves. It is difficult to know how much apparent negligence on the part of women can be traced to harassment. A woman in a graduate program, for example, hurt her career by failing to come to public lectures and departmental functions. No one knew that she was avoiding one of the faculty members who showed her unwanted attention whenever he encountered her. Indeed, the most commonly heard response to accounts of sexual harassment is, Why didn't she just quit? No doubt this is exactly what many women have done. We will never know how many excellent employees have left jobs because of harassment—resulting not only in an injustice to them, but a loss of valuable workers to the companies they leave.

If women are to be welcomed into previously male work environments, they must not be made uncomfortable by sexual references and assaults, which, surveys indicate, they frequently are. Though many incidents, maybe even most, are minor and possibly unintended, many are major and intended. And the cumulative effect of even minor offenses can wear down individuals over time and compromise their effectiveness as well as their happiness. The situation, unfortunately, will continue until people—men as well as women—feel in their hearts that pressing sexual advances on those who don't want them is an offense, and until the power of redress is vested not in members of the institution, who have so much to lose if the boat they are floating in is rocked, but in impartial panels *outside* the institution to whom victims can tell their experiences.

Only when action to remove offenders—and exonerate those falsely accused—is swift and permanent will those who are tempted to behave carelessly or maliciously find the inner strength to resist temptation, and will women cease to be sacrificed at the altar of the status quo.

Times of transition are always difficult, and recognizing that individuals have varying reactions to the same ways of talking confuses things for everyone. The awareness that many women are made uncomfortable by sexual references—and can protest them—does make things harder for some, but it makes them easier for others, who may find it easier to express their discomfort (preferably without an accusatory tone). In a parallel way, those who are told they should stop doing something they thought was harmless (or even well intentioned) should not take offense but realize such differences in sensibilities are unavoidable. There is no reason that office interaction should stop being fun. My own observations in offices across the country have convinced me they haven't. And I still kiss my dean hello—when I have not seen him for a long time, on the cheek.

NINE

Who Gets Heard?: Talking at Meetings

I have long been amazed at how often, when I call people at their offices, I am told they are "in a meeting." Do people at work spend all their time in meetings? Sometimes it seems that way, to those at work as well as to those who are trying to reach them by phone. One answer to the puzzle is that the term is used freely to refer to any focused conversation that has a specific agenda, especially but not only if it has been set up in advance: "He's in a meeting" can mean simply that he's talking to someone in his office. Yet many people spend large portions of their work time in what we think of as typical meetings: Three or more gather around a table at an appointed time to discuss business matters that have been set forth in a previously determined agenda. "Too much time spent in meetings" was one of the most common sources of dissatisfaction with work that I heard. Although I have talked to people who say they like meetings, especially if they are running them, frustration with meetings is pervasive.

Why should meetings be so frustrating? A large source of dissatisfaction is the conviction that your time is being taken up without obvious results; another is the feeling that you are not being heard. In that sense, meetings are a pressure-cooker microcosm of the workplace: A diverse group of people, with their own ideas, comes together to get a job done. Not everyone's ideas can be taken up, and individuals' styles, and how their styles interact with each others', are as influential as the quality of the ideas themselves. Furthermore, in addition to getting the job done, people are getting credit (or not getting it) for their contributions to the outcome.

"DIDN'T I JUST SAY THAT?"

Cynthia was a member of a committee to raise funds for a political candidate. Most of the committee members were focused on canvassing local businesses for support. When Cynthia suggested that they write directly to a list of former colleagues, friends, and supporters of the candidate, inviting them to join an honorary board (and inviting them to contribute), her suggestion was ignored. Later the same suggestion was made by another committee member, Barry. Suddenly, the group came alive, enthusiastically embracing and planning to implement "Barry's idea."

Some of the men I spoke to—and just about every woman— told me of the experience of saying something at a meeting and having it ignored, then hearing the same comment taken up when it is repeated by someone else (nearly always a man). At one company, I observed a related process as it happened.

A focus group was organized to evaluate a recently implemented flextime policy. People who had a variety of positions at several major divisions were gathered in a circle and asked about

277

the advantages and disadvantages of the new system. I sat in, as a neutral observer, and took running notes on who said what. The group concluded that the system was, on the whole, an excellent one, but they also agreed upon and submitted a list of recommendations to improve it. The meeting had gone well and was deemed a success by all, according to my own observations and everyone's comments to me. But the next day, when I typed up my notes, I was surprised. I had left the meeting with the impression that a particular member of the group, a man I will call Phil, had been responsible for most of the suggestions adopted by the group. But as I reread the blow-by-blow dialogue in order to type it, I noticed that almost all the key suggestions had been made by another group member, a woman I will call Cheryl. Where had I gotten the impression that they had come from Phil? He had picked up Cheryl's points and expanded them, speaking at greater length in support of Cheryl's ideas than she had in raising them.

It would be easy to regard Phil as having "stolen" Cheryl's ideas, and her thunder. But I do not think that would be an accurate assessment. As far as I could see, Phil had no intention of taking credit for Cheryl's ideas; when he talked them up, he did not claim them as his own. He was simply supporting suggestions that he recognized as valuable. Cheryl herself, as she told me later, left the meeting feeling satisfied that it had gone well, confident that she had contributed significantly, and appreciative that Phil had recognized and supported her contributions. In response to a question about how she responded to Phil speaking for her proposals, she volunteered, with a laugh, "It was not one of those times when a woman says something and it's ignored, then a man says it and it's picked up." Moreover, in terms of the group's charge—to come up with recommendations for improving the flextime system— Cheryl and Phil worked well as a team, helping the group fulfill its charge. The company got what it needed. From that point of view, it would not seem that Phil or Cheryl should do anything differently, that she push herself to talk at greater length about her ideas, or that he refrain from supporting ideas he deems worthwhile.

There would be a problem, though, if a pattern like this occurred—and I do not doubt that it often does—in a context where the individuals involved worked together over time, and the supervisor was unaware of the dynamics of their interaction, as I was unaware of them on first observation. In that case, the person who is the source of ideas that are picked up by the group but generally attributed to someone else may be ranked unfairly low. In addition to this personal unfairness, the company suffers if the contributions of its employees are not accurately perceived. When a decision has to be made about assignments in which an innovative mind is needed, it would be a loss to the company if someone who has been the unobtrusive source of innovation is passed over. In times of downsizing, such a person might even be let go, the company never knowing that the person cut loose was the source of many of its most successful projects.

It's Not What You Say but How You Say It

Many people (especially women) try to avoid seeming presumptuous by prefacing their statements with a disclaimer such as, "I don't know if this will work, but . . ." or "You've probably already thought of this, but . . ." Linguist Charlotte Baker calls these self-protective openers "butterfinger buts," drawing an analogy to the way girls use the word "butterfingers" in a game of hopscotch: You don't get penalized for dropping your token by accident if you call out "butterfingers" in time. In a meeting, beginning in this way prevents others from objecting on the grounds you have mentioned. Such disclaimers are even found on e-mail—the electronic conversation medium. An example given by linguist Susan Herring to illustrate the tone of messages typical of women who took part in an on-line discussion began, "This may be a silly naïve question, but . . ."

Some speakers (again, including many women) may also speak at a lower volume, and try to be succinct so as not to take up more meeting time than necessary. Barbara and Gene Eakins examined tape recordings of seven university faculty meetings and found that, with one exception, the men spoke more often and, without exception, spoke longer. The men's turns ranged from 10.66 to 17.07 seconds, the women's from 3 to 10 seconds. The longest contribution by a woman was still shorter than the shortest contribution by a man.

Herring found the same situation in electronic meetings. In the e-mail discussion she analyzed, which took place on a linguistics "distribution list," she found that five women and thirty men took part, even though women make up nearly half the members of the Linguistic Society of America and 36% of subscribers to the list. Men's messages were twice as long, on average, as women's. And their voices sounded very different. All but one of the five women used an "attenuated/personal" voice: "I am intrigued by your comment . . . Could you say a bit more?" The tone adopted by the men who dominated the discussion was assertive ("It is obvious that . . ."; "Note that . . .").

All these aspects of how one speaks at a meeting mean that when two people say "the same thing," they probably say it very differently. They may speak with or without a disclaimer, loudly or softly, in a self-deprecating or declamatory way, briefly or at length, and tentatively or with apparent certainty. They may initiate ideas or support or argue against ideas raised by others. When dissenting, they may adopt a conciliatory tone, mitigating the disagreement, or an adversarial one, emphasizing it.

Those who speak in ways that are more likely to claim attention may be either male or female; our cultural background, the part of the country we grew up in, and individual personality all affect the ways we speak. Either women or men who tend to be ignored at meetings could train themselves to change their ways of speaking if they wish to. But they may not wish to, since how we speak is inextricable from who we think we are. Not everyone is eager to undergo a personality-change operation. Also, as I showed in previous chapters, a man who learns to speak more forcefully will be perceived as more masculine—but so will a woman, and the consequences for her will be quite different.

SILENT BUT STRONG

Simply being quiet, not speaking a lot at meetings, not speaking in a declamatory way, and not taking the floor do not in themselves preclude being listened to. At a company where I sat in on meetings and also tape-recorded them, I was struck by the influence of a man I will call Gary who was, by any measure, "quiet." He did not often volunteer to speak. And yet it was clear that if he expressed an opinion, he was listened to, and when he didn't volunteer, his opinion was often explicitly sought. At one 2-hour meeting, for example, the group discussed how tasks would be apportioned among them in connection with a joint project, and drew up a chart that had boxes for each task. Gary spoke very little during the first hour and a half. In all that time, he made only three brief comments, one in response to a direct question asked of him by a colleague named Connie, and another in response to a general call for questions or comments. When the meeting seemed about to close, Peter, the director of the group, expressed his satisfaction with the results of their work, and another colleague, Ben, concurred. Only then did Gary speak up, expressing dissatisfaction:

> Peter: I—I mean I think that's a reasonable—I think we've done some— made some reasonable adjustments to it. What's everybody saying?
> Ben: I think it's more clear to everybody I think. /?/ every box here. It's certainly more clear to me.
> Peter: Yeah.
> Gary: Well I—I don't find it very clear actually. [Gary laughs; others laugh, too.]

Peter teased Gary by calling him "designated contrarian" but then invited him to explain what he had in mind. Gary explained that they needed more specific information in the chart:

Gary: I—I—I suppose pa—part of what Ted was saying earlier about how we've used ... just boxes ... that we haven't been clear in ...

Peter: Oh, I think the display could /?/

Gary: And also th— I guess the terminology that we've used in the box, it's not to *me* quite clear ... as to what we're doing there or who's doing it or ... what the output is and where does the output go to ... and ... my—my *own* thought is that we maybe have for each of the boxes just a simple backup. ...

Peter: I think that's a great idea.

Gary: Maybe number the boxes and say ... who—who's—

Peter: Backup sheet—

Gary: actually involved in doing the activity ... what's the output of it and where does the output go to.

As the above excerpt shows, Peter, the director, began expressing his agreement even before Gary finished, both explicitly ("I think that's a great idea") and implicitly, by repeating and building on Gary's words ("backup sheet").

As soon as Gary finished, everyone joined in approving his idea:

Peter: I agree. That's great.

Connie: Yeah.

Ben: I think it'll be really helpful for everybody. I'm sure ... yeah.

Connie: Particularly for the person who's presenting ... [She laughs.]

Ben: Especially yeah ... the one who's responsible for that box. [He laughs.]

Gary made only two more comments, and then for the rest of the meeting the other group members discussed how to implement his suggestions. Although he did no more talking, they had not forgotten whose ideas they were implementing. When they agreed on all the changes, Connie turned to Gary and asked, "Like that, Gary?"

He gave his approval: "Yeah, looks much better."

Not only did Gary talk relatively little, but he also spoke rather hesitantly, especially when he began. He stuttered ("I—I—I" and "pa—part"), he attributed what he was saying to someone else ("what Ted was saying earlier"), and he hedged ("I suppose," "I guess"). He also paused frequently (as shown by the unspaced dots). Yet none of this resulted in a lack of influence. Quite the contrary, his brief comments completely redirected the discussion and the outcome of the meeting.

Gary is British; this probably affected his hesitant-sounding style and perhaps his taciturnity: He told me that he often found it difficult to find the right moment to jump into an American conversation. Moreover, whereas many Americans begin with relatively negative expectations of nonnative speakers from some backgrounds (as demonstrated by the experiment discussed in Chapter Six in which students had trouble understanding a lecture if they thought the speaker was Chinese), they often have relatively positive expectations if they know someone is British. All these factors may well have played a role, in addition to Gary's abilities and accomplishments, which his colleagues respected based on their prior experience working with him.

It's Not How You Say It but Who You Are

It would be misleading, then, to attribute the tendency to ignore some people and pay attention to others solely to the individual's own behavior. Many factors influence how seriously someone is taken, some of which are in their control and some not. For one thing, position in the organization plays a significant role. Those of higher rank are more likely to speak up and to be listened to when they do. If the faculty at the meeting studied by Barbara and Gene Eakins was typical, the men were probably also higher-ranking than the women, and this may have played a role in the Eakinses' findings.

In the focus-group meeting, Phil and Cheryl were the highest-ranking people present, the only two whose jobs involved supervising others. Between them, Phil had a higher rank and worked in a technical area that was accorded prestige in the company. For all these reasons, not only was lending his support to ideas he felt were worthwhile not culpable; it was part of his responsibility. Furthermore, people often speak more freely in a group where they are highest in rank since others in the room are not in a position to judge them, and there can be fewer negative consequences if they don't come off well. Someone at a lower rank who speaks foolishly at a meeting attended by a boss may pay a price when the people review rolls around. Length of time in the organization, and how well a person is known, also play a role. I recall that I said little at faculty meetings during my first years in my department, and gradually increased my participation as my rank and length of service increased. Among other reasons, I didn't feel I had the experience to judge what to say. The assumption that newcomers will not speak up lay behind expressions of surprise when Ruth Bader Ginsburg asked questions on her very first day on the Supreme Court.

Although the ways women speak may contribute to their not being listened to, research shows that, all else being equal, women are not as likely to be listened to as men, regardless of how they speak or what they say. A telling backdrop to this research emerged in my investigation of the focus-group meeting at which Cheryl had originated most of the ideas picked up.

Intrigued by my own surprise on typing up my notes of the meeting, I sought out each of the six group members and the two men who had run the meeting. I was able to contact seven of the eight people present: the two leaders, the three women who had participated, and two of the three other men. I asked each participant in turn who they thought had been the most influential group member, most responsible for the ideas that had been adopted. I discovered a revealing pattern. The two other women named Cheryl as having most influenced the group. The two male leaders named Phil. Among the men, only Phil himself named Cheryl.

A closer look at the comments of each of these people is instructive. First of all, everyone commented that no one had "dominated" the meeting, and everyone agreed this was a good thing. One of the men who had led the group commented that the six nonleading participants fell into two groups: Three had been "fairly assertive in the way they put their opinions forward," and three had been relatively quiet. The three he considered "fairly assertive" were Phil, Cheryl, and another man; the other two women and one man had been fairly quiet. He responded to my prodding, however, by adding that if he had to point to one person who "dominated" (even though I did not use that word in my query), it would be Phil, "in terms of the opinions he put forward." The other leader also stressed that no one had dominated, but he added that Phil "kind of came out and set the pace. . . . Maybe he set the tone." Another man in the group did not name anyone, saying only that no one had dominated.

The other two women both named Cheryl as the one who had most influenced the group. One went on to say that Cheryl is "very confident," and that she admires women who are confident. (I suspect she got this impression precisely because Cheryl spoke up, as the other two women didn't. Once again, people tend to equate assertiveness with confidence.) The other woman's response exactly described the group process that I had been able to discern only after examining my notes. She readily answered my query about who had been particularly influential by saying "Cheryl," and when I asked, "Who else?" she identified Phil. She said that in the beginning he didn't talk that much, but later he did, and that Cheryl opened up a lot of the subjects that the group talked about. Phil, a very successful and well-liked manager, commented that Cheryl had been "insightful." He added, "She had good comments and people built on them."

The men did not actually attribute the ideas to Phil; what they attributed to him was influence: he "set the tone." In this, they were right. But what I am commenting on is that they attended to his influence more than Cheryl's, whereas the women I talked to attended more to Cheryl's.

It's Hard for Girls to Influence Boys

Why did the women at the meeting name Cheryl as the most influential, while the men (other than Phil himself) named Phil? The research of Stanford University psychologist Eleanor Maccoby may hold a clue. In an article originally presented when she received an award for Distinguished Scientific Contributions, Maccoby summarized a lifetime of her own research, much of it with her colleague Carol Jacklin, as well as key research by others. She begins by mentioning her own classic book, written with Jacklin and published in 1974, *The Psychology of Sex Differences,* which held that psychological research offered very little evidence for significant sex differences, and where differences were found, "the amount of variance accounted for by sex was small, relative to the amount of variation within each sex." Looking back in 1990, Maccoby points out, "Our conclusions fitted in quite well with the feminist zeitgeist of the times, when most feminists were taking a minimalist position, urging that the two sexes were basically alike and that any differences were either illusions in the eye of the beholder or reversible outcomes of social shaping."

In her 1990 summary, Maccoby explains that her earlier conclusion that there are few or no significant sex differences was based on the testing of individual performance in such areas as mathematical and verbal ability. But subsequent research (her own and others') has shown that significant sex differences do emerge when children are observed interacting with other children rather than being individually tested. In other words, boys and girls, and women and men, have quite similar individual abilities, but they tend to have somewhat different characteristic styles of interacting, and these style differences often put females at a disadvantage in interaction with males.

Maccoby cites numerous studies, including her own, to demonstrate that children, beginning at ages as young as three, prefer to play with other children of the same sex, and these preferences are particularly and increasingly strong in the preteen years. She suggests two reasons for this: First, that girls are "wary" of boys' "rough-and-tumble" play, and of boys' "orientation toward issues of competition and dominance." (Perhaps this resistance on the part of girls makes them less fun for boys to play with.) Second, and this is the point that is crucial for women's participation at meetings: "Girls find it difficult to influence boys."

Maccoby and Jacklin encountered dramatic evidence of this pattern when they observed children whose ages averaged thirty-three months—between two-and-a-half and three years old. When children played in pairs, one frequently objected to something another one did. The researchers found that when girls told boys to stop doing something, the boys just kept right on doing it, but boys did respond to the verbal protests of other boys. Girls, in contrast, responded to the verbal protests of both girls and boys.

The pattern by which boys tend to ignore girls could account for another phenomenon that Maccoby describes. In a study of children who did not previously know each other playing in pairs at ages around two and a half to three, she and Jacklin did not find girls to be more passive than boys in general. They rarely observed girls being passive when they played one-on-one with another girl; they observed more passive behavior in boy-boy pairs. But when girls and boys played together in pairs, girls often stood aside while the boys played with the toys. This apportionment of participation among boys and girls is exactly what researchers Myra and David Sadker have found over and over in their lifelong study of schools, which they describe in their book *Failing at Fairness:* In coed classrooms, girls often become bystanders and observers, while the boys are active participants.

When girls are not ignored by boys, the attention they get is often negative. The experience of a lone girl among boys is quite different from that of a lone boy among girls. Jacqueline Madhok compared twenty-three small groups of students working on a science problem. When a group was made up of three girls and a boy, the girls deferred to the boy, who ended up speaking twice as much as all the girls put together. But when a group was composed of three boys and a girl, the boys ignored and insulted the girl. In one such group, a girl protested, "You guys aren't even asking for my opinion, but then who cares." When she volunteered her opinion, they ganged up on her:

Boy 1: This is medium. There is no way [laughing].
Boy 2: No, up. No, down a little. Down, down, down a little. Down a little.
Girl: Up.
Boy 1: She says up a little. All three, three against one.

Simply put, male children pay less attention to females of their own age than to other males. And the experience of women at meetings indicates the same is often true for adult men and women. Susan Herring's study of the discussion on a linguistics network had similar results. Women who took part were either ignored or attacked, their opinions ridiculed and their intelligence questioned; they were even called names. This situation surely was aggravated by the anonymity of the public electronic network. But it explains why women often turn to all-women distribution lists, just as they sometimes turn to single-sex schools or start their own women-only businesses.

Most of us, however, log onto mixed-gender networks, attend coed schools, and work in environments that are inhabited also, and perhaps mainly, by men. This does not mean women cannot get heard; it just means that they start out with a handicap that may be more easily overcome if it is understood. Women—or anyone who feels ignored—may push themselves not to utter disclaimers: Just jump in and state an idea without worrying about how important it is or whether anyone else has thought of it before. They may practice speaking louder and at greater length, resisting the impulse to let their intonation rise at the end—an intonational pattern often used by women to show considerateness and invite response, but often interpreted as a sign of uncertainty and insecurity. (Note, however, that research has shown that rising intonation is interpreted as uncertainty and incompetence in women but not in men.)

Before women decide to change their styles, though, they must realize the double bind I have discussed in earlier chapters. To expand on an example I referred to earlier, Geraldine Ferraro was called by Barbara Bush "the word that rhymes with witch." Ferraro's speech style was influenced by her Italian heritage, her New York City upbringing, and her working-class roots. Any woman who tries to become more "assertive," like any woman who starts out with a more assertive style as a result of her cultural background, runs a risk of being sanctioned for being "too aggressive," just as men from the South may be seen as not masculine enough. How else to make sense of William Safire's taunting Clinton's nominee for secretary of defense, Bobby Ray Inman, "How can a grown man call himself 'Bobby'?"

Many women try to adjust to the expectation that women not appear too assertive (which will be deemed aggressive) by modulating how often they take the floor. Elizabeth Aries found, in studying discussion groups of college women and men, that women who spoke up at one discussion-group meeting would intentionally speak less at the next, so as not to appear dominating. Women students in my own classes tell me that they consciously make this adjustment as well: If they contribute a lot one week, they keep silent the next. Even Margaret Mead, according to her daughter, Mary Catherine Bateson, judiciously chose the issues on which she would speak up, so as not to come across as dominant. Such a strategy may be a wise one for everyone, women as well as men. On the other hand, it may also be wise to decide that being seen as aggressive is a price worth paying for being listened to. Finally, we can all hope that if enough women adjust their styles, expectations of how a feminine woman speaks may gradually change as a result.

UNEQUAL OPPORTUNITY

Whenever decisions are made by a group rather than by an individual, the negotiating strategies of the members of the group become crucial. This occurred in a meeting of a law-review board at a major American law school. Women were well represented on the board, but the articles that were published did not proportionately represent their judgment. One decision was particularly rancorous. An article submitted addressed issues of women in law school. The women members of the board felt strongly that the article was of high caliber and of great relevance to the readers of the review, but the men felt that although the article itself was an excellent one, it was not the type of article they should publish. At the board meeting at which the decision had to be made, the women argued more and more passionately for the importance of publishing the article, but the men were intransigent. Finally, one woman exclaimed not only in frustration but in disbelief, "Doesn't the fact that we feel this strongly about it mean anything to you? If there were something you felt as strongly about as we do about this, I would give it to you, even if I didn't agree." The men simply said no. They felt it was their responsibility to stick to their guns, regardless of how anyone else felt. In the end, the women backed down, and the article was not published.

When decisions are made by groups, not everyone has equal access to the decision-making process. Those who will take a position and refuse to budge, regardless of the persuasive power or intensity of feeling among others, are far more likely to get their way. This attitude may result from approaching the situation as a win-lose prospect: If your position prevails, you win; if you give ground, you lose—not only lose the argument but lose face, lose points, lose power. Those who feel strongly about a position but are inclined to back off in the face of intransigence or very strong feeling from others are much less likely to get their way. This attitude may result from a different approach to the meeting in the first place—for example, a feeling that "we are here to listen to each other's positions and make the best decision," or a different attitude toward conflict: "We must make peace by the end of the meeting and reach agreement; it would be too unpleasant to try to work together if we ended the meeting at loggerheads."

To the extent that these styles are likely to be apportioned by gender, adding women to decision-making bodies does not always result in women's points of view being equally represented. Processes similar to those of the law-review board take place daily in newspaper editorial meetings. Many newspapers have hired women writers in hopes of attracting more women readers. But the writers often end up writing articles that are indistinguishable from articles written by the men who were there before them, whereas the editors who hired them had hoped they would write stories of particular interest to women.

Nancy Woodhull, a consultant who works with newspapers to help them win more women readers, points out that decisions about what stories to pursue are made "democratically" at news meetings where editors argue for and against story ideas. Woodhull has observed that women editors have a harder time getting their story ideas accepted. Journalists necessarily consult their own intuition: Does this "feel" like something that "grabs" me or not? If it is true that women and men (like other culturally diverse readers) have different interests in some regards, then the "gut" feelings of the white men might not be a good indicator of what will appeal to women (or African-American or Asian) readers. So if decisions about what stories to cover are decided in group meetings, and some men in the group (it does not have to be all) argue intransigently for their own judgment, the newspaper is not taking full advantage of the potential value that hiring women (or other "diverse") journalists could offer. Instead, according to Woodhull, when women editors realize they are not rewarded for bringing different perspectives to the table, they begin suggesting story ideas they know male editors will like.

The difficulty of getting heard can be experienced by any individuals who are not as tenacious as others about standing their ground, do not speak as forcefully at meetings, or do not begin with a high level of credibility, as a result of rank, regional or ethnic style differences, or just personality, regardless of whether they are female or male. Whoever is more committed to compromise and achieving consensus, and less comfortable with contention, is more likely to give way. One woman who praised her boss to me in glowing terms remarked that his only failing was that he had no stomach for confrontation, so he allowed uncooperative managers to stonewall him and never fired anyone, even when he should have.

This is exactly the problem identified by Kunihiko Harada as a weakness inherent in the Japanese communication system, which is based on avoidance of direct conflict. In a society in which empathy is a highly valued characteristic, the person with the most empathy is likely to withdraw an opinion at the earliest chance, even if it is the best one. This is a great irony by which "democratic" principles, which seem to be self-evidently desirable, don't always end happily for everyone and—most important—may not always result in the best decisions being made. When people have different negotiating styles, a seemingly democratic structure may end up functioning on the revised principle of *Animal Farm:* "All animals are equal, but some are more equal than others."

THE UNFAIRNESS OF UNSTRUCTURED GROUPS

Elizabeth Sommers and Sandra Lawrence were interested in investigating the benefits of the wonderful-sounding "cooperative learning," by which students in composition classes meet in small groups to respond to each other's writing. Sommers and Lawrence studied the talk that went on among the students in the composition classes they taught, but since the two of them had different teaching styles, the results of the group process were different for their students. One teacher gave her students explicit instructions about how to structure their discussion, whereas the other teacher allowed the students to determine their own structure. I think many Americans would feel that allowing group members to determine the structure of their own groups is preferable; it seems more democratic, less authoritarian. Ironically, though, women fared better in the "teacher-directed" groups, in which females and males participated almost equally. In the student-directed groups, females made 17% fewer comments and took 25% fewer turns.

Sommers and Lawrence show how this happened. When the structure was prescribed, each student spoke in turn, while the others remained silent. Free discussion followed only if time remained after each student had taken a turn. In other words, the opportunity to speak was handed to each student. In this structure, the young women took their turns just as the young men did, showing that they had things to say and were willing to say them. In contrast, in the free-wheeling discussions of the other groups, speakers had to get the floor for themselves in order to speak. In this situation, the young women "tended to acquiesce more, to be interrupted more, and to initiate less." Whereas the young men in these groups interrupted each other as well, they were more likely to persist in the face of those interruptions until they made their points, whereas the young women usually just backed off and gave up when their attempts to speak were met with interruptions.

This study offers a window on what goes on when people talk to each other in offices, meeting rooms, and the corridors of power. Running a meeting in an unstructured way seems to give equal opportunity to all. But in practice, conversational-style differences result in unequal opportunity. Those who feel they should get others' agreement before taking the floor, back off when interrupted, and minimize the talking space they monopolize—or those whose culturally learned rhythms are simply different—end up speaking less. In Sommers and Lawrence's study, women fell into that category more often than men did. But men with similar conversational styles would find it equally difficult to be heard—as often happens when British men or women talk to Americans, when Californians talk to New Yorkers, or when New Englanders talk to Californians.

Simply counting up how much individuals speak does not tell much about group dynamics at a meeting. What each person says is just as important, if not more. Sommers and Lawrence examined the contributions of a woman, Meredith, who was the only female in a group of four students in a composition class. Not only did she make few comments, but when she did speak, she spent most of her time affirming the three men in the group. She agreed with their observations, reassured the writer, and remarked on the process of group interaction or the process of writing. Half her turns were agreements. For example, when Bob said, "You just got to ... elaborate more on it," Meredith said, "Yeah, I mean, you need to elaborate." There were also times that Bob echoed Meredith's words, to reassure the writer:

> Meredith: It wasn't *bad.*
> Bob: It wasn't ... no ...
> Meredith: It wasn't bad.
> Bob: I really liked the conclusion.

Meredith's own comments were often interrupted or drowned out. Six times she tried to make a contribution but backed off when interrupted:

> I think . . .
> . . . The change . . . should . . .
> Cause . . . cause . . .
> . . . Cause right on that account . . .
> . . . Or else you will be . . .
> Yeah, I . . .

Again, it would be easy to blame the young men in Meredith's group for interrupting or even "silencing" her. Clearly, they did that. But the process by which interruption occurs is very complex. Like everything else that happens in interaction, it is the doing of two people, not one. For an interruption to occur, one person has to start speaking and another has to stop. Sommers and Lawrence observe that the young men in their study also interrupt each other. When interrupted, they continued to try to speak until they got their ideas out. But Meredith gave up five out of the six times she was interrupted.

I do not know if her fellow students interrupted Meredith in the same way that they interrupted each other. (Studies have shown more *attempts* to interrupt women than men.) And Sommers and Lawrence point out that even when Meredith persisted, her voice was drowned out by the others', as it was the highest in pitch and the lowest in volume. Whether or not Meredith's own way of speaking played a part in her not speaking equally, it is clear that she did not have an equal opportunity to speak.

Another, quite similar example comes from a colleague who wrote to ask my advice about how to avoid just such a pattern in his own classes, also apparently resulting from his nonauthoritarian teaching style. He wrote to me after the class was over, but he wanted to avoid anything like this happening in the future. He explained that the students in his graduate class divided into two groups, to analyze a linguistic phenomenon in two languages:

> About half the class chose analyzing French and half worked on Spanish. Richard, the only man in the class, got in the French group. He almost immediately took over and would ask me to announce that the group was meeting after class, or even for time during class when he could take the French group aside. One time they went out in the hall, and when they came back, some of the women in the group were making wry jokes about "executive decisions."
>
> At the end of the term, they were doing course evaluations, so I left for ten minutes. On the way back, I was stopped in the hall for questions from two students who were working on Spanish. While I was talking to one of them, one of the women in the French group burst out of the room and walked past us looking straight ahead with a grim look on her face. The student I was talking to said, "She seems disgusted." When I went into the room, there was Richard, up at the board expounding while the women in the group sat in a little circle around him.

My colleague commented, "I think my natural inclination just to let people alone might not have been the right thing this time."

A similar irony emerged in the companies where I observed.

For example, one manager, a woman, typically ran meetings by throwing major decisions back on the group. In a highly democratic way, she asked her team, "Where should we go from here?" But in a somewhat undemocratic way, this opportunity tended to be seized by two of the eight team members, both men who habitually spoke up and hence disproportionately determined the direction the group would take.

"How Did I Get Here?"

An important point to keep in mind is that the men who end up taking over do not necessarily want or exult in that role (although they may). I had the privilege to glimpse the feelings of a young man who apparently did not enjoy the role he took. I had asked the students to keep notebooks in which they commented on their own experiences and observations communicating with others, as well as their analyses of them, and to hand them in at the end of the term. This articulate young man wrote about his reaction to finding himself caught in the pattern I have just described. He was a student in a very large undergraduate class I taught on cross-cultural communication. Since there were nearly eighty students in the class, I frequently divided them into smaller groups of four or five and asked them to discuss topics in their groups and then designate one member to synthesize the group discussion for the entire class. There were far more women in the class than men, so most small groups had only one man in them, if any. Yet just about without fail, when it came time to present small-group findings to the class, each group that included a man had chosen the man to stand up and be the spokesperson. This is what the young man wrote in his notebook:

> We worked in small groups today, and for the second time out . . . I ended up being the spokesperson for the group. And I find this bizarre. I don't "like" being the spokesperson—or so

I say. So if I'm exuding "not wanna do the synthesis," how come I seem so perfect to be elected for the task. Maybe it's by default; no one else wants to. I don't think I buy this. Oh, well, that's all fairly immaterial anyway.

It is anything but immaterial, to those of us who want to understand what goes on when women and men get together in groups. Why was this young man repeatedly chosen against his conscious will? What I find most interesting is that he himself didn't know how it happened—and wasn't especially pleased that it did. This is how he described the experience:

> I also wonder why I feel relatively calm in a small group. I feel like I'm myself, like I'm a personality. But when I tell the class about the small-group discussion, I feel like an abstraction.

I love this description of the alienation of speaking to a large, faceless crowd, not knowing how they are responding—and how different it is from speaking in the small group, in which this young man said he felt quite comfortable. And it is interesting to me that even though he ended up being the one to address the group, he did not feel comfortable doing it.

This young man's experience is useful to bear in mind, to remember that if you are not happy with the role taken by someone else in an interaction, it is not necessarily the case that the other person is happy with that role or necessarily set out to take it.

THE JOY OF FREE-FOR-ALL STYLES

Another researcher, Carole Edelsky, poses the question, "*Under what conditions* do men and women interact . . . more or less as equals and under what conditions do they not?" Sommers and Lawrence's research provides a partial answer: When the floor is handed to participants in turn, women and men are more likely to interact as equals. Another partial answer is provided by Edelsky in her own study of talk at meetings.

Edelsky taped and analyzed five complete meetings of a standing university department faculty committee composed of seven women (of which she was one) and four men. When she set out to measure how much women and men spoke at the meetings, she realized that the meetings broke into two different types of interactions. At times, interaction followed what one thinks of as meeting structure: One person spoke while others listened or responded. But there were times when the nature of interaction was quite different: They seemed like "free-for-alls" in which several people talked at once or seemed to be "on the same wavelength." In order to answer the question of who talked more, she first had to ask which type of interaction was going on. She found that men took more and longer turns and did more joking, arguing, directing, and soliciting of responses during the more structured segments of meetings. During the "free-for-all" parts of the meetings, women and men talked equally, and women joked, argued, directed, and solicited responses more than men. In these parts of the meeting, no one person held the floor while others sat silently listening. Instead, several voices were going at once as people either talked over each other or talked to their neighbors at the same time that other parallel conversations were going on.

This is a very different lack of structure than that of the self-structuring student writing groups, where one person at a time held the floor, but the group determined for itself who would get it. Although the question of why women talked more in the free-for-all parts of meetings is outside of Edelsky's focus in her study, I think it may be that those parts of the meetings are more like the interactional style to which many women have become accustomed in same-sex conversations.

At many different companies where I observed or taped, there happened to be meetings made up of women only. At all these meetings, there were more "multiple floors," more laughing, teasing, and overlapped speech than I observed in meetings where most or all of the participants were men. A university professor wrote to me about her experience at meetings in her university. She said that she found university-wide meetings difficult, but department meetings pleasurable. In fact, she wrote, "the most enjoyable conversations seem to be those characterized by a lot of interruption and overlapping; lack of interruption seemed to be characteristic of conversations I would characterize as stilted and uncomfortable." Two major distinctions seem to be how large the meeting is, and whether or not the people taking part in the meeting "are all fairly comfortable socially with one another"—which is the case for her with her immediate colleagues.

One meeting I sat in on at a regional human-services facility was typical. The meeting was composed of four women who were caseworkers for clients with disabilities, together with their female supervisor. Orange juice and doughnuts were available—a feature fairly common at meetings I observed in a range of businesses; what was different here was that participants interrupted the meeting from time to time to offer each other food. The topics jumped back and forth between personal and work-related matters. And much of the work got done by a system of indirect request and offer.

For example, one caseworker said, "Oh, I forgot I have to pick Dean up, but I told my family I'd be home by two." I heard this as troubles talk; I assumed she would call her family to let them know she would be late and then pick Dean up. So I was surprised when another caseworker immediately said, "I can do it." Several solutions were found that way. The one time a need was expressed and no one offered to fill it, the supervisor asked, "Can anyone help with that?"

In addition to these examples of the effectiveness of indirect communication at the meeting, I thought I observed one in which this group's style didn't work. A caseworker was reporting on a problem involving a client who kept forgetting to do some of the steps in a task he was being trained to do. When she asked him what the task entailed, he would say, "I have to tell the supervisor I'm here, wash my hands, and set up the supplies." But when he actually performed the task, he'd set up the supplies and not do the other two parts. Her colleagues told her about the usefulness of having the client check off the elements of the task in a book, but they never got her to agree to do it. Instead, she said, "We haven't gotten to that yet." This seemed to be an example of where the indirect style was not working. Perhaps they—or the supervisor—should have told her directly, "It's time to do it."

SHIFTING ALIGNMENTS

Individuals' participation in groups can change according to context and over time. One woman reported a transformation of her status over a year in an organization. At the beginning, she would make contributions at meetings and see them passed over. Occasionally, they were picked up and attributed to others. But by the end of the year, the tables had turned. She was taking part in a meeting at which a man made a comment that she thought very important, but it was ignored. So she repeated it, giving full credit to him. The group then listened to it and took it up, referring to it thereafter as her idea.

This suggests that it is not only the fact that an idea is picked up by a man that makes it listened to, but simply the fact that it is picked up. If a number of individuals agree to pick up and repeat each other's ideas at meetings, they may be able to increase the impact of all their contributions.

Those who speak up in one setting are not necessarily talkative in others. Although gender is only one of a range of influences on conversational style, the differing socialization patterns of boys and girls makes meetings a very different environment for most men and women. As previously mentioned, there has been a great deal of research by psychologists, anthropologists, and sociologists on how children speak and interact in their peer groups. I have summarized these differing styles as "report talk" versus "rapport talk." Meetings are often a paradigm case of "report talk," and therefore situations in which many men feel more comfortable speaking up than many women. In other words, the ways many men have learned to speak in a group—trying to take and keep center stage—better prepare them for talking at meetings.

It is crucial to bear in mind that not all boys excel at these skills. Since boys' groups are made up of high- and low-status boys, those who are able to hold center stage and those who can't, not all boys do well as children and not all men are comfortable or successful at getting heard at meetings. In her study of students working on a science problem in small groups, Jacqueline Madhok found that in the all-male groups there was a wide range of participation: Some boys talked a lot, while others talked very little. Recall too that Maccoby observed more passive behavior when boys played together in pairs than when girls did. But their socialization patterns as children gave men a better crack at learning the skills that are rewarded in this setting, and some men learned them well.

The skills girls are more likely to have learned, such as linking one's comments to those of others, waiting to be recognized rather than speaking out, making suggestions rather than demands, supporting others' remarks rather than making all one's comments sound original, are very constructive when everyone at the meeting is observing those rituals. But they may not help a speaker stand out—or even get the floor—at a meeting. And there are good reasons why speaking up and being the center of attention in a group, especially a group that includes men, is a more difficult and complicated matter for women, since so much of their socialization has taught them *not* to attract attention. All these patterns make meetings more congenial for more men than women.

One woman for whom this was true was a member of the focus group I discussed at the beginning of this chapter. When I asked the leaders after the fact to recall their impressions of the participants, one of them remarked that he was surprised that a particular woman didn't say more. "One-on-one," he said, "she's very full of ideas and assertive." What could have inhibited her in the group? For one thing, she was at a lower professional rank than some of the others—but that would be true when she spoke to the leader one-on-one as well. It is clear that the same person who is quiet in one situation can be talkative in another. In particular, their childhood experience talking in pairs or threes better prepares women for talking with one or a few others rather than in a larger group.

A PILOT STUDY

I have observed many of these dynamics at work in my own classes. One year, my graduate class in analyzing conversation had twenty students, eleven women and nine men. Of the nine men, four were foreign students: two Japanese, one Chinese, and one Syrian. With the exception of the four Asian men, all the men spoke in class at least occasionally. The biggest talker was a woman, but there were also five women who never spoke in class at all, only one of whom was Japanese. I decided to do something to examine and restructure patterns of participation.

I divided the class into small groups to discuss the issues raised in the readings and to analyze transcripts of conversation they had recorded. I had often used the small-group format in my teaching, but in the past I had simply told class members to count off, or to form groups with those around them. This time I devised in advance three ways of dividing the students into groups: one by the degree program they were in, one by gender, and one by conversational style. In attempting to group the students by conversational style, I put Asian students together, big talkers together, and quiet students together. The class split into groups six times during the semester, so they met in each grouping twice. I told students to regard the groups as examples of discourse, and to note the different ways they interacted in the different groups. Toward the end of the term, I gave them a questionnaire asking about their participation in the groups and in class.

I could plainly see from my own observation that women who never opened their mouths in class were talking away in the small groups. In fact, the Japanese woman commented on her question-

302

naire that she found it hard to contribute to the all-woman group because "I was overwhelmed by how talkative the female students were in the female-only group. So I couldn't say much." These were the same female students who never spoke in class. To add to the irony, one of the Asian men commented that the Japanese woman had been too talkative in the all-Asian group. This example is particularly important because it shows that the same person who can be "oppressed" into silence in one context can become the verbose "oppressor" in another. No one's conversational style is absolute; everyone's style changes in response to the context and the styles of the others in the group.

In answer to my questions, some of the students said they preferred the same-gender groups; others preferred the same-style groups. (No one preferred the grouping according to degree program.) And it was not only the quiet speakers who could feel "silenced." One woman said that when she was in a group with quiet students, she felt she had to hold herself back so as not to dominate.

Another striking outcome of this study was that, on the whole, the women in the class were more dissatisfied with their participation. In answer to the question "Would you have liked to speak in class more than you did?" six of the seven who said yes were women; the one man was Japanese. Most startlingly, this response did not come only from quiet women; it came from women at every level of class participation and included women who had indicated they had spoken in class never, rarely, sometimes, and often. Even the woman who had talked the most of anyone in the class said that she would have liked to talk more. Of the eleven students who said the amount they had spoken was fine, seven were men. Of the four women who checked "fine," two added qualifications indicating it wasn't completely fine: One wrote "maybe more," and one wrote, "I have an urge to participate but often feel I should have something more interesting/relevant/wonderful/intelligent to say!!" In other words, of the eleven women in the class, nine indicated that they would have liked to talk more than they did.

The experience of separating into groups, and of talking about patterns of participation, raised everyone's awareness about classroom participation. After we had talked about it, some of the quietest women in the class made a few voluntary contributions, though sometimes I had to ensure their participation by interrupting the students who were exuberantly speaking out to recognize someone sitting silently with her hand raised. I believe both of these procedures could be useful in a work setting. Discussing how people feel about their participation in meetings can raise everyone's awareness and make it easier for some individuals to speak up, for others to speak less, and for the person running the meeting to elicit participation from some who otherwise might not say what is on their minds. These different ethics of participation are opaque to others, so those who speak freely assume that those who remain silent have nothing to say, and those who are reining themselves in assume that the big talkers are selfish and hoggish. It may come as a surprise to some that quiet group members have something to say, and it may come as a surprise to others that the big talkers want to hear what they have to say.

GETTING HEARD

What can be done to ensure that people with varying conversational styles, including both women and men, are heard at meetings, and that companies take advantage of and recognize the contributions of all their employees? One strategy would be for quiet people to change their styles, becoming more aggressive about talking up their own ideas. This will work for some. But it may be unpleasant to others and may go against their notions of being a good team member—or a good person. And the results will not always be positive. The most important point is for managers to become skilled at observing group process and noticing the role that each group member takes. It is their job to notice, as in fact the leader of the focus group I discussed did, that the ideas that found their way into the report originated with one employee and were picked up by another.

Another possibility is for those who lead meetings to devote a portion of the meeting to going around the table and inviting all those present to express their thoughts in turn. There are drawbacks to this procedure, though. For one thing, those who speak first are likely to influence the ones who follow. Anyone planning to make comments that seem to go against what every preceding speaker has said may well decide upon a different course before speaking. And, again, once someone of high status has expressed an opinion, it may be less likely that others will express dissenting views. A way to correct for *that* would be to invite individuals to submit their opinions in writing either before or at the meeting, so they will not be unduly influenced by what others say before their turn comes.

The Japanese practice of *nemawashi,* described by sociolinguist Haru Yamada, may also be worth trying. According to Yamada, *nemawashi* is used to ensure that meetings exhibit consensus. Before an in-house meeting takes place, managers in neutral or intermediate positions go around, talk privately to each person who will be at the meeting, get everyone's opinions, and coordinate everyone's interests. The Japanese believe that people are much more likely to express their true feelings (*honne*) in private, informal conversations than they are in a meeting, which is public, formal, and likely to elicit more "false fronts" (*tatemae*), or socially acceptable feelings.

When you think about it, it is, after all, only realistic to measure one's words in public, where it is difficult to predict reactions: Others may disagree, their feelings can get hurt, and some people may feel they will lose face if they back down, so they will fight for their position even if they can see value in a different one. They may also be reluctant to bring up a new idea if they see the tide is turning in a different direction—never knowing what kind of reception they would get if they did express themselves. So *nemawashi* has advantages for everyone: It ensures that everyone's opinion is taken into account, and it saves face for those whose opinions do not carry the day. Since their opinions were not voiced publicly, they do not lose face.

The history of the Gulf War might have been different if our leaders had practiced *nemawashi*. Sidney Blumenthal wrote in *The New Yorker* that General Colin Powell foresaw the problems of entering into armed conflict against Saddam Hussein and favored continuing the sanctions of Desert Shield rather than launching the attack of Desert Storm. However, "after President Bush publicly declared his strategy of offense, Powell presented the alternative option, as if disinterestedly, to the President and his senior advisors." Blumenthal then quotes from Bob Woodward's book *The Commanders:*

> No one, including the President, embraced containment. If only one of them had, Powell was prepared to say that he favored it. But no one tried to pin him down. No one asked him for his over-all opinion. Not faced with the question, Powell was not sure what his answer would have been if he had to give it without support from one of the others.

One wonders if anyone else at the meeting—or at other meetings like it—was similarly skeptical but also waiting to be asked or waiting for someone else to express a similar opinion.

It may also be in the interest of companies to allow more decisions to be made independently by individuals whose judgment they trust, so that those judgments will not be subject to negotiation with others whose styles may give them an advantage, regardless of whose ideas are superior.

All these steps, and others that readers will think of on their own, begin with the realization that when people come together and talk to each other in groups, the results are influenced as much by the workings of conversational style as by the power of the ideas they bring to the table. Understanding and allowing for style differences should allow more truly powerful ideas to emerge—in meetings as well as other workplace conversations.

UNDERSTANDING CONVERSATIONAL STYLE AT WORK

If mixed-gender meetings in which one person at a time holds forth are settings more congenial to those with styles more common among men, then such meetings, like other work settings, are situations in which women are marked. The realization that women are marked in most work environments is crucial to understanding why more attention is paid to them in this chapter and this book.

Ways of talking do not in themselves have positive or negative value. Struggling to maintain the one-up position can work fine when everyone in the conversation is doing it, just as expending effort to maintain a conventionalized appearance of equality can work fine when everyone is doing it. But problems arise when peoples' styles differ. And styles characteristic of many women put the speaker in a one-down position in conversations with those who have styles characteristic of men—especially in a work setting, where everyone is continually laboring under scrutiny, their performance and competence subject to judgment. Not boasting, not making an effort to hide your errors or ignorance, engaging in rituals where you seem to take blame even when it is not deserved, all work against the speaker when others in the same context are not observing the same rituals.

We tend to see our own behavior as reactive: "I don't like John, so I'm curt with him; I like Jim, so I'll do anything for him." But we tend to see others as absolute: "John is a difficult person; Jim is a sweetheart." If we look for explanations, we tend to look for them in psychological makeup or background: "He has a chip on his shoulder," "She's difficult," "He's an unhappy person; maybe it's because his father died when he was young." We rarely think that the behavior we don't like in others may be a reaction to something we ourselves said or did. But this can be the case. It is always reasonable to try talking differently, though this is by no means simple. It will have to change something—and, who knows, the reaction you get may be different and more to your liking.

Most of all, we must all be aware that conversational styles can differ, so the impressions we get of others' abilities and intentions may be misleading. And others may be getting very different impressions of our own abilities and intentions than we think. We must be careful of psychological explanations, especially those that accuse women of being insecure and men of being arrogant. These are stereotypes that grow out of the characteristic ways women and men are expected to speak; overdoing it just a little bit, or doing it with others who do not share the style, can lead to those impressions.

Above all, it is important not to take ways of speaking too literally. They are rituals. And learning to understand the rituals will make it easier to understand the results that occur when the rituals others are following are not those you instinctively understand.

A woman observed by sociolinguist Shari Kendall at work felt that she had to talk like "one of the boys" in order to get the cooperation of her colleagues. But one aspect of this offended her sense of what it means to be a good person. She felt that the men she worked with frequently talked about others as if they were completely incompetent, and that she had to engage in this kind of talk when she talked to them. She commented, though, that this made her "feel dirty," since she did not consider it appropriate or justified to talk about others in this way. In a parallel fashion, a man who worked closely with a woman was put off by her desire to tell him about problems she was having with other people at the company, and problems others were having with each other. He felt this was "gossip," and he wanted no part of it. To both these speakers, and to all of us, ways of speaking are ways of being a good person—or a bad one.

Before we give anyone advice or training in how to talk in different ways, we must realize that people perceive their ways of talking to be who they are. Talk is one of the main ways people show the world their character and their worth. You may seek to change yourself, though this is risky, since your antennae are not attuned to the new style you are trying to use. Some people (with more eagerness, I suspect) will try to get others to change. But the most important key is understanding the parameters of conversational style, which provides the tools to become more flexible not only in your own way of speaking but, equally important, in interpreting how others mean what they say, and in evaluating others' abilities. Understanding what goes on when people talk to each other is the best way to improve communication—and get more work done—in the workplace as in all aspects of our lives.

Talking about patterns of behavior always runs the risk of seeming to generalize—something that, for many Americans, is a demon from which to flee. "You're generalizing" is heard as a serious criticism. Yet this view contrasts in an ironic and telling way with scientific discourse. The results of a scientific study must be "generalizable," or they are considered useless. If you can't "generalize" about your findings, you can't talk about them at all. In other words, generalizing, that great bugbear of conventional wisdom, is actually the goal of scientific research—to find a pattern in a seemingly unrelated mass of evidence, to move beyond the description of a single instance and see its relationship to other instances. That is why a scientific study must come to a conclusion that is generalizable; it can't just apply to the single instance that was studied. How can science be so at odds with common sense?

The apparent conflict can be resolved by distinguishing two different senses of "generalize." The "bad" sense of the term is the one people have in mind when they see someone observing a single instance of behavior and merrily assuming the observation applies to all instances, without evidence. The positive sense, the one scientists have in mind, refers to discerning a pattern in a single instance (a case study) or among a mass of instances and showing that the pattern holds for all or most of the instances you observed, as well as for others not in your original sample.

There are parallel positive or negative effects of having a generalization applied to you. It feels limiting to be expected to conform to a generalization that you don't think aptly describes you, but it is a relief to learn that something you thought was a personal, even a pathological, idiosyncrasy is also true of many others in your circumstances. It can be liberating to see that ways of talking for which you have been criticized are not your personal psychological problem but elements in a pattern associated with a recognizable style that make sense within that style.

When I write and talk about style differences, I am always gratified to hear people say, "I saw myself on every page," or "I was so relieved to see it isn't just me," or "just my boss," or "just my co-worker." But there are also those who say, "I fit your description of men in most ways, but as a matter of fact, I don't hesitate to ask for help," or "I'm a woman, but I'm the one who tries to give advice when people tell me their problems." This is neither surprising nor troubling. No social scientific study that describes its findings as "strong" or "statistically significant" ever finds that 100% of those in Group A did something, compared to 0% in Group B. Anything that absolute would not be the object of study; it would be self-evident. A strong finding might be 60% versus 40%. So of course there will be exceptions to the patterns observed. But that doesn't mean the description is useless—not even to those who do not fit the pattern.

For one thing, it is interesting to know the parameters of the behavior—for example, that conversational style is made up of habits with regard to pacing and pausing, indirectness, use of questions, apologizing, and so on. Knowing the patterns makes it possible to understand others as well as yourself and to be flexible in your style. But it is also useful to know when your own behavior is different from the expected. The woman who said it is her habit to offer solutions when other women tell her about problems said it has been enormously helpful to understand why her habitual responses tend to annoy some people. Once she realized that her pattern was not expected by most women, she was able to modify her behavior to improve relations with women at her job.

A complaint related to "generalizing" is "stereotyping." This too is a familiar demon for Americans, widely agreed to be a bad thing. But, like generalizing, the term "stereotyping" is sometimes applied to the results of research that bear any relation to stereotypes. In other words, if you do a study that finds women are more likely than men to make suggestions rather than give orders, you risk being accused of reinforcing stereotypes of women as manipulative and of men as bullies.

There is an irony here too. It is as if the only research that can be accepted is research that proves the opposite of what everyone previously believed. Whereas such research is surely delightful, it is, unlikely that most research will fall into this category. More commonly, research uncovers patterns of behavior that have contributed to a stereotype and helps us understand the behavior (for example, indirectness)—and eventually dispel the stereotype (for example, that women are manipulative). That is why I believe it is not only useful but necessary to understand the cultural patterns that influence our ways of speaking. Not talking about them doesn't make the stereotypes go away. It just gives them freer rein to affect our lives and robs us of the understanding necessary to change them.

I want to emphasize again that style differences are not a matter of right or wrong, though individuals may use their own styles for good or ill. I have received letters and queries from men saying, "I could see you were trying to be fair in your book, but don't you really believe that men's styles are better?" I have also received letters and queries from women who said, "I understand that you were trying to be neutral and fair in your book, but surely in your heart you know that women's styles are better." I have to respond to all these readers that, although I personally prefer one style to another—like everyone else, I prefer my own style, which makes the most sense to me—I do truly believe that all styles are equally valid *as styles,* and that they can all work well in some situations *with others who share that style.* But this does not mean that all styles work equally well in every situation. And that is why, in the end, the best style is one that is flexible.

That conversation is, at heart, a ritual is at the heart of this book. I have not provided a bilingual dictionary in which you can look up a phrase and find out what it means in the foreign country inhabited by the other gender. Much as I'd like to offer one—as I'd like to own one—language just doesn't work that way. Instead, I have offered a way of understanding how conversation works, including characteristic rituals that many (not all) women and men take for granted, rituals that, when they differ from those familiar to the people we are talking to, can lead to misunderstandings. I have shown that even though both styles are equally valid and logical in themselves, styles common among women often put them at a disadvantage in the workplace as it is currently run, according to styles more common among men. But quick tips cannot be given to fix the resulting misunderstandings, because interaction is too complicated for that, with all the subtleties of context, personality, and style that are necessarily at play wherever human beings work together. Yet experience has shown that given the tool of understanding, individuals are able to devise ways of addressing and often solving their problems.

Toward that end, I have made many statements about women and men, being cautious always to modify these statements with "typically," "many," "most," "often," and so forth. At the same time, it is crucial to bear in mind that the influence of gender is just one of many influences, and that patterns are just that—patterns to which individuals may adhere more or less or not at all, not templates that can be placed over every individual, as if each of us could be stuffed into a single mold. Nor would we want to be, even if we could. A description of how "most" or "many" women or men tend to speak should not be taken as a statement of how anyone *ought* to speak. Tendencies should not be mistaken for norms. If a study finds that 70% of women spoke in one way and 30% another, the 30% should not be seen as abnormal. There are many men and women who are not "typical" yet are extremely effective in what they do. My hope is that an understanding of conversational style will make the world safe for individuals with a vast range of styles, including styles that mix elements commonly associated with one gender or the other.

When I talk about ways of speaking that pattern by gender, the question I am most frequently asked is, "Are these differences biological or cultural?" The answer I give is that patterns I describe are characteristic of female and male styles in a particular time and place. There is no inherent, biological reason for them, as evidenced by the range of cultural variation, some of which I have described in this book. In other words, many of the ways of speaking I describe that typify women or men in our culture are characteristic of both men and women, or would be unexpected in anyone, in other cultures.

There are those who hear any reference to differences as implying that they result from biology, and there are those who regard any hint of a biological basis for differences as demonic. This is understandable, because so many foolish things have been said in the past—by "experts" as well as lay people—about the biological basis of sex differences, and often they are said in order to explain why women should be held back. Rosalind Rosenberg reminds us that in 1872 a prominent physician and Harvard trustee used biological differences to explain why women should not be permitted to attend college. He felt that the intellectual demands of higher education would threaten their ability to bear children. With the memory of such egregious history in mind, some women hear any reference to differences in how women and men tend to behave as synonymous with implying that women are less capable than men and therefore deserve to be subordinate.

Everyone knows that women and men, boys and girls, are not

the same; if they were, we wouldn't be able to tell them apart. But we can describe patterns of behavior without addressing the question of where they came from—a complex issue that will take a great deal of research to figure out, if it ever is figured out. In the meantime, however, it will not improve our situation to forbid discussion of differences as they are observed. To say that women and men tend to speak in different ways in this culture and in this time does not mean that they must go on speaking that way, or that biology is destiny.

Anthropologist Marjorie Harness Goodwin shows that girls *can* use boys' styles—for example, the girls in her study argued angrily with boys, and they gave orders when taking the role of mother while playing house. Sociologist Donna Eder showed that some girls in junior high school got into loud mutual-insult exchanges, whereas others didn't; those who did were able to issue caustic comebacks when insulted by boys, whereas those who didn't, couldn't. Obviously, women and men *can* talk like the other gender if they want to. Otherwise, we couldn't have movies like *Tootsie* and *Mrs. Doubtfire*.

Another anthropologist, Keith Basso, has spent his career working with the Western Apache. He tells of his shock when one day he heard what sounded to him like typical "white men" talking, but a glance around revealed only a group of Apache young men. After a moment of confusion, he realized they were *imitating* what white men sound like—and doing such a good job of it that it fooled Basso. These Apache men were perfectly able to talk like whites. But they rarely chose to, because they believed it was a shallow, insincere way to talk, and not their way. If women and men talk differently, it is not because they can't talk any other way but because they don't want to. Our ways of talking reflect the ways we assume a good person talks—and we get our sense of how we should be a good person by observing the others we talk to *with whom we identify*.

In these days of tightening budgets, "restructuring," and downsizing, few companies have time or money for nonessential projects. Some regard projects they think of as "communication" in this category. I have heard the complaint "I don't have time to think about communication. I have more important things to do, like my job." I have also heard, "I have to worry about the bottom line—making money for my firm." And: "Never mind ways of talking, it's *power* that counts."

But what is power? The ability to influence others, to be listened to, to get your way rather than having to do what others want. How you talk creates power, both by gaining influence within the role you have, ensuring that you are given the responsibility to make decisions, and earning promotions to higher levels of institutional power. But no matter how high up you go, you have to maintain your position and credibility with others, and this means talking in ways that bolster rather than undercut your influence.

I have heard people say, "We don't worry about communication here—if you get the job done, you're rewarded." But in order to get recognized for the work you do, others have to know you've done it. In extreme form, it is even possible to not do the work at all and yet get credit for it. (If you see someone working busily at a computer, you may not know whether he is drafting a monthly report or talking on a computer network that has a utility called "boss" that can be activated in an instant, replacing the electronic-mail conversation with an impressive-looking graph.)

A physicist pointed out to me that looking at communication from the point of view of differing conversational styles is reminiscent of complementarity in physics, which was fundamental to the work of Niels Bohr. You have to look at things from two points of view, he explained, to really understand it. It is in this spirit that I offer my work on gender and conversational style: not to say that one way is right and the other wrong; not to drive a wedge further between the sexes; but to help us all understand the conversations we find ourselves in—and, in the end, the lives that those conversations constitute.

NOTES

Full bibliographical information for all sources is given in the References section that follows the Notes.

PREFACE

Page
14 *"there is always an equally natural and opposite way of responding to the same environment."* For example, I have been told by people, "The reason I learned to interrupt and talk along with others is that I grew up in a large family, so if you didn't talk over someone, you never got a chance to talk at all." Yet others

have told me, "The reason I learned never to interrupt or talk when someone else is talking is that I grew up in a large family, so if everyone didn't wait their turn, no one would ever have been heard—it would have been pandemonium." The same environment—a large family—seemed obviously to lead to opposite attitudes toward interruption. In a similar spirit, I have heard people suggest that the reason New Yorkers tend to talk over each other, evidencing their great discomfort with silence in a friendly conversation, is that New York City is so crowded. My response is to point out that it is not more crowded than Tokyo, where long silences are expected and appreciated in conversation.

CHAPTER 1:
WOMEN AND MEN TALKING ON THE JOB

22 ". . . *the ritual nature of conversation* . . ." As my colleague Rom Harré pointed out to me, it would be useful to note, for readers interested in finer distinctions, that I am using the term "ritual" rather loosely to capture the automatic, nonliteral, conventionalized nature of conversational language. There are, of course, a number of different levels on which this operates. Technically, a "ritual" per se is a symbolic means of accomplishing a social act. Other ways in which talk is not meant literally include what scholars refer to as "phatic speech," which refers to relatively "empty" verbiage whose main purpose is the maintenance of social relations, or recognizing the other as a person.

28 "Incorrect Prices Turn Fidelity's Face Red." *The New York Times,* June 22, 1994, pp. D1, D8.

31 *"Marjorie and Lawrence Nadler suspected . . ."* Nadler and Nadler, p. 189.

36 *"girls criticize other girls who stand out . . ."* Marjorie Harness Goodwin spent a year and a half observing the girls and boys in her inner-city black Philadelphia neighborhood and found the girls sanctioning other girls who seemed to stand out by saying, in the dialect of their community, "She think she cute." Goodwin

found, for example, that girls criticized a girl who dressed too well and did too well in school.

36 The article about ten-year-old Heather DeLoach appeared in *People* magazine, November 29, 1993, p. 102. The letter criticizing her for not being humble was published in the same magazine, December 20, 1993, p. 8.

37 The crisis of confidence that girls undergo during adolescence was first brought to public attention by psychologist Carol Gilligan and her colleagues (see the essays in *Making Connections*, edited by Gilligan, Lyons, and Hanmer). Journalist Judy Mann discusses the evidence for and causes of this troubling phenomenon in *The Difference*, and provides an eloquent personal expansion on it with reference to her own daughter. Psychotherapist Mary Pipher tells the stories of adolescent girls she has seen in psychotherapy in *Reviving Ophelia*.

38 *". . . have noted that the pattern is not necessarily found, or is not as strong among black American teenage girls."* See, for example, The AAUW Report, *How Schools Shortchange Girls*, p. 13.

39 *"She feared it would 'look like bragging.' "* *Newsweek*, March 14, 1994, p. 79.

CHAPTER 2:
"I'M SORRY, I'M NOT APOLOGIZING"

43 *"And Americans in Burma are puzzled when Burmese ask, 'Have you eaten yet?'—and show no sign of inviting them to lunch."* My source for the Burmese greeting ritual is personal conversation with A. L. Becker.

44 *". . . Americans, who don't realize that the only reply expected is, 'Over there.' "* Mary Catherine Bateson mentions this Philippine greeting ritual in *Peripheral Visions*.

46 *" 'I'm sorry' can be an expression of understanding—and caring—about the other person's feelings rather than an apology."* Linguist Amy Sheldon uses the term "double-voice discourse" to

describe how the little girls in a day care center talked in ways that took account of both their own and others' interests and goals. She contrasts this with the "single-voice discourse" that typified the boys' talk: Each pursued his own goal, leaving it to others to pursue theirs. (Sheldon, "Preschool Girls' Discourse Competence")

46 My information about and quotation from pool champion Ewa Mataya are taken from "Pool's Reigning Hot Shot," by Marcia Froelke Coburn," *Know-How* magazine, Fall 1993, pp. 58–60. The quotation is from p. 60.

56 *". . . it could only be a ritual way of making her exit."* One colleague suggested to me that Evelyn's "Thanks" could be a sarcastic indication of her annoyance at being hauled to a meeting at which she wasn't needed, but the way she spoke did not give that impression.

56 *". . . she found herself positioned as the one-down recipient of a favor."* I am using the term "positioned" in much the same way that I have previously used the term "framed." In other words, I could have said, "She found herself framed as the one-down recipient of a favor." I am borrowing the term "positioning" from Bronwyn Davies and Rom Harré, who explain their use of it in an article entitled "Positioning: Conversation and the Production of Selves." I prefer this term here because its meaning is more self-evident than that of "framing," which takes quite a bit of discussion to make clear—discussion that is provided in *That's Not What I Meant!* (Chapter Five: "Framing and Reframing") and *You Just Don't Understand* (pp. 33–36) but that it seems superfluous to recapitulate here. Those interested in a more technical discussion of this phenomenon should consult my academic book, *Framing in Discourse.*

57 Gregory Matoesian's book about rape trials is entitled *Reproducing Rape.* The quotation comes from p. vii.

58 *"I would announce changes and see if anyone said anything. No one ever did."* "Souped-Up Scholar," *The New York Times Magazine,* May 3, 1992, pp. 38, 50–52. The quotation is from p. 51.

67 *"I never heard anyone say they resented receiving praise."*

Actually, there was one exception: One woman said she cried when, on her first job, all she got from her boss was praise. Since she couldn't believe she was doing everything right, she took the unalloyed praise as lack of caring.

72 *"You know, when you work with men, there's a lot of joking and teasing."* The talk show was *The Diane Rehm Show,* WAMU, Washington, DC, December 1, 1993.

72 *"When I am with my women friends, however, there's no hold on puns or cracks and my humor is fully appreciated."* This comment was in a letter written to me by Barbara Mathias, author of *Between Sisters.* I thank her for letting me quote it here.

72 *"The types of humor women and men prefer tend to differ."* Anthropologist Mahadev Apte summarizes research on gender and humor.

CHAPTER 3:
"WHY DON'T YOU SAY WHAT YOU MEAN?"

85 Kunihiko Harada was a member of a seminar I taught at Georgetown University in fall 1993. This example is taken from the paper he wrote for the seminar. I have reworded his translation of the Japanese to make it sound more idiomatic to American ears.

90 This excerpt comes from Ainsworth-Vaughn's article, "Topic Transitions in Physician-Patient Interviews," which will be incorporated in her forthcoming book, *Power in Practice.*

91 *". . . at least one study found the woman to be more focused on information than the man, not less."* In a similar spirit, a congressman observed that the women in Congress are more focused on the content of their jobs than the men: "To too great an extent," he said, "men view politics as a game and we get caught up in the game. Women see it as a service to the country or to the community, and they're more focused on solving the problems." This observation seems to contrast directly with my own observations about "troubles talk": that often women want to talk about

problems and become annoyed with men who want to solve them. The answer is that neither women nor men are more interested in solving problems in all situations. Perhaps it is because men are less likely to be engaged by the "troubles talk" ritual that they tend to take complaints as requests for solutions. And because women in Congress are less likely to be caught up in competitive game-playing, they are more likely to focus on solving the country's problems. (The congressman's observation is quoted in Congresswoman Margolies-Mezvinsky's book, p. 81.)

91 It was Charlotte Linde who called my attention to the role of indirectness in airplane crashes. (See her article "The Quantitative Study of Communicative Success: Politeness and Accidents in Aviation Discourse.") Her analysis of the "black box" recordings retrieved from the Air Florida crash site was the result of work she did, together with Joseph Goguen, for the Ames Research Center of the National Aeronautics and Space Administration. In their report on this research, which is published by NASA's Scientific and Technical Information Branch, Goguen and Linde describe the cause of the Air Florida crash this way:

> The National Transportation Safety Board determines that the probable cause of this accident was the flight crew's failure to use engine anti-ice during ground operation and takeoff, their decision to take off with snow/ice on the airfoil surfaces of the aircraft, and the captain's failure to reject takeoff during the early stages when his attention was called to anomalous engine instrument readings. Contributing to the accident were the prolonged ground delay between deicing and the receipt of ATC takeoff clearance during which the airplane was exposed to continual precipitation, the known inherent pitchup characteristics of the 737 aircraft when the leading edge is contaminated with even small amounts of snow or ice, and the limited experience of the flightcrew in jet transport winter operations (p. 106).

I want to stress that it was Linde who discovered and called my attention to the role of indirectness in the Air Florida crash, but the research report from which the above quotation is taken does not present excerpts from the black-box conversations. I identified the indirect statements myself in the transcript of the dialogue between captain and co-pilot as presented in the Aircraft Accident Report NTSB-AAR-82-8 published by the United States Government National Transportation Safety Board, Washington, DC 20594.

93 The symbol "#" that appears three times in the transcription of the conversation between pilot and co-pilot is explained by Linde in a footnote to her article "The Quantitative Study of Communicative Success": "# is a transcription convention of the NTSB [National Transportation Safety Board], indicating 'nonpertinent word.' Its various placements suggest that it is used to indicate the presence of obscenity or profanity." I presume that the question mark in place of a speaker indicates that it was not possible to ascertain with certainty who spoke that line.

95 "*A similar explanation was suggested by Kunihiko Harada.*" Harada made this observation in my Georgetown University seminar. Much has been written about the importance of unstated meaning in Japanese conversation by Sachiko Ide, Satoshi Ishii, Takie Sugiyama Lebra, Yoshiko Matsumoto, Shoko Okazaki, Patricia Wetzel, Haru Yamada, and many others.

96 "*whereas Americans believe . . .*" I first heard these two sayings contrasted by communications researcher Gary Weaver.

96 " '*The Japanese believe that only an insensitive uncouth person needs a direct, verbal, complete message.*' " Lebra, *Japanese Patterns of Behavior*, p. 47.

96 "Sasshi, *the anticipation of another's message through insightful guess work, is considered an indication of maturity.*" See, among others, Ishii and Yamada.

97 " '. . . Mr. Apple says, "Ouch"!' " Clancy, p. 234.

98 The long excerpt is from Clancy, p. 243.

99 The quotations are from Wetzel, p. 561.

104 My article comparing the use of indirectness by Greeks, Americans, and Greek-Americans is entitled "Ethnic Style in Male-Female Conversation."

105 "*. . . she was being attacked—indirectly.*" I have a lot to say about indirect criticism in a chapter titled "The Intimate

Critic" in *That's Not What I Meant!* as well as in my scholarly book *Talking Voices: Repetition, Dialogue, and Imagery in Conversational Discourse* (pp. 105–110).

105 *"Robin Lakoff . . . identified two benefits of not saying exactly what you mean in so many words."* Lakoff, *Language and Woman's Place*.

CHAPTER 4: MARKED

107 The material beginning this chapter about gender markers was published as an article in *The New York Times Magazine* (June 29, 1993, pp. 18–19) which the editors titled "Wears Jump Suit. Sensible Shoes. Uses Husband's Last Name." It was taken from a slightly longer essay I wrote under the title "There is No Unmarked Woman." The longer essay has not yet been published.

109 The quotation from Alfre Woodard appeared under the headline "As the Academy Hails Women, Women Talk Back," by Caryn James. *The New York Times*, March 28, 1993, p. 15H.

110 The anecdote from *Women Lawyers* appears on p. 103.

111 Robin Lakoff's *Face Value* is co-authored by Raquel Scherr.

112 *". . . the woman's multiple name stands out. It is marked."* A man who uses a hyphenated last name is also marked; people may variously assume he's a feminist, a henpecked husband, or British. But the point is that, unless he is born with a double-barreled name, he has the option of using an unmarked surname, the one he was born with. In the case of a married woman, every surname she could choose is somehow marked.

112 Mühlhäusler and Harré, p. 231.

118 *"We approach new perceptions by measuring them against our past experience."* I have written quite a few scholarly articles about "frames theory," the academic name for the theory that I am talking about here. This is a slightly different notion of "frames" than the type of "framing" I have previously referred to in this and my other nonacademic books. Anyone interested

should see my articles "What's in a Frame?" and "Interactive Frames and Knowledge Schemas in Interaction: Examples from a Medical Examination/Interview," in a book I edited entitled *Framing in Discourse*.

119 The quotation is from Maccoby, "Gender and Relationships: A Developmental Account," p. 518.

121 *"Author Mark Richard recalls . . ."* Michael Norman, "Reader by Reader and Town by Town, a New Novelist Builds a Following," *The New York Times Book Review,* February 6, 1994, pp. 3, 28–30. The quotation is from p. 29.

122 *". . . Rita Dove, compared a poem to a bouillon cube . . ."* This comes from an interview of Ms. Dove with Susan Stamberg on "Morning Edition," National Public Radio, February 21, 1994.

122 The quotation from the brigade commander about the photograph of Captain Barkalow appears on p. 230 of *In the Men's House*.

127 The quotation from *Somebody Somewhere* appears on pp. 91–92.

130 *". . . they risk making things worse, because they don't understand all the elements in the system and how they work."* This phenomenon was the topic of a conference that Bateson organized, the proceedings of which were written up by Mary Catherine Bateson in a book entitled *Our Own Metaphor: A Personal Account of a Conference on Conscious Purpose and Human Adaptation*.

130 The survey of Stanford MBAs was published in the *Stanford Graduate School of Business Alumni Magazine* in March 1993. I am grateful to Stanford professor Joanne Martin for calling this statistic to my attention.

131 *". . . if you try to adopt a style that does not come naturally to you, you leave behind your intuitions . . ."* My thanks to Shari Kendall for pointing this out.

CHAPTER 5: THE GLASS CEILING

133 These statistics are taken from "A Report on the Glass Ceiling Initiative," issued by the United States Department of Labor, which cites as their source "a 1990 survey done by the UCLA Anderson Graduate School of Management and Korn/Ferry International, an executive search firm."

140 Sharon E. Barnes, "The White Knight Methode," *Executive Female,* January/February 1991, pp. 40–42.

142 The article about a pediatrician talking to a mother is "Interactive Frames and Knowledge Schemas in Interaction: Examples from a Medical Examination/Interview," by Deborah Tannen and Cynthia Wallat.

144 Befu, 119.

148 Again, for the research on boys' and girls' patterns of socialization, see the summaries by Maltz and Borker and by Maccoby, as well as the work of sociologist Barrie Thorne.

149 The source of this information on abolitionist Abby Kelley is Dorothy Sterling, *Ahead of Her Time: Abby Kelley and the Politics of Antislavery.* Sterling has much to say about then-current opposition to women as public speakers, especially if their audiences included men.

154 "*. . . women gossip about trivia and keep their real secrets.*" "That's Bond, Jane Bond," by William Tuohy, *Los Angeles Times,* December 28, 1991, p. A3.

154 Eckert makes the observation about boys and girls keeping secrets in *Jocks and Burnouts.*

156 *"Eve tells Sara that 'it is absolutely intolerable . . .'"* Binchy, p. 176.

156 The excerpt is from Binchy, p. 179.

CHAPTER 6: "SHE'S THE BOSS"

162 Ochs's observations on how Samoan mothers talk are taken from her article "Indexing Gender." For her observations

about how American mothers talk to children, she cites the articles "Language Socialization" by Schieffelin and Ochs and "Language Acquisition and Socialization: Three Developmental Stories" by Ochs and Schieffelin.

164 *"You get out from under there right now!"* Adger's account of what African-American teachers and speech pathologists told her is included in a report she co-authored with Walt Wolfram (Wolfram and Adger, *Handbook on Language Differences and Speech and Language Pathology*).

164 Carolyn Adger presented the example of the teacher who characterized herself as a "mother bear" in her paper "Empowering Talk: African-American Teachers and Classroom Discourse." The phrase "nurturing and fierce" is hers.

165 The article about Dawn Clark Netsch appeared under the headline "Illinois Candidate Transforms Herself," *The New York Times,* March 21, 1994, p. A12.

166 The review of Margaret Thatcher's memoir, written by Russell Watson, was published under the heading "Has the 'Iron Lady' Gone Soft?" *Newsweek,* November 1, 1993, p. 41.

168 Harada gives this example and identifies the source as: "M. Chikamatsu, *Nihongo ni okeru danseigo ni kansuru ikkosatsu: Wakai danjo ni mirareru shu-joshi no shiyo no sai ni tsuite* (A study of male and female language in Japanese: Differences in the use of sentence-final particles between young males and females). Unpublished A.B. thesis, International Christian University, Tokyo."

170 *". . . actual authority has to be negotiated day to day, moment to moment."* Some researchers who discuss this phenomenon include Charlotte Linde (see her articles on police-helicopter discourse) and Carol Myers Scotton (in her article "Self-Enhancing Code-Switching as Interactional Power," she makes the distinction between "institutional power," which is provided by rank, and "interactional power," which results from ways of talking).

172 These excerpts come from Ainsworth-Vaughn's article "Topic Transitions in Physician-Patient Interviews." The material in this article will be included in her book, *Power in Practice.*

172 "... *female patients were more satisfied with interactions with women doctors than with men doctors."* Ainsworth-Vaughn attributes this finding to Linn, Cope, and Leake, "The Effect of Gender and Training of Residents on Satisfaction Ratings by Patients."

173 Goffman discusses his concept of "demeanor," along with the related concept, "deference," in his essay "The Nature of Deference and Demeanor."

174 Smith cites as the source of the epigram with which she began her essay: *Steps to the Sermon: A Plan for Sermon Preparation* by H. C. Brown, Jr., Gordon Clinard, and Jesse J. Northcutt (Nashville, TN: Broadman Press, 1963).

175 Kuhn, pp. 318, 323.

184 The quotations from Ainsworth-Vaughn that appear in this section come from a conversation we had on e-mail. The article in which she presents excerpts from this patient's conversations with this doctor is entitled " 'Is That a Rhetorical Question?': Power and Ambiguity in Medical Discourse."

186 " *'Hey, lady, you can't tell me what to do.'* " This comment by Lynn Wilson was quoted in *Newsweek,* August 24, 1992, "Now: The Brick Wall," pp. 54–56. The quote is from p. 56.

187 " *'I don't care to have that type of attitude ...'* " Statham, p. 417.

187 " *'If my people are happy ...'* " Statham, p. 418.

187 The quotations from men in Statham's study come from p. 421.

188 I discuss in detail the research finding that men are likely to place relatively more value on independence, while women are more likely to place relatively more value on involvement in *You Just Don't Understand.*

188 " *'She doesn't question what I do ...'* " Statham, p. 418.

190 Meg Greenfield, "The Epidermis Issue," *Newsweek,* January 21, 1994, p. 66.

190 "... *according to the mother's 'My Turn' column in* Newsweek.)" "Learning by Intimidation," by Rosemary Parker. *Newsweek,* November 8, 1993, p. 14.

190 Philip Levine, "Why I'm the Poet I've Become: Berryman and the Lucky 13," *The New York Times Book Review,* December 26, 1993, pp. 3, 16–17. The quote is from p. 17.

191 The quotation from Oprah Winfrey appeared in *People* magazine, November 29, 1993, p. 111.

196 Statham, p. 424.

197 I have taken the quotation from p. 22 of Case, "Gender, Language and the Professions: Recognition of Wide-Verbal Repertoire Speech," a paper Case delivered at a conference. The material in her paper was based on her doctoral dissertation, *A Sociolinguistic Analysis of the Language of Gender Relations, Deviance and Influence in Managerial Groups.*

198 The remarks made about the woman by men in the group appear in Case's conference paper on p. 25.

198 " '. . . I can't be what I am . . . I'm damn uncomfortable.' " Although Case does not state this explicitly, I gather that the group members were invited to express their opinions of each other, and that something went awry in this process. In addition to the extreme hostility of the opinions voiced about the woman discussed, Case quotes another woman who said, "Please, stop it, we're ganging up on her," and a man who said, "It's very demeaning. Like making love to someone, then getting a rating on a 10 point scale when you walk out of the bedroom."

201 The quotation from Caryl Churchill's *Top Girls* (London and New York: Methuen, 1982) is from p. 76.

202 ". . . *a male colleague will wander over and ask what they're doing . . .*" David Finkel, "Women on the Verge of a Power Breakthrough," *The Washington Post Magazine,* May 10, 1992, pp. 15–19, 30–34. The quote is from p. 17.

CHAPTER 7: TALKING UP CLOSE

205 ". . . *according to sociologists and anthropologists who have studied them.*" Some researchers who have written about this are Donna Eder, Penelope Eckert ("Cooperative Competition in

Adolescent 'Girl Talk' "), Daniel Maltz and Ruth Borker, and Eleanor Maccoby. Sociologist Donna Eder, for example, in her article "Serious and Playful Disputes: Variation in Conflict Talk among Female Adolescents," shows that some of the junior high school girls in her study who came from working- or lower-class backgrounds engaged in a kind of ritual insulting that was competitive in the sense that they tried to top each other's insults but was not a means to maintain or subvert status hierarchies, as was the boys' characteristic use of ritual insults.

206 *"The linguistic term for meaning more than one thing at the same time is 'polysemy' . . ."* Although she does not use this term, linguist Sally McConnell-Ginet makes a similar observation about intonation.

206 *". . . it's up to you to see that he's enjoying every minute."* Judith Unger Scott, *The Art of Being a Girl.* New York: Grosset & Dunlap, p. 177. Thanks to Shari Kendall for calling this to my attention.

208 The Miss Manners column quoted appeared under the heading "Physician Excuse Thyself," *The Washington Post,* March 9, 1980. This column is quoted in Michelina Bonanno, "Women's Language in the Medical Interview." I have not noticed any change in this practice or the feelings of patients about it in the years since this column appeared. The radio talk show on which I heard Judith Martin discuss this phenomenon was *The Diane Rehm Show* on WAMU, Washington, DC, several years later.

209 *"Ms. Martin said she was not at all surprised; she knew how strongly feelings ran on this topic."* It is not only women who resent being addressed by first name, and not only doctors who unwittingly offend. An amusing and enlightening series of columns plus letters to the editor appeared on the topic in *The Washington Post,* sparked by a column by William Raspberry (November 29, 1993) under the title "My Not So Lightly Given Name." Raspberry complained about "strangers helping themselves to my first name," especially when he feels they do so in order to gain an advantage—like insurance agents, stockbrokers, and used-car salesmen who (he surmises) think positioning themselves as his friend

will make it harder for him to say no to them. A letter writer (Gwendolyn Hackley Austin, December 14, 1993) expressed the opinion that use of first name for people outside the immediate family was unthinkable in the black culture in which she was raised. "I don't think that many whites are aware," she wrote, "that calling adult African Americans by their given names, unless the speaker knows them well, is one of the most offensive things they could possibly do." (Raspberry's follow-up column on the topic appeared December 20, and a second series of letters appeared on December 27.)

210 " 'We have not had any direct contacts with Hillary's commission.' " "Old-Fashion Liberalism—With No Apologies," by Robert Pear, *The New York Times*, February 9, 1993, p. A9.

210 "... she had actually been calling some senators by their first *names?*" "Hillary Clinton's Debut Dashes Doubt on Clout," by Maureen Dowd, *The New York Times*, February 8, 1993, C9.

211 The excerpt of girls arguing comes from Donna Eder, "Serious and Playful Disputes," pp. 70–71. See also Penelope Eckert, "Cooperative Competition in Adolescent 'Girl Talk.' "

212 The review of *The Late Shift: Letterman, Leno and the Network Battle for the Night* by Bill Carter was written by Jay Rosen and appeared under the heading "How Letterman (and CBS) Won," *The New York Times*, February 22, 1994, p. C20.

218 The example of a graduate student whose supervising professor reminded her of her football-coach father comes from an article entitled "A Most Dangerous Method," by Margaret Talbot, *Lingua Franca* January/February 1994, p. 33.

220 The quotation from Thurgood Marshall is from " 'Oh, Yipe!' Said Thurgood Marshall," *The New York Times*, February 8, 1993.

221 The supervisor's observation that men are more likely than women to put off doing what they are asked is exactly parallel to a personal observation made by Mary Catherine Bateson in her book *Composing a Life*: For years, when her husband asked her to do something, Bateson would drop what she was doing and fulfill his request immediately. But when she asked him to do something,

he invariably said he would do it as soon as he finished his current task. Bateson says they have both worked to change her behavior to be more like his rather than the other way around.

222 Herbert (p. 220) cites an article by Herbert and Straight for the finding that American compliments tend to "flow from above." The etiquette book from which he takes the quotation reproduced here is J. H. Young, *Our Deportment: The Manner, Conduct, and Dress of the Most Refined Society* (Springfield, MA: W. C. King, 1882), p. 90.

223 Linde's examples of the pilot beginning free conversation, and her comments on them, appear in her articles "Who's in Charge Here?" and "Linguistic Consequences of Complex Social Structures: Rank and Task in Police Helicopter Discourse."

223 I have taken Janice Hornyak's observations from her dissertation proposal.

227 *"What happened next is interesting."* Gavruseva's analysis did not extend to this part of the exchange. The following is my interpretation of the conversation she taped and transcribed.

228 *"... they were both men and could bond on that basis."* Gavruseva pointed out to me, though, that John is still presenting himself as someone who does not need help, which still positions him as one-up.

234 *"... men talk more than women and thereby dominate interactions."* See Deborah James and Janice Drakich for a summary of research comparing women and men with regard to who talks more.

235 The quotation comes from Cheney and Seyfarth, p. 66. The authors define a *wrr* call as "a loud, relatively long, trilling call given by females and juveniles when they spot another group" (p. 65).

235 *"which were faster-paced than those he was used to."* Yet I should note that at least one British colleague told me he finds American speech slow but inexorable. It turned out that he had in mind some particular Midwesterners whom he knew. Because of the range of styles in both the United States and the United Kingdom, I want to stress that I am not suggesting that all Britons speak

more slowly than all Americans, but only that this individual Briton had a sense of conversational rhythm that differed from his American co-workers', and this made it hard for him to find the right moment to enter a conversation.

236 "*. . . the impression of dominance might result from style differences.*" In their book *Narrative, Literacy, and Face in Interethnic Communication,* Ron and Suzanne Scollon show how these dynamics operate between Athabaskan Indians and Anglos in Alaska. The Scollons and I have discussed them so much that I surely owe to them some of my understanding of these phenomena.

236 The research on male and female styles of conflict is summarized by Maltz and Borker and by Maccoby. Many researchers who study children at play have documented that boys of all ages engage in conflict that is physically rougher and takes up more of their time than girls' conflicts. In her article "Pickle Fights: Gendered Talk in Preschool Disputes," Amy Sheldon both presents evidence from her own research to support this and summarizes other research.

236 " '*adversativeness is a larger element in the lives of males than of females.*' " Ong, p. 51.

237 " '*The bonding of men at war was the strongest thing I'd felt in my life.*' " *People* magazine, March 21, 1994, p. 110. The man is Paul Mahar. He showed up to be shipped to Vietnam in his best friend's place because he was sure they would send him home when they discovered a metal plate in his arm. They didn't. They sent him to Vietnam.

237 " '*. . . and the two become inseparable friends.*' " Bly recounts this story in *Iron John: A Book About Men* (Reading, MA: Addison-Wesley, 1990), pp. 243–244. He cites as his source Joseph Campbell's *The Masks of God: Occidental Mythology* (New York: Viking, 1964).

238 My paper, written with Christina Kakava, is "Power and Solidarity in Modern Greek Conversation."

CHAPTER 8:
WHAT'S SEX GOT TO DO WITH IT?

246 *" 'Men can be sexually harassed too . . .' "* Throughout this chapter, I focus on sexual harassment in which the harasser is male and the harassed female. All evidence is that the vast majority of cases fit this constellation. But this is not to imply that women never sexually harass men. I have no doubt that this sometimes occurs, but, as I show here, the dynamics would be extremely different in such cases. I should also mention that those who have told me about personal experiences in which they felt they were sexually harassed by a woman were all women—a situation I do not discuss here because its dynamics, too, are very different from the most common constellation.

246 Maureen Dowd's review of *Disclosure* appeared under the heading "Women Who Harass Too Much" in *The New York Times Book Review,* January 23, 1994, p. 7.

247 The quotation about Bob Packwood comes from "The Trials of Bob Packwood" by Trip Gabriel, *The New York Times Magazine,* August 29, 1993, pp. 30–33, 38–43. The quote is from p. 30.

249 Keller, p. 60.

251 *"it is far more common for women to be physically assaulted or sexually harassed than for them to bring false charges."* The frequency of violence against women and the pervasiveness of sexual harassment have been much discussed in the media. For the first topic, see, for example, Ann Jones, *Next Time, She'll Be Dead: Battering and How to Stop It.* About the second, there has been a flood of books on the subject of sexual harassment at work, ranging from Catherine MacKinnon's landmark legal treatise *Sexual Harassment of Working Women* published by Yale University Press to William Petrocelli and Barbara Kate Repa's practical guide *Sexual Harassment on the Job* published by Nolo Press. Everyone seems to agree that false charges are relatively rare because, as Petrocelli puts it, a woman who files formal charges or complaints

can expect to suffer a "hellish" ordeal. (Petrocelli is quoted as offering this insight in "Publishing's Best Kept Secret" by Maureen O'Brien, *Publishers Weekly,* April 25, 1994, pp. 32–34.) On the other hand, it must be acknowledged that the more seriously sexual-harassment charges are taken, the more tempting it may be for someone to try to destroy a rival or enemy by encouraging a woman to file a sexual-harassment complaint against him—as many feel is the case with Paula Jones's belated suit against President Clinton. In these scenarios, the woman becomes a pawn in a power play.

252 *". . . the fear of male violence is the nub."* Of course, there are American neighborhoods in which men, even more than women, live in constant fear of violent attack, though not rape. One place where some men do experience the fear—and the reality—of rape is prison. Wilbert Rideau, a prisoner in the Louisiana State Penitentiary at Angola, describes a horrific social structure (according to him, "a feature of prison life everywhere") in which large, experienced prisoners force physically smaller newcomers to become their slaves by raping them. The act of rape establishes the rapist's ownership of his victim. But, although this is an all-male system, gender is still at its core. The enslaved prisoners are referred to as "wives," as "old ladies" to their "old men." Rideau explains that being raped "redefines" a prisoner as female. Chillingly, he observes that this two-tiered system of male masters and "female" slaves conquered by rape simply reflects the men's attempt to function as "normally" as possible in the abnormal prison world.

253 *". . . the act of throwing someone down mixes passion with physical assault."* A friend of mine, a gay man, upon hearing this incident, laughed and said, "I'd love it if a man said that to me!"

253 William King was a student at Skagit Valley College in Oak Harbor, Washington. I am grateful to him for permission to quote from his essay, and to his professor, Les Stanwood, who sent me King's essay along with a selection of essays his students had written in answer to a question on a midterm exam asking them to

synthesize their readings of *You Just Don't Understand* and their classroom discussion of rape.

254 *"Erving Goffman points out that the threat of violence is the flip side of chivalry . . ."* In his essay "The Arrangement Between the Sexes," Goffman observes that because of their greater size (reinforced in individual couples by "selective mating"), and their greater training in "outdoor competencies" and fighting, "displays by men to women of physical help and physical threat will be widely possible" (p. 321). In other words, "Males . . . can physically threaten present females, as well as come to their aid should others threaten" (p. 320).

254 *". . . the awareness of the possibility is there."* There are neighborhoods where girls do fight physically with each other and beat up other girls. Physical violence from girls is becoming an increasing problem in cities too.

255 *". . . I found the presence of boys I didn't know intimidating."* Boys beat up other boys too. But it seems that the presence of violence is more a part of routine socialization among boys in some cultures, at least. Attacks on girls are less frequent, but when they occur, they come more out of the blue, and girls in most cultures are less prepared to fight back.

255 The quotation is from Barkalow, p. 196.

256 *". . . she had never experienced physical violence."* A British colleague tells me that the level of emotion expressed by Americans at work is surprising to him and his compatriots.

256 The review of *That's Not What I Meant!* appeared in *The Washington Times,* March 10, 1986. The author, Philip Nicolaides, was identified as someone who "drafts presidential messages and proclamations at the [Reagan] White House" and "taught psychology at Fordham University."

258 The quotation from Congresswoman Jill Long appears in David Finkel, "Women on the Verge of a Power Breakthrough," *The Washington Post Magazine,* May 10, 1992, pp. 15–19, 30–34. The quote is from p. 15.

258 *". . . 73% of female residents said they had been sexually harassed by male physicians."* This finding is attributed by Phillips

and Schneider to M. Komaromy, A. B. Bindman, R. J. Haber, and M. A. Sande, "Sexual Harassment in Medical Training," *New England Journal of Medicine* 328(1993):322–26.

259 The quotation from Congresswoman Margolies-Mezvinsky is from her book *A Woman's Place*, p. 47.

260 Goffman introduces the term "faultable" in his essay "Radio Talk," p. 225.

261 That a visitor to Congresswoman Rosa DeLauro's office signed her guest book in this way was reported by David Finkel in "Women on the Verge of a Power Breakthrough," *The Washington Post Magazine*, May 10, 1992, pp. 15–19, 30–34. The quote is from p. 15.

262 "*. . . and do their dirty work for them.*" "Consecration of Woman Bishop Will Be Anticlimax," by Jack Kapica, *The Toronto Globe and Mail*, December 29, 1993, p. A6.

265 "*. . . press sexual advances on women in their charge.*" Cases involving these professionals have been much reported in the press. The problem of male coaches and female athletes was brought to my attention by Mariah Burton Nelson's *The Stronger Women Get, the More Men Love Football.*

265 "*. . . subjected to sexual abuse by Dr. Masserman.*" Thirteen people had come forward by the time of the book's publication; the rest spoke up after, according to Ms. Watterson. Five out-of-court settlements had resulted from suits brought by former patients before publication.

265 "*. . . 77% of women doctors surveyed felt they had been sexually harassed by male patients.*" Susan Phillips and Margaret Schneider, "Sexual Harassment of Female Doctors by Patients."

266 "*the emphasis this patient placed on the need to avoid being intimidated by doctors . . .*" For example, he gave this as a reason for addressing the doctor by first name ("Hi, Sue!"), even though this office had an explicit policy by which staff addressed patients by title–last name. "[W]hen I was younger," he told Ainsworth-Vaughn, "I was intimidated by the people in white coats. But over the years you start to learn . . . and you suddenly realize that yeah, they're no big deal. They're like everybody else, and you

make a point of, uh, calling them, speaking to them with their first name. Never call them doctor. Don't let the ego get in there."

267 " 'They have to put you down to make you lower than them.' " "Hey Doc, You Got Great Legs!" *Newsweek,* January 31, 1994, p. 54.

269 ". . . 42.3% of Japanese marriages are between couples who meet at work." This statistic is cited by linguist Shoko Okazaki in her study of communication between Japanese spouses. The source she cites is: Ministry of Public Welfare *(Koseisho). Nohonjin-no Kekkon-to shussan (Marriage and Childbirth of the Japanese).* Tokyo: *Kosei tokei kyokai,* 1993.

269 ". . . the military ban on fraternization of any sort within a chain of command." Captain Barkalow mentions this regulation (p. 182). On the other hand, as anthropologist Edward T. Hall shows, the ban is often violated. (See Chapter Eleven, "Army Life," in his book *An Anthropology of Everyday Life,* pp. 150–152.

270 Alice Mattison's "The Crossword Puzzle" appears in her short-story collection, *The Flight of Andy Burns* (New York: William Morrow, 1993). The quotation is from p. 148.

CHAPTER 9: WHO GETS HEARD?

277 ". . . saying something at a meeting and having it ignored . . ." Among academics, there is a written counterpart to this phenomenon: being "cited"—that is, having another scholar refer to your work in print. Anthropologist Catherine Lutz counted the proportion of articles written by women and men in four major academic journals in her field, and then counted how many times women and men were cited. She discovered that whereas women had written 30% of the articles, citations to their work accounted for only 18% of works cited in the journals.

279 " 'This may be a silly naïve question, but . . .' " Herring, p. 7.

284 ". . . when Ruth Bader Ginsburg asked questions on her very first day on the Supreme Court." The reactions I read were

not critical, just surprised. Justice Ginsburg was called "rude," however, for "interrupting" other justices when they were questioning presenting attorneys. (*Newsweek,* April 11, 1994, p. 6). I am convinced that the source of both behaviors was a style difference based on geographic and ethnic background. In my research on regional style differences, I describe a style I call "high involvement," in which speakers show their enthusiasm and interest by speaking up without necessarily waiting for others to finish their turns. I describe this in detail in a book entitled *Conversational Style: Analyzing Talk Among Friends,* and I discuss the phenomenon in *That's Not What I Meant!* as well.

286 The quotations are from Maccoby, 1990, p. 513.

286 "*. . . and these style differences often put females at a disadvantage in interaction with males.*" Maccoby's conclusions are similar to those I arrived at in writing *You Just Don't Understand: Women and Men in Conversation:* that boys and girls develop different styles of interacting as they grow up playing with other children of the same sex; that the environment they grow up in can therefore be thought of as "different cultures"; that each style works well in interaction with others who share it; but that the style differences put females at a disadvantage in interaction with males. I was (to my chagrin) unaware of Maccoby's work when I wrote *You Just Don't Understand,* a lapse I attribute to my focus on studies of ways of speaking, whereas her work and that of those she cites is concerned with nonverbal types of behavior. Nonetheless, the similarity in theme is evidence of the validity of the framework. There are, of course, overlaps in the research we cite, such as Maltz and Borker, so the similarity in our frameworks may have something to do with this.

287 " 'Girls find it difficult to influence boys.' " Maccoby, p. 515.

289 "*. . . according to her daughter, Mary Catherine Bateson.*" Bateson makes this point in her book *With a Daughter's Eye.*

294 These excerpts come from Sommers and Lawrence, p. 23.

294 Sommers and Lawrence, p. 22.

297 " '. . . *and under what conditions do they not?*' "
Edelsky, p. 221.

300 I discuss "report talk" and "rapport talk" in *You Just Don't Understand.*

301 ". . . *their socialization has taught them* not *to attract attention.*" In "The Arrangement Between the Sexes," Goffman points out that the meaning of visual attention paid to women is inextricable from the courtship ritual that is fundamental to the sexes' impressions of each other. In courtship:

> The female adorns herself in terms of received notions of sexual attractiveness and makes herself available for review in public, semi-public, and restricted places. Males who are present show broadcast attention to females held to be desirable, and await some fugitive sign that can be taken as encouragement of their interest. . . . [T]he male's assessing act—his ogling—constitutes the first move in the courtship process (p. 309).

Furthermore:

> Given that males will be watching for encouragement, looking to some lapse in the female's wonted reserve as a sign of this, it follows that any forwardness on her part, any initiative, insobriety, aggressiveness, or direction-giving, can be seen as sexually inviting, a sign, in short, of accessibility (pp. 312–313).

According to Myra and David Sadker, a reluctance to attract attention, to being the focus of all eyes, is one of many reasons that girls become "onlookers" rather than full participants in coed classrooms. The Sadkers quote a mother who says, "When our daughter Lara was in high school, she was extremely reluctant to speak out in class. In fact, she refused to wear red (a color that accentuates her dark hair and coloring) to school because it made her too noticeable" (p. 273).

306 Sidney Blumenthal, "Why Are We in Somalia?" *The New Yorker*, October 25, 1993, pp. 48–60. The quote is from p. 57.

AFTERWORD

315 "*. . . threaten their ability to bear children.*" Rosenberg, p. 5.

317 The physicist was Freeman Dyson, to whom I offer thanks.

REFERENCES

AAUW Report, The. 1992. *How Schools Shortchange Girls: A Study of Major Findings on Girls and Education.* Washington, DC: The American Association of University Women Educational Foundation.

Adger, Carolyn. 1993. "Empowering Talk: African-American Teachers and Classroom Discourse." Paper presented at the 1993 Annual Meeting of the American Education Research Association in Atlanta, Georgia.

Ainsworth-Vaughn, Nancy. 1992. "Topic Transitions in Physician-Patient Interviews: Power, Gender, and Discourse Change." *Language in Society* 21: 409–26.

Ainsworth-Vaughn, Nancy. 1994. " 'Is That a Rhetorical Question?': Power and Ambiguity in Medical Discourse." *Journal of Linguistic Anthropology* 4:2.

Ainsworth-Vaughn, Nancy. In preparation. *Power in Practice: Control and Identity in Physician-Patient Discourse.* New York and Oxford: Oxford University Press.

Apte, Mahadev L. 1985. *Humor and Laughter: An Anthropological Approach.* Ithaca, NY: Cornell University Press.

Aries, Elizabeth. 1976. "Interaction Patterns and Themes of Male, Female, and Mixed Groups." *Small Group Behavior* 7:1.7–18.

Baker, Charlotte. 1975. "Butterfinger *Buts.*" *San Jose State Occasional Papers in Linguistics,* Vol. 1, 18–24. Linguistics Program, San Jose State University, San Jose, California.

Barkalow, Carol, with Andrea Rabb. 1990. *In the Men's House: An Inside Account of Life in the Army by One of West Point's First Female Graduates.* New York: Poseidon.

Basso, Keith. 1979. *Portraits of "The Whiteman."* Cambridge: Cambridge University Press.

Bateson, Gregory. 1972. "A Theory of Play and Fantasy." *Steps to an Ecology of Mind,* 177–93. New York: Ballantine.

Bateson, Mary Catherine. 1972. *Our Own Metaphor: A Personal Account of a Conference on Conscious Purpose and Human Adaptation.* New York: Knopf. Reprinted by Smithsonian Institution Press, 1991.

Bateson, Mary Catherine. 1984. *With a Daughter's Eye: A Memoir of Margaret Mead and Gregory Bateson.* New York: William Morrow.

Bateson, Mary Catherine. 1990. *Composing a Life.* New York: Atlantic Monthly Press, Plume.

Bateson, Mary Catherine. 1994. *Peripheral Visions: Learning Along the Way.* New York: HarperCollins.

Becker, A. L. 1994. *Beyond Translation: Essays Toward a Modern Philology.* Ann Arbor: University of Michigan Press.

Beeman, William O. 1986. *Language, Status, and Power in Iran.* Bloomington: Indiana University Press.

Befu, Harumi. [1974] 1986. "An Ethnography of Dinner Entertainment in Japan." *Japanese Culture and Behavior: Selected Readings* (revised edition), ed. by Takie Sugiyama Lebra and William P. Lebra, 108–20. Honolulu: University of Hawaii Press.

Bellinger, David, and Jean Berko Gleason. 1982. "Sex Differences in Parental Directives to Young Children." *Sex Roles* 8:1123–1139.

Binchy, Maeve. 1978. "King's Cross." *London Transports,* 172–192. New York: Dell.

Bonanno, Michelina. 1982. "Women's Language in the Medical Interview." *Linguistics and the Professions,* ed. by Robert J. Di Pietro, 27–38. Norwood, NJ: Ablex.

Bookchin, Murray. 1989. *Remaking Society.* Montreal: Black Rose Books.

Bowman, Garda W., Beatrice B. Worthy, and Stephen A. Grayser. 1965. "Problems in Review: Are Women Executives People?" *Harvard Business Review* 43:4.14–28, 164–178.

Byrnes, Heidi. 1986. "Interactional Style in German and American Conversations." *Text* 6:2.189–206.

Carli, Linda L. 1989. "Gender Differences in Interaction Style and Influence." *Journal of Personality and Social Psychology* 56:565–576.

Case, Susan Schick. 1985. "A Sociolinguistic Analysis of the Language of Gender Relations, Deviance and Influence in Managerial Groups." Ph.D. dissertation, State University of New York at Buffalo.

Case, Susan Schick. 1991. "Gender, Language and the Professions: Recognition of Wide-Verbal Repertoire Speech." Fifth Annual International Conference on Pragmatics and Language Learning. Parasession on Gender and Language. University of Illinois, Urbana-Champaign.

Cheney, Dorothy L., and Robert M. Seyfarth. 1990. *How Monkeys See the World.* Chicago: University of Chicago Press.

Churchill, Caryl. 1982. *Top Girls.* London and New York: Methuen.

Clancy, Patricia. 1986. "The Acquisition of Communicative Style

347

in Japanese." *Language Acquisition and Socialization Across Cultures,* ed. by Bambi B. Schieffelin and Elinor Ochs, 213–50. Cambridge: Cambridge University Press.

Cose, Ellis. 1994. *The Rage of a Privileged Class.* New York: HarperCollins.

Cox, Joe A., Raymond L. Read, and Philip M. Van Auken. 1990. "Male-Female Differences in Communicating Job-Related Humor: An Exploratory Study." *Humor* 3:3.287–295.

Davies, Bronwyn, and Rom Harré. 1990. "Positioning: Conversation and the Production of Selves." *Journal for the Theory of Social Behavior* 20:1.43–63.

Doi, Takeo. 1973. *The Anatomy of Dependence.* Tokyo and New York: Kodansha. Japanese edition: *Amae no Kozo.* Tokyo: Kobundo, 1971.

Duncan, Starkey S., Jr., and Donald W. Fiske. 1977. *Face-to-Face Interaction: Research, Methods and Theory.* Hillsdale, NJ: Erlbaum.

Eakins, Barbara Westbrook, and R. Gene Eakins. 1976. "Verbal Turn-Taking and Exchanges in Faculty Dialogue." *The Sociology of the Languages of American Women,* ed. by Betty Lou Dubois and Isabel Crouch, 53–62. Linguistics, Trinity University: San Antonio, TX.

Eckert, Penelope. 1989. *Jocks and Burnouts.* New York: Teachers College Press.

Eckert, Penelope. 1993. "Cooperative Competition in Adolescent 'Girl Talk.'" *Gender and Conversational Interaction,* ed. by Deborah Tannen, 32–61. Oxford and New York: Oxford University Press.

Edelsky, Carole. 1981. "Who's Got the Floor?" *Language in Society* 10.383–421. Reprinted in *Gender and Conversational Interaction,* ed. by Deborah Tannen, 189–227. Oxford and New York: Oxford University Press, 1993.

Eder, Donna. 1990. "Serious and Playful Disputes: Variation in Conflict Talk Among Female Adolescents." *Conflict Talk,* ed. by Allen Grimshaw, 67–84. Cambridge: Cambridge University Press.

Eder, Donna. 1993. " 'Go Get Ya a French!': Romantic and Sexual Teasing Among Adolescent Girls." *Gender and Conversational Interaction,* ed. by Deborah Tannen, 17–31. New York and Oxford: Oxford University Press.

Ekman, Paul. 1991. "Who Can Catch a Liar?" *American Psychologist* 46:9.913–20.

Ekman, Paul. 1992. *Telling Lies.* New York: Norton.

Eskilson, Arlene, and Mary Glenn Wiley. 1976. "Sex Composition and Leadership in Small Groups." *Sociometry* 39:183–94.

Fink, Cynthia. 1982. "Perceptions of Women's Communication Skills Related to Managerial Effectiveness." Fifth Annual Communication, Language, and Gender Conference, Athens, OH.

Gavruscva, Lena. 1993. "Constructing Interactional Power in Employer-Employee Discourse." Paper written for seminar, "Language in Hierarchical Settings," Georgetown University Linguistics Department.

Gilligan, Carol, Nona P. Lyons, and Trudy J. Hanmer (eds.). 1990. *Making Connections: The Relational Worlds of Adolescent Girls at Emma Willard School.* Cambridge, MA: Harvard University Press.

Gleason, Jean Berko. 1987. "Sex Differences in Parent-Child Interaction." *Language, Gender, and Sex in Comparative Perspective,* ed. by Susan U. Philips, Susan Steele, and Christine Tanz, 189–99. Cambridge: Cambridge University Press.

Goffman, Erving. 1967. "The Nature of Deference and Demeanor." *Interaction Ritual,* 47–95. Garden City, NY: Doubleday.

Goffman, Erving. 1977. "The Arrangement Between the Sexes." *Theory and Society* 4:3.301–331.

Goffman, Erving. 1981. "Radio Talk." *Forms of Talk,* 197–327. Philadelphia: University of Pennsylvania Press.

Goodwin, Marjorie Harness. 1990. *He-Said-She-Said: Talk As Social Organization Among Black Children.* Bloomington: Indiana University Press.

Goguen, J. A., and C. Linde. 1983. *Linguistic Methodology for the*

Analysis of Aviation Accidents. Report prepared for the Ames Research Center and published by the National Aeronautics and Space Administration Scientific and Technical Information Branch.

Hall, Edward T. 1992. *An Anthropology of Everyday Life*. New York: Doubleday.

Hall, Judith A., and Karen G. Braunwald. 1981. "Gender Cues in Conversation." *Journal of Personality and Social Psychology* 40:99–110.

Harada, Kunihiko. 1993. "Gender in Japanese Hierarchical Settings." Paper written for seminar, "Language in Hierarchical Settings," Georgetown University Linguistics Department.

Harrington, Mona. 1994. *Women Lawyers: Rewriting the Rules*. New York: Knopf.

Heatherington, Laurie, Kimberly A. Daubman, Cynthia Bates, Alicia Ahn, Heather Brown, and Camille Preston. 1993. "Two Investigations of 'Female Modesty' in Achievement Situations." *Sex Roles* 29:11/12.739–54.

Herbert, Robert K. 1990. "Sex-Based Differences in Compliment Behavior." *Language in Society* 19:2.201–24.

Herbert, Robert K., and H. Stephen Straight. 1989. "Compliment-Rejection Vs. Compliment-Avoidance." *Language and Communication* 9:35–47.

Herring, Susan. 1992. "Gender and Participation in Computer-Mediated Linguistic Discourse." ERIC Clearinghouse on Languages and Linguistics (October).

Holmes, Janet. 1986. "Compliments and Compliment Responses in New Zealand English." *Anthropological Linguistics* 28:4.485–508.

Holmes, Janet. 1989. "Sex Differences and Apologies: One Aspect of Communicative Competence." *Applied Linguistics* 10:2.194–213.

Hornyak, Janice. In preparation. *Shifting Between Personal and Professional Frames in Office Discourse*. Ph.D. dissertation, Georgetown University Linguistics Department.

Ide, Sachiko. 1990. "How and Why Do Women Speak More Politely in Japanese?" *Aspects of Japanese Women's Language,* ed. by Sachiko Ide and Naomi Hanaoka, 63–79. Tokyo: Kuroshio Publishers.

Irvine, Judith. 1974. "Strategies of Status Manipulation in the Wolof Greeting." *Explorations in the Ethnography of Speaking,* ed. by Richard Bauman and Joel Sherzer, 167–191. Cambridge: Cambridge University Press.

Ishii, Satoshi. 1984. "Enryo-Sasshi Communication: A Key to Understanding Japanese Interpersonal Relations." *Cross-Currents* XL:1 (Spring).49–58.

James, Deborah, and Sandra Clarke. 1993. "Women, Men, and Interruptions: A Critical Review." *Gender and Conversational Interaction,* ed. by Deborah Tannen, 231–80. Oxford and New York: Oxford University Press.

James, Deborah, and Janice Drakich. 1993. "Understanding Gender Differences in Amount of Talk." *Gender and Conversational Interaction,* ed. by Deborah Tannen, 281–312. New York and Oxford: Oxford University Press.

Johnson, Donna M., and Duane H. Roen. 1992. "Complimenting and Involvement in Peer Reviews: Gender Variation." *Language in Society* 21:1.27–57.

Johnstone, Barbara. 1993. "Identity, Ideology and Women's Public Speaking in Contemporary Texas." Paper delivered at the annual meeting of the American Anthropological Association, November 1993, Washington, DC.

Jones, Ann. 1994. *Next Time, She'll Be Dead: Battering and How to Stop It.* Boston: Beacon Press.

Kakava, Christina. 1993. "Aggravated Corrections as Disagreement in Casual Greek Conversations." Proceedings of the First Annual Symposium about Language and Society—Austin (SALSA). *Texas Linguistic Forum* 33:187–95.

Kawakami, Itoko. 1993. "Address Forms as Indexing Markers of Gender, Age, and Hierarchy: Analysis of Address Forms in Conversations Among Japanese Teachers." Paper written for seminar, "Language in Hierarchical Settings." Georgetown University Linguistics Department.

351

REFERENCES

Keller, Evelyn Fox. 1985. *Reflections on Gender and Science*. New Haven: Yale University Press.

Kendall, Shari E. 1993. "Talking Competence: Gendered Discourse Styles in the Construction of Competence in a Work Setting." Paper written for seminar, "Language in Hierarchical Settings," Georgetown University Linguistics Department. Also presented as "Constructing Competence: Gender and Mitigation at a Radio Network." American Association for Applied Linguistics Annual Conference, March 7, 1994, Baltimore, Maryland.

Kochman, Thomas. 1981. *Black and White Styles in Conflict*. Chicago: University of Chicago Press.

Kuhn, Elisabeth D. 1992. "Playing Down Authority While Getting Things Done: Women Professors Get Help from the Institution." *Locating Power: Proceedings of the Second Berkeley Women and Language Conference*, Vol. 2, ed. by Kira Hall, Mary Bucholtz, and Birch Moonwomon, 318–25. Berkeley, CA: Berkeley Women and Language Group, University of California, Berkeley.

Lakoff, Robin. 1975. *Language and Woman's Place*. New York: Harper and Row.

Lakoff, Robin Tolmach, and Raquel L. Scherr. 1984. *Face Value: The Politics of Beauty*. Boston and London: Routledge and Kegan Paul.

Lakoff, Robin Tolmach. 1990. *Talking Power: The Politics of Language in Our Lives*. New York: Basic Books.

Leaper, Campbell. 1991. "Influence and Involvement: Age, Gender, and Partner Effects." *Child Development* 62:797–811.

Lebra, Takie Sugiyama. 1986. *Japanese Patterns of Behavior*. Honolulu, HI: University of Hawaii Press.

Lebra, Takie Sugiyama. 1987. "The Cultural Significance of Silence in Japanese Communication." *Multilingua* 6:4.343–57.

Linde, Charlotte. 1988. "The Quantitative Study of Communicative Success: Politeness and Accidents in Aviation Discourse." *Language in Society* 17:375–99.

Linde, Charlotte. 1988. "Who's in Charge Here?: Cooperative

Work and Authority Negotiation in Police Helicopter Missions." Second Annual ACM Conference on Computer Supported Collaborative Work.

Linde, Charlotte. 1988. "Linguistic Consequences of Complex Social Structures: Rank and Task in Police Helicopter Discourse." *Proceedings of the Fourteenth Annual Meeting of the Berkeley Linguistic Society,* ed. by Shelley Axmaker, Annie Jaisser, and Helen Singmaster, 142–152. Berkeley, California: Berkeley Linguistics Society.

Linn, Lawrence S., Dennis W. Cope, and Barbara Leake. 1984. "The Effect of Gender and Training of Residents on Satisfaction Ratings by Patients." *Journal of Medical Education* 59:964–66.

Lutz, Catherine. 1990. "The Erasure of Women's Writing in Sociocultural Anthropology." *American Ethnologist* 17:611–27.

Maccoby, Eleanor E., 1990. "Gender and Relationships: A Developmental Account." *American Psychologist* 45:4.513–20.

Maccoby, Eleanor E., and Carol Jacklin. 1974. *The Psychology of Sex Differences.* Stanford, CA: Stanford University Press.

MacKinnon, Catherine. 1979. *Sexual Harassment of Working Women.* New Haven, CT: Yale University Press.

Madhok, Jacqueline J. 1992. "The Effect of Gender Composition on Group Interaction." *Locating Power: Proceedings of the Second Berkeley Women and Language Conference,* Vol. 2, ed. by Kira Hall, Mary Bucholtz, and Birch Moonwomon, 371–85. Berkeley, CA: Berkcley Women and Language Group, University of California, Berkeley.

Magenau, Keller. 1993. "More Than Feminine: Attending to Power and Social Distance Dimensions in Spoken and Written Workplace Communication." Paper written for seminar, "Language in Hierarchical Settings," Georgetown University Linguistics Department.

Maltz, Daniel N., and Ruth A. Borker. 1982. "A Cultural Approach to Male-Female Miscommunication." *Language and Social Identity,* ed. by John J. Gumperz, 196–216. Cambridge: Cambridge University Press.

353

Mann, Judy. 1994. *The Difference: Growing Up Female in America*. New York: Warner Books.

Margolies-Mezvinsky, Marjorie, with Barbara Feinman. 1994. *A Woman's Place: The Freshmen Women Who Changed the Face of Congress*. New York: Crown.

Mattison, Alice. 1993. *The Flight of Andy Burns*. New York: William Morrow.

Matoesian, Gregory. 1992. *Reproducing Rape: Domination Through Talk in the Courtroom*. Chicago: University of Chicago Press.

Matsumoto, Yoshiko. 1988. "Reexamination of the Universality of Face: Politeness Phenomena in Japanese." *Journal of Pragmatics* 12:403–26.

McConnell-Ginet, Sally. 1983. "Intonation in a Man's World." *Language, Gender, and Society,* ed. by Barrie Thorne, Cheris Kramarae, and Nancy Henley, 69–88. Boston: Newbury House.

Mead, Margaret. 1977. "End Linkage: A Tool for Cross-Cultural Analysis." *About Bateson,* ed. by John Brockman, 171–231. New York: Dutton.

Mülhäusler, Peter, and Rom Harré, with Anthony Holiday and Michael Freyne. 1990. *Pronouns and People: The Linguistic Construction of Social and Personal Identity*. Oxford and Cambridge, MA: Basil Blackwell.

Nadler, Marjorie, and Lawrence Nadler. 1987. "The Influence of Gender on Negotiation Success in Asymmetric Power Situations." *Advances in Gender and Communication Research,* ed. by Lawrence B. Nadler, Marjorie Keeshan Nadler, and William R. Todd-Mancillas, 189–218. Lanham, MD: University Press of America.

Nelson, Mariah Burton. 1994. *The Stronger Women Get, the More Men Love Football: Sexism and the American Culture of Sports*. New York: Harcourt Brace.

Nieva, Veronica, and Barbara Gutek. 1980. "Sex Effects on Evaluation." *Academy of Management Review* 5:2.267–76.

Noël, Barbara, with Kathryn Watterson. 1992. *You Must Be Dreaming*. New York: Poseidon.

Ochs, Elinor. 1992. "Indexing Gender." *Rethinking Context: Language As an Interactive Phenomenon,* ed. by Alessandro Duranti and Charles Goodwin, 335–358. Cambridge: Cambridge University Press.

Ochs, Elinor, and Bambi B. Schieffelin. 1984. "Language Acquisition and Socialization: Three Developmental Stories." *Culture Theory: Essays in Mind, Self and Emotion,* ed. by Richard A. Schweder and Robert A. LeVine. Cambridge: Cambridge University Press.

Okazaki, Shoko. 1994. "Ellipsis in Japanese Conversational Discourse." Ph.D. dissertation, Georgetown University Linguistics Department.

Olsen, Jack. 1989. *Doc: The Rape of the Town of Lovell.* New York: Atheneum. Paperback: Dell, 1990.

Ong, Walter J. 1981. *Fighting for Life: Contest, Sexuality, and Consciousness.* Ithaca: Cornell University Press.

Pan, Yuling. 1994. "Politeness Strategies in Chinese Verbal Interaction: A Sociolinguistic Analysis of Official, Business, and Family Settings." Ph.D. dissertation, Georgetown University Linguistics Department.

Paules, Greta Foff. 1991. *Dishing It Out: Power and Resistance Among Waitresses in a New Jersey Restaurant.* Philadelphia: Temple University Press.

Petrocelli, William, and Barbara Kate Repa. 1992. *Sexual Harassment on the Job.* Berkeley, CA: Nolo Press.

Phillips, Susan P., and Margaret S. Schneider. 1993. "Sexual Harassment of Female Doctors by Patients." *The New England Journal of Medicine* 329:26.1936–939.

Pinter, Harold. 1975. *No Man's Land.* New York: Grove Press.

Pipher, Mary. 1994. *Reviving Ophelia: Saving the Selves of Adolescent Girls.* New York: Putnam.

Remlinger, Kate. In preparation. "The Socio-linguistic Construction of Gender and Gender Relationships in a University Community." Ph.D. dissertation, Michigan Technological University.

Rideau, Wilbert. 1992. "The Sexual Jungle." *Life Sentences: Rage and Survival Behind Bars,* by Wilbert Rideau and Ron Wikberg, 73–107. New York: Times Books.

Rosenberg, Rosalind. 1982. *Beyond Separate Spheres: Intellectual Roots of Modern Feminism.* New Haven: Yale University Press.

Ryan, Ellen Bouchard, Linda H. Boich, and Laura Klemenchuk-Politeski. 1994. "Patronizing Behavior in Health Care: Is Ignoring the Older Accented Speaker Excusable?" International Conference on Communication, Aging and Health, Hamilton, Ontario, May.

Rubin, Donald. 1992. "Nonlanguage Factors Affecting Undergraduates' Judgments of Nonnative English-Speaking Teaching Assistants." *Research in Higher in Education* 33:4.511–31.

Sadker, Myra, and David Sadker. 1994. *Failing at Fairness: How America's Schools Cheat Girls.* New York: Scribners.

Schieffelin, Bambi, and Elinor Ochs. 1986. "Language Socialization." *Annual Review of Anthropology* 15.163–246.

Schiffrin, Deborah. 1984. "Jewish Argument as Sociability." *Language in Society* 13:3.311–35.

Scollon, Ron, and Suzanne B.K. Scollon. 1981. *Narrative, Literacy and Face in Interethnic Communication.* Norwood, NJ: Ablex.

Scotton, Carol Myers. 1988. "Self-Enhancing Code-Switching As Interactional Power." *Language and Communication* 8:3/4.199–211.

Sheldon, Amy. 1990. "Pickle Fights: Gendered Talk in Preschool Disputes." *Gender and Conversational Interaction,* ed. by Deborah Tannen, 83–109. New York and Oxford: Oxford University Press.

Sheldon, Amy. 1992. "Preschool Girls' Discourse Competence: Managing Conflict." *Locating Power: Proceedings of the Second Berkeley Women and Language Conference,* Vol. 2, ed. by Kira Hall, Mary Bucholtz, and Birch Moonwomon, 528–39. Berkeley, CA: Berkeley Women and Language Group, University of California, Berkeley.

REFERENCES

Smith, Frances Lee. 1993. "The Pulpit and Woman's Place: Gender and the Framing of the 'Exegetical Self' in Sermon Performances." *Framing in Discourse,* ed. by Deborah Tannen, 147–75. New York: Oxford University Press.

Sommers, Elizabeth, and Sandra Lawrence. 1992. "Women's Ways of Talking in Teacher-Directed and Student-Directed Peer Response Groups." *Linguistics and Education* 4:1–36.

Statham, Anne. 1987. "The Gender Model Revisited: Differences in the Management Styles of Men and Women." *Sex Roles* 16:7.409–29.

Sterling, Dorothy. 1991. *Ahead of Her Time: Abby Kelley and the Politics of Antislavery.* New York and London: Norton.

Stewart, Lea P. 1982. "Women in Management: Implications for Communication Researchers." Eastern Communication Association Convention, Hartford, CT.

Tannen, Deborah. 1979. "What's in a Frame? Surface Evidence for Underlying Expectations." *New Directions in Discourse Processing,* ed. by Roy O. Freedle, 137–81. Norwood, NJ: Ablex. Reprinted in *Framing in Discourse,* ed. by Deborah Tannen, 14–56. New York and Oxford: Oxford University Press, 1993.

Tannen, Deborah. 1982. "Ethnic Style in Male-Female Conversation." *Language and Social Identity,* ed. by John Gumperz, 217–31. Cambridge: Cambridge University Press. Reprinted in *Gender and Discourse,* 175–94. New York and Oxford: Oxford University Press.

Tannen, Deborah. 1984. *Conversational Style: Analyzing Talk Among Friends.* Norwood, NJ: Ablex.

Tannen, Deborah. 1986. *That's Not What I Meant!: How Conversational Style Makes or Breaks Your Relations with Others.* New York: William Morrow, Ballantine.

Tannen, Deborah. 1989. *Talking Voices: Repetition, Dialogue, and Imagery in Conversational Discourse.* Cambridge: Cambridge University Press.

Tannen, Deborah. 1990. *You Just Don't Understand: Women and*

Men in Conversation. New York: William Morrow, Ballantine.

Tannen, Deborah (ed). 1993. *Framing in Discourse*. Oxford and New York: Oxford University Press.

Tannen, Deborah, and Christina Kakava. 1992. "Power and Solidarity in Modern Greek Conversation: Disagreeing to Agree." *Journal of Modern Greek Studies* 10:1.11–34.

Tannen, Deborah, and Cynthia Wallat. 1987. "Interactive Frames and Knowledge Schemas in Interaction: Examples from a Medical Examination/Interview." *Social Psychology Quarterly* 50:2.205–16. Reprinted in *Framing in Discourse,* ed. by Deborah Tannen, 57–76. New York and Oxford: Oxford University Press, 1993.

Thorne, Barrie. 1994. *Gender Play: Girls and Boys in School.* New Brunswick: Rutgers University Press.

Tracy, Karen, and Eric Eisenberg. 1990/1991. "Giving Criticism: A Multiple Goals Case Study." *Research on Language and Social Interaction* 24.37–70.

Ueda, Keiko. 1974. "Sixteen Ways to Avoid Saying 'No' in Japan." *Intercultural Encounters with Japan: Communication— Contact and Conflict,* ed. by J. C. Condon and M. Saito, 184–92. Tokyo: Simul.

Watanabe, Suwako. 1993. "Cultural Differences in Framing: American and Japanese Group Discussions." *Framing in Discourse,* ed. by Deborah Tannen, 176–208. New York: Oxford University Press.

West, Candace. 1984. *Routine Complications: Troubles with Talk Between Doctors and Patients.* Bloomington: Indiana University Press.

Wetzel, Patricia J. 1988. "Are 'Powerless' Communication Strategies the Japanese Norm?" *Language in Society* 17:555–64.

Williams, Donna. 1992. *Nobody Nowhere: The Extraordinary Autobiography of an Autistic.* New York: Random House, Avon.

Williams, Donna. 1994. *Somebody Somewhere: Breaking Free From the World of Autism.* New York: Times Books.

REFERENCES

Winter, Joanne. 1993. "Gender and the Political Interview in an Australian Context." *Journal of Pragmatics* 20.117–39.

Wolfowitz, Clare. 1991. *Language Style and Social Space: Stylistic Choice in Suriname Javanese*. Urbana and Chicago: University of Illinois Press.

Wolfram, Walt, and Carolyn Adger. 1993. *Handbook on Language Differences and Speech and Language Pathology:* Baltimore City Public Schools. Washington, DC: Center for Applied Linguistics, 1993.

Wolfson, Nessa. 1984. "Pretty Is As Pretty Does: A Speech Act View of Sex Roles." *Applied Linguistics* 5:3.236–44.

Yamada, Haru. 1992. *American and Japanese Business Discourse: A Comparison of Interactional Styles*. Norwood, NJ: Ablex.

Yerian, Keli. 1993. "Being Funny, Being Heard: Gender, Language and the Workplace: Gaining Interactional and Organizational Power Through Strategic Uses of Humor." Paper written for seminar, "Language in Hierarchical Settings," Georgetown University Linguistics Department.

Grateful acknowledgment is made to the authors and publishers for permission to reprint previously published materials from:

"Topic Transitions in Physician-Patient Interviews: Power, Gender and Discourse Change" by Nancy Ainsworth-Vaughn in *Language in Society*. Copyright © Nancy Ainsworth-Vaughn. Reprinted by permission of Cambridge University Press.

"Why Are We in Somalia" by Sidney Blumenthal. Copyright © Sidney Blumenthal. Reprinted by permission of *The New Yorker*.

Top Girls by Caryl Churchill. Copyright © Caryl Churchill. Reprinted by permission of Reed Consumer Books.

"The Acquisition of Communicative Style in Japanese" by Patricia Clancy in *Language Socialization Across Cultures*, ed. Bambi B. Schieffelin and Elinor Ochs. Copyright © Patricia Clancy. Reprinted by permission of Cambridge University Press.

"Serious and Playful Disputes: Variation in Conflict Talk Among Female Adolescents" by Donna Eder in *Conflict Talk*, ed. Allen Grimshaw. Copyright © Donna Eder. Reprinted by permission of Cambridge University Press.

"Women on the Verge of a Power Breakthrough" by David Finkel. Copyright © David Finkel. Reprinted by permission of *The Washington Post Magazine*.

"Playing Down Authority While Getting Things Done: Women Professors Get Help from the Institution" by Elisabeth Kuhn in *Proceedings of the Second Berkeley Women and Language Conference*. Copyright © Elisabeth Kuhn. Reprinted by permission of Elisabeth Kuhn.

"Gender and Relationships: A Developmental Account" by Eleanor Maccoby in *American Psychologist*. Copyright © Eleanor Maccoby. Reprinted by permission of *American Psychologist*.

"Women Who Harass Too Much" by Maureen Dowd in *The New York Times Book Review*. Copyright © Maureen Dowd. Reprinted by permission of *The New York Times*.

"The Trials of Bob Packwood" by Trip Gabriel in *The New York Times*. Copyright © Trip Gabriel. Reprinted by permission of *The New York Times*.

"Book of the Times: How *Letterman (and CBS) Won*" by Jay Rosen. Copyright © Jay Rosen. Reprinted by permission of *The New York Times*.

"Women's Ways of Talking in Teacher-Directed and Student-Directed Peer Response Groups" by Elizabeth Sommers and Sandra Lawrence in *Linguistics and Education*. Copyright © Elizabeth Sommers and Sandra Lawrence. Reprinted by permission of Ablex Publishing Corporation.

"The Gender Model Revisited: Differences in the Management Styles of Men and Women" by Anne Statham in *Sex Roles*. Copyright © Anne Statham. Reprinted by permission of Plenum Publishing.

"The Crossword Puzzle" by Alice Mattison in *The Flight of Andy Burns*. Copyright © Alice Mattison. Reprinted by permission of William Morrow and Company.

"Giving Criticism: A Multiple Goals Case Study" by Karen Tracy and Eric Eisenberg in *Research on Language and Social Interaction*. Copyright © Karen Tracy and Eric Eisenberg. Reprinted by permission of Boreal Scholarly Publishing.

In the Men's House: An Inside Account of Life in the Army by One of West Point's First Female Graduates by Carol Barkalow with Andrea Rabb. Copyright © Carol Barkalow and Andrea Rabb. Reprinted by permission of Carol Barkalow and Andrea Rabb.

"King's Cross" by Maeve Binchy in *London Transports*. Copyright © Maeve Binchy. Reprinted by permission of Christine Green, Ltd.

"Aggravated Corrections as Disagreement in Casual Greek Conversations" by Christina Kakava in *Proceedings of the First Annual Symposium About Language and Society*. Copyright © Christina Kakava. Reprinted by permission of Christina Kakava.

"Miss Manners" by Judith Martin. Copyright © Judith Martin. Reprinted by permission of *The Washington Post*.

INDEX

accommodating ways of speaking, 146–147,
    163–164
adaptation of styles, 119–125
address forms, *see* forms of address
Adger, Carolyn, 164
admitting fault, 46
adolescents, 154–166, 211–212, 320–321,
    332, 342
adversativeness, *see* fighting
African-Americans, 38, 164, 260, 333
aggressiveness, 36, 39–42, 57
    see also fighting
Ainsworth-Vaughn, Nancy, 90, 124,
    171–173, 184–185, 265, 266–267
Air Florida Flight 90 crash, 91–94
Ali, Muhammad, 38
Allason, Rupert, 154
Allegheny Airlines Flight 453, 93–94
alliances, networks of, 211–213
amae, 215
Anatomy of Dependence, The (Doi), 215
anger, 88–90, 189–190
    fear of violence and, 255–256
    indirectness and, 88–89
anticipation, 96
Apache, imitation and, 316
apologizing, 44–51, 56–57, 76
application forms, women's choices on,
    111
Apte, Mahader, 323
arguing, friendly, 238–240
Aries, Elizabeth, 289
"Arrangement Between the Sexes, The"
    (Goffman), 15, 338, 342
arrogance, 23, 41, 42
art installations, 88–89, 140–141
asking questions, *see* questions
assertiveness, 199
attention, women avoiding, 301, 342
attorneys, *see* lawyers, women
audience:
    authoritative questions from, 149–150
    hostile questions from, 145–146
authority, 134, 160–203
    demeanor and, 173–177
    direct speech and, 98, 99
    of doctors, 171–173, 184–185
    downplaying of, *see* authority,
        downplaying of
    female stereotypes and, 164–166
    holding vs. seeking of, 191–193
    home problems and, 199–200
    images of, 193–194

maleness associated with, 167–169
    negotiating of, 170–171
    same words, different reactions and,
        195–198
    special challenge of women in, 202–203
    women in, 72, 171–189
authority, downplaying of, 171–189
    effect of, 184–185
    equality and, 177–178
    of preachers, 173–175
    of professors, 175–176
    reasons for, 185–189
    saving face and, 179–183
authors, *see* editor-author relationship
autism, 42, 127
"autonomy-invested" management style,
    187–188

baby talk, 163
Baker, Charlotte, 279
bantering, 23, 73, 74
Barkalow, Carol, 121, 122–123, 255
Barnes, Sharon, 140
Basso, Keith, 316
Bateson, Gregory, 130, 234
Bateson, Mary Catherine, 289, 333–334
Becker, A. L., 242
Beeman, William, 216
Befu, Harumi, 144
Bellinger, David, 84–85
Berryman, John, 190
Binchy, Maeve, 156–157
black-box conversations, 91–94
blame:
    assigning and assuming of, 51–52
    sharing of, 46–47
Blumenthal, Sidney, 306
Bly, Robert, 237
boasting (bragging), 153–155
    by females, 23, 36–39, 153
    by males, 153–155
    recognition and, 153–155
Bogarde, Dirk, 219
Bohr, Niels, 317
Bonanno, Michelina, 332
Bookchin, Murray, 215
Borker, Ruth, 40, 332
Bowman, Garda, 158
bragging, *see* boasting
Braunwald, Karen, 119
British style, 235, 334–335, 338
Burma, greetings in, 43
Bush, Barbara, 289

INDEX

INDEX

pronouns, 112, 137
Pronouns and People (Mühlhäusler and Harré), 112
psychological treatment, 102
Psychology of Sex Differences, The (Maccoby and Jacklin), 286
public speaking, 148–150
    opposition to women's, 328
Public Welfare Ministry, Japanese, 269
publishing, 53–54, 127–128, 263–264

questions, 284
    asking vs. not asking, 26–29
    authoritative, 149–150
    competence and, 144–145
    hostile, 145–146

Rage of a Privileged Class, The (Cose), 117
raises, asking for, 31–32, 39
rape, false accusations of, 249–250
rape, of men, 337
rapport, 61, 67, 71, 105
rapport-talk, 71
Raspberry, William, 332–333
recognition:
    boasting and, 153–155
    performance vs., 135–137, 155–157, 159
    public speaking and, 148–150
    self-promotion and, 151–152
    special, 152
recruitment policies, 155
Reflections on Gender and Science (Keller), 249
regional differences, 102–104, 341
Remaking Society (Bookchin), 215
Remlinger, Kate, 26–27
Repa, Barbara Kate, 336
research method, 16–17
resignation, as threat, 33–34
"respect/deference," 216
Reviving Ophelia (Pipher), 321
Richard, Mark, 121
Rideau, Wilbert, 337
Rimington, Stella, 154
Rising Sun (film), 260
ritual, *see* conversational ritual(s)
    definition of, 320
Roen, Duane, 120
Rollins, Ed, 153–154, 155
Rosenberg, Rosalind, 315
Rubin, Donald, 194–195
rudeness, compliments as, 223
Russell, Bertrand, 254
Ryan, Ellen, 144

Sachs, Jacqueline, 167
Sadker, David, 287, 342
Sadker, Myra, 287, 342
Safire, William, 289
Samoan mothers, 162–163
sasshi, 96
sassuru, 96

saving face, 146–147, 179–183
Scalettar, Raymond, 210
Schenk, Lynn, 114
Schieffelin, Bambi, 163
Schiffrin, Deborah, 238
Schneider, Margaret, 266
schoolmarm image, 165–166
Scollon, Ron, 214, 215, 335
Scollon, Suzanne Wong, 214, 335
Scotton, Carol Myers, 329
secretaries, 100–102
    indirectness when talking to, 78–79, 100
    indirect speech used by, 101–102
    professional women mistaken for, 115–116
secret-keeping habits, 154–155
self-depreciation, tone of as apology, 45
self-mocking, as humor, 73
self-protection, 147
Senate, New York State, 257–258
Senate, U.S., women in, 203
sensitivity, 21–22, 27–28
sermons, giving of, 173–175
Servant, The (film), 219
servants, indirect communication with, 84
sex-class-linked behavior, 15
sexism, 114–117, 133
sexual harassment, 242–275
    cultural scripts and, 268
    doctors and, 258–259, 264–267
    false accusations and, 249–251, 273
    "faultable," female as, 260–262
    men's vs. women's perspective on, 251–254
    of men, 246–248
    power and, 248, 249, 257–260, 263–267
    violence and, 249–257, 273
    woman as witch and, 248–251, 273
    women's vs. men's perspective on, 251–254
Sexual Harassment of Working Women, 336
Sexual Harassment on the Job, 336
Seyfarth, Robert, 211, 234–235
Sheldon, Amy, 321–322, 335
Shepherd, Karen, 260
shoes, 108, 109, 110
sibling relationship, 215
silence, 61, 96, 234, 235
small talk, 63–66, 196, 223–224
    balance of power and, 223–224, 227–230
Smith, Frances Lee, 173–175
Somebody Somewhere (Williams), 42, 127
Sommers, Elizabeth, 292–295, 297–298
sports, 64, 65
    abuse and insults in, 190
    humor and, 74
    male authority and, 161
    metaphors at work, 113, 121–122, 218
    workplace language and, 121

INDEX